D1276598

Someone To Tell It To:
Moved with Compassion

MICHAEL GINGERICH AND TOM KADEN

Nate,

Compassion is alive
in you!

Michael Gingerich + Tom Kaden

Someone To Tell It To:
Moved with Compassion

by Michael Gingerich and Tom Kaden

Copyright © 2017

Library of Congress Number: 2017913522
International Standard Book Number: 978-1-60126-546-3

Published by

Masthof Press

219 Mill Road | Morgantown, PA 19543-9516
www.Masthof.com

About Someone To Tell It To, the ministry:

"Just a brief word of congratulations for the work that you're doing for Christ and the Kingdom. You obviously have tapped into something very precious and wonderful in the way of ministry. May God continue to bless you, your work, and supply all of the needs to make your ministry more extensive and more powerful than ever before."

"Someone To Tell It To is one of the most compassionate outreaches by the church to those who are troubled by groanings that cannot be uttered. The prayerful listening and counseling that these two men do is one of the most effective instruments for the healing of minds and souls that I know about anywhere in the world. What a treasure it is for us to have these men serving so faithfully at work that is essential and, yet, has been left largely undone."

Dr. Tony Campolo, author, Eastern University Campolo Center for Ministry

"To listen to another's story is to accept an audacious invitation onto holy ground. By their example, Someone To Tell It To teaches us how to take off our shoes, open our hearts and change the world."

Wm. Paul Young, author *The Shack, Crossroads* and *Eve*

About the authors' previous book,
Someone To Tell It To: Sharing Life's Journey:

"Dear 'Listeners' -

We just finished reading your book and LOVED it! The book is alive with kindness, wisdom, and loads of grace. You have been so transparent and honest. Our reaction from the heart is simply that we like what God has called you to do. What a good fit that you can offer the gift of being 'someone to tell it to.'"

"We have often said that one of the greatest gifts we can offer a child is to really see them. What we really meant is listen to them. Clearly it is something we all need throughout our entire lives."

"We can see how the writings and teachings of Henri Nouwen have influenced you and are woven throughout your book."

"We are sure Henri would have enjoyed and encouraged your ministry. We do think we should find ways to work together. Once again, congratulations on this very inspiring and life-giving book and on your obedience to God's call. You are truly faithful listeners to those who need be met with authenticity, kindness and encouragement."

Karen Pascal, Executive Director, The Henri Nouwen Society

"Someone to Tell It To represents one of the most compassionate outreaches by the Church to those who are troubled by groanings that cannot be uttered. The prayerful listening and counseling that these two men do is one of the most effective instruments for the healing of minds and souls that I know about anywhere in the world. What a treasure it is for us to have these men serving so faithfully at work that is essential and, yet, has been left largely undone."

Dr. Tony Campolo, author, Eastern University Campolo Center for Ministry

"Relationships, the kind that connect people in ways only the Gospel makes possible. That's what Someone To Tell It To is all about. And that's why their vision has my support."

Dr. Larry Crabb, Author, Psychologist

"Too often we suffer alone, afraid to share the truth of our insides, afraid to be authentic with others, particularly when we are suffering. That greatly exacerbates pain and prolongs it. A big part of my message, when discussing my friendship with Mister Rogers, is to encourage people to come out of their hiding. Cop to their pain. There are people out there who will listen with healing presence and compassion, and I have just discovered two more. They are Michael Gingerich and Thomas Kaden, who have recently embarked on a mission they have named, brilliantly enough, Someone To Tell It To. I learned of their hopes to help coax people out of their isolation, as Fred coaxed me out of mine. I believe one of the greatest struggles of humankind is individual isolation, particularly with suffering. With great personal courage themselves, these two guys are committed to tackling that struggle head on. I endorse them without reservation, and admire them both greatly. I am proud to call them my brothers, my friends."

Tim Madigan, Author of *I'm Proud of You: My Friendship with Fred Rogers*

*F*or Kathy and Sarah, for their limitless patience and unending belief in what we've been called to do. For Adam, David, Matthew, Lillian, Luke, Madelyn, Mya, Kate, Janelle, Lilyanna, Emma, Emmett, Elle and Milo, who enable our legacy to live on.

Compassion is alive in each of you.

To our parents and siblings:

For giving us the permission to be who we are—and who God has created us to be—the often quiet, introspective, introverted, sensitive, gentle people we are. Your security in us helps us overcome our insecurities.

To everyone in our families:

For giving us the permission to tell "our stories," from our experiences and perspectives—and for doing so with grace, kindness, forgiveness and unwavering unconditional love. Your courage in the process, trusting that our stories can bring hope and redemption to our beautiful, broken world—gives us hope too! We love you so much it hurts.

Acknowledgements

To Michele Eby, who once again gave her valuable time to make our words readable and our message coherent. We could not accomplish this without you and your gifts, offered so freely and generously. We will be always grateful for you. Without you, the first to read our thoughts, no publication of ours would be possible.

To everyone who opened up your lives and souls to us—and who wanted your stories to be told so others might find redemption in theirs, we offer you our profound respect. By telling your stories you enable a view into compassion's limitless heart. You show a hurting, anguished world how it was created to be—kind, gentle, forgiving, peaceful and marked by love.

Someone To Tell It To: Moved With Compassion is meant to be read slowly, in small portions. Each of the stories we tell is intimate; they invite readers to reflect deeply on the examples they offer. Compassion requires an intentional consideration of another's circumstances, a grace that recognizes our common humanity in all its beauty and brokenness. While not every story may resonate personally and strongly with every reader, we pray that intentional consideration will move you toward a more empathetic response to the ever-present realities of the human experience.

All proceeds of this book will be used to help the ministry of Somone To Tell It To—"To create a caring culture that accompanies others on the path toward meaningful connections."

We also thank Albert Sarvis for the cover photo, taken by him at Cadillac Mountain Acadia National Park, in Maine, and Christopher Heberlig Hoke for the cover design. Your work is striking. We appreciate your artistic eyes and the creative gifts you each share every day to help make this world a more beautiful place.

Table of Contents

SECTION 1

"What Did You Guys Do to Form Such a Solid Friendship?"

SECTION 2

*"How Do You Create and Foster Healthy Relationships
of Depth and Intimacy?"*

SECTION 3

"What Makes a Good Listener?"

SECTION 4

"When Have You Not Seen the Presence of Compassion?"

SECTION 5

"What Does It Mean to Be Compassionate?"

CONCLUSION

"And Jesus went about all the cities and the villages, teaching in their synagogues, and preaching the gospel of the kingdom, and healing all manner of disease and all manner of sickness.

But when he saw the multitudes, he was moved with compassion for them, because they were distressed and scattered, as sheep not having a shepherd."

MATTHEW 9:35-36
AMERICAN STANDARD VERSION (ASV)

Introduction

"ONE'S LIFE HAS VALUE so long as one attributes value to the life of others, by means of love, friendship, indignation and compassion."
-SIMONE DE BEAUVOIR

"I finished your book the other day and I have some questions for you." Our curiosity was piqued.

What was he going to say? Did he like the book? Had we written something offensive in it? Our palms got sweaty and our hearts skipped a few beats as we waited to hear what would follow.

"I loved it! It genuinely spoke to me."

Phew! We both took a deep breath and let out a huge sigh of relief. Writers never know how their work will be received, especially because our writing opens our lives to the world. Because we wrote about so much of our own stories in the book, *Someone To Tell It To: Sharing Life's Journey*, we had considerable apprehension about what others would think of us. Would telling several vulnerable moments in our lives (many, few others were intimately aware of) open us up to hurtful criticisms and judgments? Would opening up about some of our insecurities, fears and wounds heap more insecurities, fears and wounds upon us?

Would the very thing we, in our ministry, encourage so many others to do with us—acknowledge their brokenness, take off their masks and embrace their humanness—backfire on us when we opened up to the world?

When relief replaced our uncertainty and uneasiness in the coffee shop one autumn afternoon, we became curious about what our friend would say. He loved it! Now, what? The conversation following was instrumental in forming the focus of this new book.

A week earlier he had led a book discussion on *Someone To Tell It To: Sharing Life's Journey* at his church. He said the group liked the book also and he told us some of the things people said during the discussion. He said many were expecting a "how to" or "self-help" book, which would offer five to 10 steps for becoming more compassionate and empathetic with others. Our friend indicated, at first, he too was looking for a progression through the book ultimately leading to clear-cut, definitive answers to his theological and philosophical questions. His analytical approach to life naturally steered him in that direction.

But, he soon realized the book wasn't written with absolute answers—intentionally—because life isn't absolute. Becoming more compassionate and empathetic with others is not just a matter of internalizing half a dozen steps to take; it's more complicated. Even so, he said he still wondered:

"Just what can I do to lead a more compassionate life?"

So we asked him: "What exactly would you like us to write about in our next book, as a follow-up to the first? What do you think people would like, or need, to hear knowing the answers aren't so clear-cut? What would help you better respond to life's mysteries and ambiguities?"

He began talking about his relationship with his wife and how he tries to live authentically with her, a theme we wrote about throughout our first book, but how "most" people don't seem to know how to have genuine, authentic, healthy relationships.

Since we started our non-profit, Someone To Tell It To, in 2012, we have been asked countless times:

"So how did you come to know each other? How do you work so well together? Why are you such great friends, especially given the two-decade age gap between you?"

Well, we sit with one another, walk beside one another, pray with, and for, one another, listen to one another, commiserate with one another, encourage one another and remind one another— especially on those days when we feel alone— we are beloved children of God—which is precisely how Someone To Tell It To was born. We have been each other's "someone to tell it to" through some of the most tense moments and seasons of our lives. It is what we are for one another, literally, every day.

It is our deepest hope this book will help to consider these questions posed by our friend: "What Did You Guys Do to Form Such a Solid Friendship?" "How Do You Create and Foster Healthy Relationships of Depth and Intimacy?" "What Makes a Good Listener?"

"When Have You Not Seen the Presence of Compassion?" And, answer in the end, **"What does it mean to be compassionate?"** May these stories help you understand what being more compassionate and emphatic can mean for your life and for the lives of those you encounter every day.

Building a Home There

THE EVENING NEWS runs in the background. We listen intently as the newscaster reviews the day's headlines: suicide bombers, earthquakes, the death penalty debate, toxic race relations, lack of safe water, AIDS, cancer, Ebola. The list goes on and on.

A commercial break interrupts the broadcast and grabs our attention. A statistic citing the number of children who perish every minute from malnourishment flashes across an image of a starving, dying African infant held in his mother's arms. Another advertisement asks for donations to support The Red Cross and its outreach around the world in times of crisis. As a third commercial rolls, we hear Sarah McLachlan's beautiful voice singing the haunting song *Angel*:

In the arms of the angel fly away from here, from this dark cold hotel room and the endlessness that you fear, you are pulled from the wreckage of your silent reverie, you're in the arms of the angel, may you find some comfort here...

The pictures of abused animals on the screen are anything but angelic. Our heads turn away.

Our hope for this book is to help move people toward compassion, while at the same time embrace our humanness – including our imperfections and our shortcomings.

One November morning several years ago, we spoke to a group of 25 pastors about our mission. After our talk, during a time of questions and answers, one pastor quietly mentioned,

"What you are doing is impressive. It seems you're doing what the church is supposed to be doing . . . but isn't."

His words continue to reverberate in our minds and in part, are the reason we are writing this book, *Someone To Tell It To: Moved with Compassion*.

Saint Mother Teresa's life, with its selfless, ceaseless works of charity, was—and continues to be—an inspiration to countless people of all faiths. The way she lived her life was her greatest message. It was the embodiment of the merciful life and our faith, and who, we believe, Jesus Christ calls us to be. But even she was not perfect; no human being is. All we are asked to do is try to be our best in responding to the invitation to live a life of goodwill.

We don't have to give up everything we know today and go to Calcutta to live the very unique life Saint Mother Teresa did. But each of us in our own distinctive ways can embody sensitivity and warmth every day. Too often, we look at people such as her, Gandhi, Martin Luther King, Jr., Nelson Mandela, or Malala Yousafzai and think their examples of service and humanity are not something we can follow. People often view them as saintly people who are unlike the rest of us—people to be admired, not possibly emulated. While their specific circumstances and lives of poverty, sacrifice or heroism are not for everyone, we all might consider these two questions:

How can I live compassionately with the gifts and opportunities I have been given?
What is unique to me that I can share with those whom I meet each day?

We have more than one friend, who has said to us, "I'm not compassionate. I'm not an empathetic person. I couldn't do what you do every day."

We wonder what they think compassion is. We want this book to awaken the goodwill we believe abides in all of us as children of God. It's the divine and sacred spark called love.

The sense of tenderness we feel and try to respond to comes from this,

"You must be compassionate, just as (God) is compassionate." Luke 6:36 (New Living Translation)

Some translations use the word "merciful" or "mercy," others use the word, "kind." Beautiful words. Beautiful concepts: to be generous, humane, gracious, forgiving, understanding, caring, gentle, thoughtful, benevolent, considerate and empathetic.

They are all variations of the word "compassion"—in the Latin, *pati cum*, which means "to suffer with."

Yet "suffering with" and being benevolent is taxing. There's no doubt about it. This may be why there is so little compassion evident in our world, and in so many of our lives.

Why do we witness and experience so much the opposite—inhumanity, meanness, cruelty, coldheartedness, mercilessness, brutality, callousness, intolerance, evil, disdainfulness and indifference?

In the Bible, according to Luke 6:36, Jesus's words are more than a suggestion. They are a command—*You must be compassionate*—gracious, forgiving, empathetic, etc. It's not "be compassionate if you feel like it," but a direct mandate. For most of us, we don't like hearing the word "command." We immediately think of someone standing over top of us shouting if we don't accomplish what we are "commanded" to do; but this is not how we view this passage. Yes, we believe Jesus commands us to be as generous in graciousness as God is toward us. But at the same time we realize the impossibility of being as generous as God. We strive to accept our humanness, to respond with grace toward everyone, including ourselves, when we don't carry out the mission as well as we could. Actually, we like to use the word invitation, rather than command. God invites us, we believe, to be part of an outreach of love, grace and sensitivity, as a response, because we have first been shown an outreach of love, grace and sensitivity by God.

Every time we give a talk at a church, civic organization or to a staff of caregivers, someone invariably asks us:

"How do you guys do what you do all day long and not get burned out? I don't think I could do what you do."

Certainly, there is considerable merit to this question, as it is commonplace for caregivers, pastors, counselors and others who are in helping professions, to run themselves into the ground extending mercy.

At times, we appreciate the question and the compliment coming with it. Who doesn't like a pat on the back and being acknowledged for a job well done? Who isn't appreciative when others show concern for his or her welfare and well-being?

But more and more, it troubles us when others state, in essence, **"It's notable what you are doing. Keep up the good work! But don't expect me to do the same."**

Our spiritual hero, the late theologian Henri Nouwen, described compassion as "full immersion into the condition of being human." Compassion requires us to imagine ourselves in another's circumstances, to try to feel another's pain, sorrow, fear, uncertainty or insecurity. It's not an easy thing to imagine. In fact, as Nouwen wrote, along with Donald McNeill and Douglas Morrison, it is human nature to try to avoid suffering; it's not among our most natural responses. We desire strongly, reflexively to stay away from pain (*Compassion: A Reflection on the Christian Life,* 1982, p 4,). Suffering with another, much less ourselves is not attractive and we can easily be repelled by it. Yet, as they write, it is the very thing we, as followers of Jesus, are mandated to do.

In *The Message* version of the Bible, Eugene Peterson translated John 1:14 as, "The word became flesh and blood and moved into the neighborhood."

We treasure the image of God's love moving into the neighborhood, putting up permanent residence to show us how much God cares—It is precisely this presence which really counts in moments of distress and anguish—It is the one who stays with us showing us that our pain and suffering matter. After all, isn't knowing that we are innately significant, regardless of who we are, what all of us most inherently desire and need? To be shown that we all are of consequence is compassion.

Years ago, I (Michael) officiated at a wedding in which an honored guest was the sister of the late vice president of the United States, Hubert Humphrey. At the rehearsal dinner, the groom introduced my wife Kathy and me to her; she was a long-time family friend. She graciously asked us if we had children and wanted to know a little about them. When we spoke of our son Matthew who has severe intellectual disabilities and autism, she quickly exclaimed in a paraphrase of one of her brother's most famous quotes, "My brother so often said, 'The moral test of society is how that society treats those who are in the dawn of life, the children; those who are in the twilight of life, the elderly; and those who are in the shadows of life, the sick, the needy and the handicapped'."

Her words were an act of compassion to us, a recognition and acknowledgement that it is relentless parenting a child such as Matthew, who has so many needs and such profound dependency on us. Her words reassured us that someone noticed, and that others recognized the weight involved in raising a child with disabilities. So often, a simple gift such as her recognition provides encouragement to continue on. She reminded us that our care giving for Matthew is respected. She reminded us that Matthew is innately respected, too.

Our hope, in this book, in our ministry, and how we have decided to intentionally live, is to provide a glimpse into the different faces of compassion and what it is. Compassion is not about drawing attention to us, but to God, who is the source of all compassion, grace and unconditional love.

But as best we can, we strive to show solidarity with the condition of being human, made in the image of God, by entering the "dark uncharted spaces" of others' lives. We try to live out the words of Nouwen, McNeill and Morrison, who wrote,

"More important than any particular action or word of advice is the simple presence of someone who cares . . . we have lost the simple gift but difficult gift of being present to each other . . . we have been led to believe that presence must be useful . . . we have forgotten that it is often in 'useless,' unpretentious, humble presence to each other that we feel consolation and comfort." (*Compassion*, p 11-12). **It is this very presence that we hope to articulate throughout this book.**

The Gospels continuously portray Jesus as being "moved with compassion." In the Greek in which the Gospels were originally written, "compassion" is literally translated as a deep feeling "within the bowels" (for the bowels were thought to be the seat of love and pity). (*Thayer's Greek Lexicon*) That's how deep and strong the feeling is.

The travail of Jesus doesn't make sense to us as rational beings. Couldn't there have been a better way? Did he have to experience all that we experience, all of the pain, heartache, loss, fear, loneliness, sadness, despair, highs and lows, peaks and valleys?

To us, and to many, many others around the world, this is what makes Jesus so special—this is good news! This idea of Jesus willingly giving up his rights and privileges is a foreign concept to many of us. Most of us operate, without even knowing it, in a "kill or (we will) be killed" mode. Life is a giant competition, and in order to win the game, we have to be on the offensive; we must compete at the highest level making all the correct and shrewd moves if we expect to win and be successful.

The idea of being compassionate as opposed to doing acts of compassion makes all the difference.

To truly "be compassionate as God is compassionate" we look toward the example of Christ. Jesus didn't simply mandate us, his followers, to live a life of humility and surrender; he lived it himself, perfectly. For Jesus, "being compassionate" meant that he embodied mercy—all the time! As we read the Gospels, we don't find Jesus saying: "You know what, today I feel like doing an act of compassion for another human being." No! He always, always, embodied the humane way. Jesus was never about getting ahead or getting his own way; he didn't operate under the model of "kill or be killed" or in competition. In fact, he willingly, as the Apostle Paul writes, chose to be killed, "When he appeared in human form, he humbled himself in obedience to God and died a criminal's death on a cross."(Philippians 2:7-8).

"Here we see what compassion means. It is not a bending toward the underprivileged from a privileged position; it is not a reaching out from on high to those who are less fortunate below; it is not a gesture of sympathy or pity for those who fail to make it in the upward pull. On the contrary, tenderness means going directly to those people and places where suffering is most acute and building a home there. God's compassion is total, absolute, unconditional, without reservation. It is the compassion of the one who keeps going to the most forgotten corners of the world, and who cannot rest as long as there are still human beings with tears in their eyes. It is the compassion of a God who does not merely act as a servant, but who expresses the divinity of God through servanthood." (*Compassion*, p. 25)

Compassion, as we understand it, is simply a response to God's love. Our aim is to awaken that response in each of us, a response to this crazy generosity of the love of God. God gives unremittingly, infinitely, and extravagantly.

Someone To Tell It To: Moved with Compassion shares the stories of God's love—and the natural outpouring and overwhelming reaction to such a love. Because we are loved, we are inspired to share love with one another. If this book can help us to love God and to love each other, as we would like to be loved ourselves, then it has served its purpose.

"What Did You Guys Do to Form Such a Solid *Friendship*?"

A Friend Is . . . (Michael)

"A friend is more than a therapist or confessor, even though a friend can sometimes heal us and offer us God's forgiveness. A friend is that other person with whom we can share our solitude, our silence, and our prayer. A friend is that other person with whom we can look at a tree and say, "Isn't that beautiful," or sit on the beach and silently watch the sun disappear under the horizon. With a friend we don't have to say or do something special. With a friend we can be still and know that God is there with both of us."
- HENRI J. M. NOUWEN

ONE SPRING, after six and a half years providing spiritual and emotional care to people who lived with cancer, I learned my job would end due to cuts in funding. Of all the responses to the news that I would be losing my job, Tom's was the most out of the ordinary. Everyone I told was supportive. They expressed their concern. They encouraged me. They offered words of hope. But, Tom declared something in addition to the encouragement, something engaging and touching:

"Now we'll be able to hang out more together!"

Tom's response still resonates with me more than six years later because he made good on his declaration.

My job eventually ended and spring turned into summer and summer into fall, and we did hang out a great deal together. We talked on the phone almost every day. Even though we live 45 minutes apart, we saw each other at least once a week. I regularly ran over my phone texting limits at the time, which prompted me to get an unlimited plan. Tom was, and continues to be, a true constant for me.

As one season evolved into the next, I began to understand the deeper meaning of Tom's words.

"Now we'll be able to hang out more together!" meant—"I treasure spending time with you and now, at least for a while, I can. I'm not going to let you walk through this valley alone. I'm going to help you to figure out what's next. I love you."

And he's meant all of it. He's said each of those things. In saying them and living them, Tom was offering his compassion with me.

3

Tom is, most definitely, a friend who cares. He steps in and offers to stand with me in all life presents—its delight and its distress, its triumphs and its defeats, its illuminating moments and its foreboding shadows. He steps in and stays when life is happy and light, but also when it is scary and grim.

Tom helped me to face an uncertain future with certainty, certainty that along with my family and others in my life, I have a best friend who will insure I have— another arm around me to calm me when I'm unsettled, another pair of legs to walk beside me as I forge another a new path, another set of ears to listen when I simply need to be heard, another kindred spirit to reassure me that my hopes and dreams are worth pursuing, and another soul open to exploring a deeper faith, a closer and intimate connection, and a more complete and richer life.

We've taken countless long and strenuous walks and more than a few long runs. We've played tennis, gone swimming, ridden bikes, eaten many meals, toasted with many beers, and seen many movies together. We've worshiped together and read countless books and discussed them together. We've developed a profound trust. We have both been intentional about nurturing a relationship speaking to the need for males to support one another on their common as well as uncommon journeys. Not just as "buddies who hang out together" or pals who seldom reach below the surface. But as men who are committed to exploring a depth rarely reached. We've lain open our souls and allowed each other in.

We asked each other deep and penetrating questions, which have enabled us to talk about the most essential aspects of who we are. As a result, we have grown to know each other—and ourselves—better and more intimately.

Someone To Tell It To was birthed from this intentional time.

In a September 2014 commentary in the *New York Times,* "Startling Adult Friendships," David Brooks wrote about being asked what he would do if he had $500 million to give away. His dream, he offered, would be to affect people in a "personal and profound way." In particular, he'd want to affect friendships. Ancient authors such as Aristotle and Montaigne, he indicated, have written about friendship as the "cornerstone of society," spreading "universal warmth."

Brooks believes companionship offers many significant benefits - helping people make better judgments, allowing us to see our own lives with a second sympathetic self, and enabling us to bring out better versions of each other.

"People behave better if they know their friends are observing," he wrote. "People tend to want to live up to their friends' high regard." We have close friendships "simply for the pleasure itself of feeling known and respected."

But Brooks lamented: studies show friendship is not in great shape in America today. In 1985, a General Social Survey showed people tended to have about three close friends; by 2004, research at Duke University and the University of Arizona indicated people tended to have only two close confidants, and the number of people who say they have no close confidants (at all) had tripled over time.

The creation of Someone To Tell It To came about because we, too, saw – and at times felt - this phenomenon happening. So we made a covenant to do this for ourselves, as well as for others.

One of the covenants we made for the time we would spend together in that season was to visit places holding special—actually spiritual—meaning for each of us. We went overnight to New York City, a magical, energizing city we both enjoy immensely. We've spent time on the beach in Ocean Grove, New Jersey, where Tom's family had a summer home when he was growing up, which holds deeply warm and beautiful memories for him. We enjoyed a respite at my family's mountain cabin near the New York/Pennsylvania border, a place that has been a very sacred place in my life since I was born.

Each visit together drew us further into each other's past. Each visit shed a brighter light into understanding each other's present. Each visit, ultimately, enabled both of us to see with greater confidence and reassurance the possibilities inherent in each other's future. Our 25-year age difference, manifested only occasionally in generational cultural reference points, was virtually rendered moot by so many mutually resonant feelings. New York City's ability to energize us and to give us the anonymity pastoral work in smaller communities takes away, the beach's overwhelming power to relax and restore us, the mountain woodland's isolated peacefulness brings wonder and softens the world's problems away when we are there.

In New York, we sat on a rock outcropping, in the Central Park sun, amidst a grove of trees. For several hours we found reprieve in the rustic calm muting the traffic's din and relieving the city's frenetic pace. Our conversation was personal, each of us revealing moments of hurt and apprehension in our youth, divulging details that few beyond our wives and another friend or two had ever heard before. It was the place where I felt safe enough with Tom to answer his question, "What is something very few people know about you?" with a disclosure about the sexual harassment and abuse I received as a teenager.

And as we walked miles and miles throughout the streets, and later reveling in the most expensive dinner we had ever had, our ever-deepening connection made our time together in the city absolutely sublime.

In Ocean Grove, we spent the day at the beach with our children. Tom brought Lilly, who was four at the time, and Luke, who was two. I brought Matthew. We loaded down my minivan with strollers, toys, extra clothes and diaper bags. Two dads and their kids. We packed so much stuff it looked as if we were going for a week. Keeping the kids happy and occupied was constant. But it was well worth the energy as Tom proudly showed me the place meaning the most to him growing up, the town where his family was at its most cohesive, where time spent together brought lasting memories of simple joy, contentment and love. As Tom discussed stories of his many trips to this beach town, I felt heartened he brought me to a sacred place for him.

We experienced a moment on the boardwalk cementing our connection as dads. On a hot, sunny day, ice cream seemed like a great idea. But the heat and the bright sun predictably turned the ice cream into a flowing volcano. Within minutes, Lilly, Luke, and Matthew were covered in chocolate, sticky and wet, and as happy as they could be. We had a real mess to clean up and none of the kids made it easy to accomplish.

Tom and I laughed and lamented at the same time. We expressed a few whispered curses between us, which helped discharge some tension. We also admitted, as much as we love our children, being a parent is a tremendous responsibility, a responsibility neither of us could have prepared for. While there are countless moments of laughter and enjoyment, there are often untidy and fatiguing moments to manage as well, which we talked about for most of the ride home, while Lilly and Luke slept and Matthew looked excitedly at lights on the cars going by. The common topsy-turvy boardwalk moment gave us an opening to talk vulnerably about the irritations of parenthood, along with the blisses, and helped us both to understand what we each live and grapple with as dads every day.

At my family's mountain cabin, there isn't much to do. That's the point. Tom and I simply went to walk and talk. A lot. To tell each other more of our stories. Four hours driving there. Four hours back. No TV. No radio. No Internet. Not even reliable cell service. It was the perfect two days to either come away more closely bonded or with a newly found disdain for one another. Thankfully, our bond of friendship grew stronger.

I asked Tom to tell me about all the injuries, surgeries and physical pain he's endured since he was a teenager. Previously, he had told me bits and pieces of that aspect of his life. But on this trip we had the time and space to talk about it in detail. It helped me grasp what he went through as a teenager and what he still lives with every day. The visit there was revealing, helping me, at least, to be more sensitive to Tom's chronic pain and discomfort.

On each of our personal pilgrimages, Tom and I took paths one or the other, or both, had never traveled before. In New York we ventured into a corner of Central Park new to both of us. We visited the World Trade Center site together. I had been there several times since the gruesome day in 2001. But Tom, who grew up in the New York suburbs had literally been eating lunch on the Center's plaza just one week before the September 11 attacks. For 10 years he couldn't bring himself to go back to a place of such ghastly death and devastation. But he decided he was ready to go with me. Tom took me to the beach in Ocean Grove because he wanted me to know his roots and his history. It is a mystical spot for him and he wanted me to know the place, which meant so much. We hiked through sections of woods and fields near my family's cabin—in all my years of going there—I had never ventured into or seen before. We discovered a beautiful valley and a rushing stream, following the season's incessant rains, and took in its sedative sounds, its refreshing sight. So many memories grow from that place for me. I wanted Tom to know them too.

When I'm with Tom, time stands still. Our conversations transport us beyond the immediate world surrounding us and take us to places in which we can both open up as much as we do with our wives. We are two brothers in the spirit, craving the intimacy of knowing another deeply and being known in return. Between us there is absolute confidence, complete grace enabling us to be. We know we can bare our insides and there will be no judgment. We can be unashamed of who we are and what we experience. Tom helps me to be a better husband and father, a better friend, a better man. We explore our faith together and inspire each other to be better at living out our values. We both believe all of us in life crave lasting and consequential connections with others. And we also both believe men, especially, so often don't know how to open up enough, to connect on a deeper level, to break the bonds of separation all of us fight in some way every day. Men need other men to help show each other a better way.

But together Tom and I have made the covenant to be the kind of man, the kind of friend, who our mutual spiritual hero, Henri Nouwen, describes . . . the friend with whom,

. . . *we can be still and know God is there with both of us.*

Between us there are very few walls, little pretense, and barely a facade. Just a welcome security and familiarity, another safe place to go to be appeased when we are disturbed, to walk beside one another as we forge another path, to listen when we simply need to be heard, to reassure each other our hopes and dreams are definitely worth pursuing, to explore . . . a deeper faith, a closer and intimate connection, more substantial, purposeful lives.

That is a friend who is in it with me.

It is in asking questions of one another beyond "How's it going?" or "Did you see the play in the bottom of the eighth inning last night?" or "Can you believe how hot it is today?" where deeper friendships are created. It is in recognizing we all have trials and tribulations lying buried within. It is offering to explore those darker, often secret places, allowing one another to bring them into the light, where mending and liberation is found. It is being willing to enter into rough territory with someone else, which helps us, strip away the layers of guilt and shame cloaking us in varying degrees of agony and sorrow. Being a friend who stays in it with us isn't always easy. But being a friend who cares is always more fulfilling and rewarding.

We all need friends such as these. We pray every life could have those kinds of connections. For they give life its richness and relevance.

"All we see is sky for forever, we let the world pass by for forever, feels like we could go on for forever this way; two friends on a perfect day."
Benj Pasek and Justin Paul, "For Forever," from *Dear Evan Hanson*

Calling (Tom)

"God often uses our deepest pain as the launching pad
for our greatest calling."
-Unknown

"Out of our deepest pain comes the greatest sense
of the presence of God and the love of God."
-Elisabeth Elliot

"I WOULD HAVE GONE through all of the pain again just to have been able to meet you and start this friendship and journey together."

The words rolled off my tongue as if I had rehearsed them hundreds of times before. But I hadn't. It was a Friday afternoon and we were concluding our work-week together. We were taking some time, as we often do, to express gratitude, as well as to pray for those individuals who had reached out to us in their deepest distress. We talked about our plans for the weekend, as well as about the monumental event happening on the coming Sunday morning.

It had been a very full and active month. We hadn't had the opportunity to reflect deeply on the importance of what was about to occur: I was about to walk into the church where I served as a youth pastor in my first position out of seminary— the place where my deepest pain began.

For 18 months I felt as though I walked on eggshells in the church. If it wasn't an issue about one matter, it was an issue with another. And if it wasn't an issue with one specific individual, then it felt like it was an issue with someone else. Every day, a new problem arose; I felt more and more alone.

What kept me going was a suggestion from the previous youth pastor: "If you need to vent about the trials of ministry or needed someone to remind you of your worthiness and positive contributions to the church when you are feeling devalued, there is a person who will listen."

Michael was that person.

I can't remember the specifics of our first meeting together; maybe he can. But I do remember the many evenings we spent together on the deck at his home in the first year, as I opened up about the highs and lows of life in ministry. We dreamed together about what a "perfect" ministry could be like and talked about the kind of role we both loved playing in others' lives. We talked about our love of being "mentors" and "shepherds," caretakers of God's flock. We agreed that there is nothing we enjoyed more than sitting with someone and listening intently to who they are, what they believed and what made them who they are today. We loved cultivating deep friendships with others, the kind of deep friendship we were fostering with each other.

In a year and a half, Michael did far more listening to me than I probably did for him. Having served as a pastor for more than 20 years himself, he understood what I was going through. He consoled me when I needed consoling, encouraged me when I needed encouraging and allowed me to be angry when I needed to be angry. He loved me.

There were many moments when I thought seriously about giving up. There were constant adversities and I could sense more and more things weren't quite "right" (which may be the understatement of my life). A year and a half into the job, I received a message from a superior about meeting first thing the next day. Speculating about the meeting, I couldn't sleep. My mind churned with the probabilities and none of them were positive; deep inside my heart I knew the result.

It was a Tuesday morning. On Tuesday mornings I would join a group of "prayer partners." We would get together to pray for each other, to pray for our families, to pray for church and whatever was on our hearts. One of the "prayer partners" could sense my edginess as soon as I opened the door to the room. She asked openly, "What's wrong?"

Tears started streaming down my face as I explained the email and how I could sense it was the beginning of the end for me. She listened and asked if we could pray together. I started praying, and surprisingly, prayed a version of the prayer Jesus prayed in the Garden of Gethsemane the night before his death.

"God, I don't know why this is happening. I don't know why this has to be so excruciating and if there is a way to take this cup from me . . . please take it!"

Sensing the cup wasn't going to be taken, I continued, "Surely this isn't my will, but I trust you can bring good out of it."

The other "prayer partner" prayed for me too. She prayed for the meeting and what lay ahead, she prayed for me to sense the abiding presence and love of God, she prayed for my family.

Later in the morning, the meeting went down. For nearly two hours I felt as if I was told everything I had done wrongly. More tears. I asked if I could close the door. My superior said no. I couldn't hide my tears from others walking by in the church hallway.

When the "trial" ended I walked home and went straight to our bedroom and pulled the covers over my head. I didn't—couldn't—move for the rest of the day. There has never been a time in my life, and I pray there never will be again, when I doubted my belovedness like I did then. When things spiral so violently out of control in our lives, it's common to question our identity.

"God uses our deepest pain as the launching pad for our greatest calling," someone has said, and I've found it to be the case in my own life. Someone To Tell It To, my calling, was launched out of immeasurable strain.

Through such an immensely agonizing season of my life, Michael, my wife Sarah, and several others reminded me, when I needed to be reminded most, how I had made a lasting difference in dozens of young persons' lives, that I was a reputable, faithful youth pastor. It was then Michael uttered those four little words drastically shaping the direction of both our lives: "I'm proud of you!"

"I'm proud of you for taking this step and I'm so glad we can deal with it together."

Fast-forward several years from that heart-wrenching day. We were each other's "someone to tell it to" through some of the most demanding moments of our lives. It was the day when our calling began.

And on this particular Friday afternoon I marvel at what has come to pass—so much of it positive—since that fateful day and I can hardly believe I will be returning to the place where so much trouble was caused for me.

Michael had been invited to preach and I wanted to be there to support him. In addition, the church was going to hold a book signing for our first book a few weeks later, as well as to offer us financial support for our ministry.

Talk about a miraculous, unexpected gift! I needed to be there. We prayed for the worship service and to experience a monumental day, for both of us.

I arrived at church several minutes early. I didn't want to walk in late. I didn't want the moment to be any more stressful or uncomfortable than it already was. Looking across the parking lot, I saw another of my closest friends walking toward my car. He knew how important a day this was for me and he wanted to be there too. Michael greeted us at the door with a warm embrace.

"I just want to remind you, one more time, how deeply proud of you I am for taking this step to be here today."

We opened the doors. The very same doors I once viewed as prison doors now gave me a sense of peace and freedom. My mind reeled with all the possibilities I had built up in my mind. I had dreams of what it would be like to enter the church again. For several years when I would drive by the highway exit leading to the church, my mouth would get dry, a knot formed in my stomach, I'd start to sweat and I'd have shortness of breath. I remembered well the deep depression I spiraled down into following my tenure there. I never thought I'd go through those doors again. Would the story of the "12 Days of Christmas" unfold before my very eyes? Would there be trumpets blaring, choirs singing, and lords leaping? How about an army of people ready to greet me with hugs as if the prodigal son had just returned home? Maybe?

No. What I experienced was anything but that. Instead, it was ordinary.

I smelled the same familiar smells. I walked past the same bulletin boards. I was greeted by the same people who often worked at the coffee table. I heard the same sounds. Everything was "normal;" just like it had ever been before.

Perhaps forgiveness is like that sometimes; it's quiet like a summer afternoon breeze. There aren't necessarily any lightning bolts. There aren't necessarily any mountains falling into the heart of the sea. There aren't necessarily any rainbows or rays of sunshine. There is only the still, small voice of God inspiring us quietly from a distance.

Ever since, the church has cheered us on too. We have become a mission of the congregation, which comes with generous financial support. There have been some leadership changes and the pastors have given us unqualified affirmation. Many people from the congregation have referred others to us. And we trust the relationship will only become even more fruitful.

That's redemption. That's forgiveness. God is in the business of restoring that, which has been shattered. That is what God does. And God invites us to be a part of the repairing and reconciling process. I can honestly acknowledge my own responsibility for brokenness during my time there. I can also recall many good moments and people in the church, too.

Following the service, Michael and I went out to lunch together. He asked me how I felt. I told him it was more unglamorous than what I had expected; but it was acceptable. We continued our conversation from the previous Friday afternoon about how grateful we were to have been able to meet each other in the deepest, darkest of moments—and, how, as a result, we have had the gift of exploring other dark moments of our lives. We reflected on how stunning God is and how God can use our deepest hurt to be a source of hope and healing for others.

A friend of mine bought a copy of our first book. He said that the husband of one of his co-workers was going through a very similar situation at their church. My friend gave the book to his co-worker, recommending the story detailing my experience as youth pastor might bring some reassurance to her husband. She in turn offered it to her husband, who wrote me a very kind message in response, thanking me for having written it.

Author and theologian Frederick Beuchner, in his book *Wishful Thinking: A Theological ABC* wrote, "The place God calls you to is the place where your deep gladness and the world's deep hunger meet."

The world is hungry for people who can take their brokenness, with gladness, to others who need it most. True compassion, as Jesus exemplified, is allowing God to bring redemption through our hurt, because we all hurt about some things. We are equals. Compassion is a relationship between equals, those who have been wounded and those who need healing. May God help you to use your sore spots as a source of fulfillment to a world in need.

"The Church often wounds us deeply. People with religious authority often wound us by their words, attitudes, and demands. Precisely because our religion brings us in touch with the questions of life and death, our religious sensibilities can get hurt most easily. Ministers and priests seldom fully realize how a critical remark, a gesture of rejection, or an act of impatience can be remembered for life by those to whom it is directed.

There is such an enormous hunger for meaning in life, for comfort and consolation, for forgiveness and reconciliation, for restoration and healing, that anyone who has any authority in the Church should constantly be reminded that the best word to characterize religious authority is *compassion*. Let's keep looking at Jesus whose authority was expressed in compassion." Henri Nouwen

What Does *Success* Mean to You?
(An Essay in Four Parts)

SUCCESS (MICHAEL)

> *"Birthdays need to be celebrated . . . Because to celebrate a birthday means*
> *to say to someone: 'Thank you for being you.' Celebrating a birthday is*
> *exalting life and being glad for it. On a birthday we do not say: 'Thanks*
> *for what you did, or said, or accomplished.' No, we say: 'Thank you for*
> *being born and being among us.'"*
> -HENRI NOUWEN

IT WAS TOM'S BIRTHDAY. His mood was reflective.

Birthdays can do it to both of us. The end of one year of life and the beginning of another causes us to take stock of what has been and what might yet be. We consider the year's thrills and setbacks and the future's prospects and trials.

We were in the car together, driving to lunch to celebrate the day—Tom's life—when he turned to me and said, "There is a question I want to ask you. Maybe it's because it's my birthday that I'm thinking about this. But it's definitely been on my mind today." He paused and then, continued.

"What does 'success' mean to you? For you individually and for us and our ministry?"

Pondering for just a second or two, I responded, and was shocked by how much I had to say. I told him how I loved the question but didn't have a quick sound bite answer. I went on to explain.

For me, it's absolutely about relationships. It's about creating and nurturing relationships that are deep, intimate, and mutual. With Kathy, with (my oldest sons) Adam and David, and their growing families. There's a different kind of intimacy with Matthew. But it's just as profound. With you, surely, certainly. With others in our lives.

For me, success is about being the best husband, father, son, brother and friend I can be. It's about creating connections allowing me to know another and be known. It's about a relationship with God sustaining and inspiring me. That's part of it.

It's about the world around me being better than when I entered it. I think it's about my presence and making a difference to help to make the world a little less dark, less scary, and less threatening because I was in it.

It's about recognizing the gifts I was given and using those gifts as fully and completely as I possibly can, to enhance the people and the world around me. It's about not squandering them.

About knowing who I was created to be and then actually being that person, about being my very best self.

"It's about leaving a legacy, isn't it?" Tom asked me as he continued to reflect. In one question Tom summed up what I was trying to put into words.

"Exactly! Yes. You got it!" I said. "That's what I'm talking about. It's about fostering the kind of relationships to leave a good legacy. It's about taking my gifts and allowing them to be used to help make this world a little better."

Too quickly, we arrived at the restaurant, ending our conversation and interrupting my thoughts as we parked, walked into the restaurant, and were seated at a table. Hungry as we were to eat, we were both even hungrier to continue the conversation.

Those are the discussions we savor. Those are the kinds of conversations serving as the foundation for our marriages, as well as our friendship, and with others. It's those philosophical reflections connecting us ever more eternally to one another—and sharpening, ultimately, our relationship with God, whom we believe created us to have those kinds of relationships.

While we thoroughly enjoyed red beet and blue cheese salads with grilled salmon, we picked up the discussion again.

"So, you answered what success means to you personally," indicated Tom. "But, what about professionally? What does it mean to you in the work we do every day?"

My answer was very simple.

It's pretty much the same. It's about the relationships we develop and nurture and the legacy of grace and love we create through them.

Let me give an example. Years ago I had a girl approach me and ask if I would perform her wedding ceremony. The members of her immediate family were prominent members in my church and in the local community. They were very well to do. She and her fiancé started meeting with me regularly. During one of our conversations about their upbringings, I could sense something was wrong. I asked her what was troubling her.

She said, "I've never had a relationship with my dad; he's basically a stranger to me. He is nothing more than a paycheck. For as long as I can remember, my dad would leave for work before the sun came up and wouldn't arrive home until after I had already gone to bed. I don't know anything about him."

Her strong words were marked with sadness and anger, along with pain. I think the void she felt speaks to what we are trying to model for others. I'm reminded of two quotes from Saint Mother Teresa.

She would often say: "If you want to bring happiness to the whole world, go home and love your family." She would also say, "What can you do to promote world peace? Go home and love your family."

We both took a moment to consider her words. Nurturing relationships—is success. Developing and nurturing relationships, and offering grace and love through those relationships, is complicated. To do it well, to maintain healthy relationships, to extend grace and love—especially unconditional love as God has extended it to us—is a cosmic choice.

It's not a choice easily made; we often have to consciously follow through with it. It's not always natural, sometimes it's painful. Often we have to swallow pride and our egos; it requires us to see a situation from another person's perspective.

Throughout the rest of the afternoon, our discussion continued during our free moments after we left the restaurant and went about our day's work.

Success for us, we agreed, is not an accumulation of a certain amount of money or titles or degrees or positions to impress. All of those things can help us in some ways. But none of it matters to us if grace and love are not present over the entire journey. We want to be extenders of God's joy, grace, peace, compassion, and love to the best of our human ability. It begins within our own families and continues in every relationship we nurture. That's success.

———

DOWNWARD MOBILITY (MICHAEL)

*"The compassionate life is the life of downward mobility! In a society
in which upward mobility is the norm, downward mobility is not only
discouraged but even considered unwise, unhealthy, or downright stupid."*
-HENRI NOUWEN

A chapter from the book Tom and I were currently reading together, *Here and Now*, by Henri Nouwen, offers a small gem of wisdom about success.

Throughout his life, well-meaning people who encouraged him to go "higher up" had surrounded Nouwen. But, according to him, those voices, calling him to upward mobility, are completely absent from the Gospels. Instead, he contends, Jesus actually extended a message of downward mobility. Nouwen writes:

*This is the way of downward mobility, the descending way of Jesus. It is
the way toward the poor, the suffering, the marginal, the prisoners, the refugees, the lonely, the hungry, the dying, the tortured, the homeless—toward all
who ask for compassion.*

For many years, Henri Nouwen lived and served in a community for people living with intellectual disabilities, called Daybreak. One of his daily responsibilities was to minister to a man named Adam. Nouwen would get Adam up each morning, bathe him, shave him, dress him, comb his hair and feed him. It wasn't always a routine easy to administer. But he came to love it and find gladness in it. He even began to look forward to it. Nouwen writes about the cheer he experienced:

*The joy that compassion brings is one of the best-kept secrets of humanity.
It is a secret known to only a very few people, a secret that has to be rediscovered over and over again . . . Each time we return to where there is pain, we
get a glimpse of the joy that is not of this world.*

He and Adam developed a real love for one another. He said that the morning routine with Adam brought him some of the most precious moments of each day. Nouwen's words resonate with me and touch my heart.

I think of them as I begin my morning routine. It is a routine I have almost every morning with my son Matthew.

I help to get him up, change his often soaked pajamas, strip his wet bed, dress him, feed him breakfast, and walk him to the van that takes him to his day program.

Kathy and I give him a shower, shave him, feed him his meals, brush his teeth, change his diapers, trim his nails and generally attend to all his daily and personal needs. He requires complete attention. With tenderness and patience, we do our best to give him what he needs. To echo Nouwen's sentiment, most times it is a delight, a delight not of this world.

Sometimes, though, I am impatient and sometimes it's bothersome to be tender. When he won't cooperate or when he clings defiantly to the bed because he doesn't want to get out of it in the morning, it's trying to be patient. Or when he pees all over the floor or gets me all wet after I've taken a shower and dressed for the day, it's nearly impossible to feel pleasure. When he refuses to wear any of the clothing choices we offer him in the morning, when he flings his breakfast yogurt onto the floor, the wall, himself or us, or when he is banging his forehead until it's red and raw, it is not easy to see the beauty in the routine.

Love is not always appealing or pretty.

I have days with many tense and irate moments. There are tussles taking all my strength as I try to keep Matthew from hurting him or the house or us. There are nights when Kathy and I sigh with great exoneration when he is in bed and won't be driving us to aggravation again until the next day. I don't want to pretend that love keeps me feeling utterly satisfied and at peace all the time. Sometimes, daily life feels as if it's too much to handle. Some days, the first words out of my mouth are "bad" ones when he gets me all wet, smacks me and knocks my glasses off or stomps on my toes. All of it's inadvertent on his part. But still, it's often too much to take.

But those moments subside. Those moments drift away. Matthew's steel blue eyes—in those rare moments when he actually makes eye contact with me—are the most beautiful eyes I've ever seen. Maybe that's because eye contact with him (or any person with autism) is rare.

Matthew loves to go somewhere, anywhere, every day. To see his excitement when he understands we're preparing him for a car ride and time on the go is unparalleled. To hear his exuberant laugh when the car door opens for him to get in is truly music to our ears.

Understanding his needs and being patient with them and him can bring immense joy and I am grateful for that gift.

Downward mobility, as Nouwen describes it, is a descent toward those who need compassion. And, it can lead to a joy not of this world—if we let it.

One of the very important things Tom and I do for each other is to remind one another of where our core values lie. Success, we both believe, isn't just about material or financial acquisitions; it's about embodying an intimately relational way of living. It's being intentionally sensitive to others' needs, sacrificial, servant-minded, vulnerable in nature and generous in sprit. Our mutual reading and studying is about these values and others who embody them. We constantly strive to encourage each other as we both do our best to live these values in our personal and professional lives. Neither of us is impeccable at it. But knowing neither of us is alone in the striving certainly enables the effort to be much easier.

And the result is continually discovering this kind of downward mobility to be a deeply cherished way of life.

THIS MOMENT (TOM)

> *"Your greatest contribution to the kingdom of God*
> *may not be something you do, but someone you raise."*
> -ANDY STANLEY

Just before my head hit the pillow I opened Facebook one last time. I was hoping for an important message from a friend but it hadn't yet arrived. I quickly scanned the latest news feed for the day and a post by a girl, about my age, caught my eye.

She has been coping with cancer for many months and frequently writes about her journey and the lessons she is learning about gratitude along the way. I read her post and think about her incredible courage. I say a prayer for her. Then I fall fast asleep.

A few hours later, I wake up in a cold sweat. The clock reads 4:51a.m. As my mind registers the time—it's way too early to be awake on a Saturday morning—I consider the vivid details of my dream, or nightmare.

I rarely remember my dreams. But this one, I couldn't forget.

"I was in the doctor's office surrounded by close family members and friends. Sarah and our kids were there. My dad was there. Michael was there. Everyone in the waiting room seemed intense. A few people were in the corner of the room, huddled together, eyes closed, praying fervently. Some others, especially my dad, kept looking at me, trying to gauge my emotions at such a pivotal moment in my life. I kept thinking to myself, "Guys, this isn't a big deal. Nothing is wrong. I'm still too young for anything to BE wrong."

Normally, I'm the emotional one! These people are the ones I lean on in my most troublesome moments. Even Sarah, who is normally far more emotionally stable than I am, is crying and concerned. The more I look at her, with tears running down her face, the more anxious I get. The moment is a serious one. It feels like we are waiting in line for a funeral service. Are we waiting in line for a funeral service?

Luke, our five-year-old son at the time, asks if he can sit on my lap. Madelyn and Mya, our two-year-old twins, are still too young to have any idea what is happening. They continue coloring in their coloring books.

My mind starts wandering to the responsibilities demanding my attention. It's a Saturday. It's early November and winter is almost here; I have leaves to rake, grass to mow, wood to chop for the wood stove. I have writing to do. I have a sermon to finalize for Sunday morning. I have a huge list of emails that need responses. The list goes on and on.

"Can we just go home already!?" I restlessly think to myself.

I keep looking at the clock on my cell phone. How much longer do we have to wait!!!? This is crazy.

Our children are being more patient than I am—which rarely, if ever, happens. The door to the waiting room opens.

The doctor enters. His face tells the story. He walks up to me. He grabs my hand. "Mr. Kaden." I want to turn around and look at my Dad; no one ever calls me Mr. Kaden. But, he is looking at me. He can't be talking to me, I think. He must be talking to my Dad. Right? But, no. He is talking to me.

"You are dying," the doctor says. "It won't be long now. I'm terribly sorry."

Several "ughs" and "awes" and "no's" are expressed out loud by everyone in the room. One person screams. Sarah and the kids cluster around me. Many tears are shed.

And, then I wake up.

I lie in bed staring in the dark at the ceiling. The only sound I hear is the sound of Sarah's deep inhales and exhales, asleep next to me.

I hear a whisper in my ear: Don't miss THIS moment. I look around the room; it's dark and cold and scary. "Who said that?" I say out loud. I hear the voice again.

Don't miss THIS moment.

I grab the flashlight sitting on my nightstand. Other than the two of us, the room is empty and silent.

My head hits the pillow again. I hear the same voice: Don't miss THIS moment. My mind wanders.

At once, like rapid-fire snapshots of my life, my mind shows me situations having come and gone, no longer to be re-lived again. Missed opportunities. Missed moments. Missed memories.

In each circumstance, joy, happiness, and goodness was standing in front of me, ready to be received and embraced, but I didn't notice.

I think of innocent little Luke, tapping my shoulder several times, begging me to look at his dinosaur painting.

Not right now, Luke, I need to get this email finished.

I think of Lillian, who was seven, standing in front of me in her *Frozen* costume, wanting me to tell her how she looks better than Elsa did in the movie.

I'm on an important phone call. Just give me a few minutes.

I think of Madelyn, standing in the playroom, yelling loudly, as she mispronounces words: "Daddy, do yew want to do dis puzzew wit me?"

I need to finish the dishes now, Madelyn, and then we can play.

I'm not sure how long I lay in bed, before heading downstairs to write, but it was long enough for the lesson to be felt, learned, and—I pray—grasped.

I grab my journal.

> *God, I'm thankful to be alive. I'm thankful to be awake!*
>
> *I want to thank you for moments such as this. Thank you for always "speaking" even at the most random times and in the most random situations.*
>
> *The message I sense you are trying to convey is an important one; sometimes I need to feel certain things before responding. I need to feel things "deep within my bowels," like Jesus felt things "deep within His bowels."*
>
> *I've been living life in the fast lane, zooming in and out of lanes, hoping to arrive at my destination as rapidly as possible. You know my areas of weakness and brokenness. You know I'm wired as a "results guy" (because you wired me).*
>
> *Sometimes, my motives are the right ones. I want so badly to see the kingdom expanded. I want to see the kingdom come here upon the earth as it is in heaven. I want my life to make a difference and I want to be a part of movement and activity and seeing lives changed by the power of love—the same love I have received. The challenge for me though, is that so much of life in the kingdom comes slowly, like a small mustard seed, growing up from the ground over many years. I don't often get to look at the corn I've planted or the fields I have mowed . . . and it seems impossible for me to simply LET GO. I need to be reminded, daily, my worth doesn't come from what I accomplish or produce. It comes from loving the person in front of me.*

Someone sent me two quotes yesterday about parenting.

"Your greatest contribution to the kingdom of God may not be something you do, but someone you raise."—Andy Stanley

"Parenting: The days are long but the years are short."—Anonymous

I've had an impossible time "leaving work at work." I've been finding myself becoming emotionally disconnected to the people closest to me, the ones you have called me to love the most. Sometimes the days seem to go on forever, especially with our kids, but the years are going by in a blink of an eye . . . and I don't want to miss them.

The many images of my children replaying in my head last night after the dream were harsh images to see, but I'm so grateful to see them and feel them. I've extended so much energy focusing on the things of the past, things I can't change, and things of the future, things I can't control; I'm missing the precious moments right in front of me.

I'm asking for you to show me how to live in the present, being grateful for what IS, rather than what COULD be or SHOULD be, and receiving THIS moment. "THIS is the day the Lord has made, let (me) rejoice and be glad in it." THIS is the only day I have!

I'm reminded of a statement of Jesus': "For what do we have if we get all the world and lose our own souls? What can we give to buy back our souls?."

What good is it if I extend all this energy for "the kingdom" but miss the small things (or the small ones) before me?

Lord, have mercy.

Lord, hear my prayer.

I finish writing and grab a second cup of coffee. I pick up my Bible and open to the Psalms. Most mornings I read two Old Testament passages and one New Testament passage. I start with a passage from the Psalms, which reads:

"Children are a gift from the Lord; they are a reward from him. Children born to a young man are like arrows in a warrior's hands. How joyful is the man whose quiver is full of them!" Psalm 127:3-5 (NLT)

I then open to Matthew's Gospel, chapter 18. Here is what I read: "About that time the disciples came to Jesus and asked, "Who is greatest in the King-dom of Heaven? Jesus called a little child to him and put the child among them. Then he said, 'I tell you the truth, unless you turn from your sins and become like little children, you will never get into the Kingdom of Heaven. So anyone who becomes as humble as this little child is the greatest in the Kingdom of Heaven.'"

It's still early but with the most recent clock change, all four of our children are awake. Sarah worked the evening shift at the hospital. She needs space to rest. I close the bedroom door and turn my attention to the kids.

Madelyn sits down on her potty in the middle of our dining room. Trying to be helpful, she accidently dumps her filled potty across the hardwood floor. She then tries to clean herself to prove to the world she is, in her words, "a big girl now." She has never tried to clean herself before, so it doesn't end well.

Mya says she needs to go potty. Sadly, I'm too late sitting her down and she relieves herself in her pants.

I clean up both messes, wash my hands, and start making breakfast. We don't have too many free and unscheduled mornings together these days, so I want it to be a special one. Pancakes and eggs.

The kids ask to help. "Okay," I say unenthusiastically.

The words I hear in the middle of the night cross my mind again.

"Don't miss THIS moment."

A glass of orange juice gets knocked over by one of the children, splashing all over my shirt and pants.

"Seriously!" I want to scream, but refrain. I pull some clean clothes out of the laundry basket and quickly change my clothes.

The pancake batter requires several eggs. "I want to do it!" Lillian yells.

"This isn't going to end well." I prophetically think for the second time and whisper under my breath. She doesn't hear me.

It doesn't end well. Several eggshells end up in the bowl. Or does it end, well?! "Don't miss THIS moment." I hear the faint voice one more time, ringing in my ears and in my heart.

My mind wanders for a moment to dinner out the previous night. An older couple sat at a table next to ours. They made a comment to me, which bothered me at the time, because it's something everyone says. But they were speaking about the very same principles I am trying desperately to follow this morning:

"Those moments are precious! Don't miss them. Trust us. They come and go in a blink of an eye."

The rest of my day, I focus on admiring my kids, genuinely admiring them. Every mispronounced word the twins yell out, all the smiles, all the laughter, all the simplicity only kids with no worries can express, I soak it all up. I celebrate each child's own sense of individuality and uniqueness.

To be compassionate is to receive each moment, both joyful and sorrowful, with open arms, open eyes, and open hearts. THIS moment is the legacy. THIS moment is the only one I have. God is here and God is present, as God is in every moment and every situation, so THIS moment is a momentous one. I vow to try to remember that. THIS moment is all any of us have.

Here is another one of those lessons Michael and I strive to remember and encourage in one another. THIS moment is truly the only one we have. Being present—truly, completely, purposefully—is not only something we try to personify in our own lives; we also try to model it and encourage it in every speaking engagement, every message we express in every interaction with those to whom we listen. THIS moment is a gift. That presence has bound and grown our friendship into a place of unreserved trust and sanctuary. We want everyone to have that kind of confidence and refuge in their lives, in their relationships, too.

According to Dr. Laura Cartensen, a psychology professor at Stanford and the author of *A Long Bright Future: Happiness, Health, and Financial Security in an Age of Increased Longevity,* men, on average, die five years younger than women, and researchers believe a big part of the reason is social isolation. In other words, men are dying, to some extent, because they undervalue friendship.

It saddens us when people don't have at least someone in their lives who is a beacon of light, a safety valve, a reminder of our value, a convey of unrelenting love. It is especially important as males, who far too often don't have anyone who can be with them in THIS moment, to savor and cherish the gift THIS moment, every moment, can be.

———————

HOW CAN I LOVE YOU BETTER? (MICHAEL)

"Your sacred space is where you can find yourself again and again."
- JOSEPH CAMPBELL

We've written about our annual December 23 Christmas celebrations, a sacrosanct and cherished ritual for us. We'd like to describe our tradition as it unfolded one year. We hope to offer an example of how we aim to love the important people in our lives—our family and our friends—better. Our conversation wasn't planned. But getting to know one another in a deeper way is commonly intentional.

It is two nights before Christmas 2014. We are sitting in front of the huge stone fireplace in the Iberian Lounge at the Hotel Hershey, in Hershey Pennsylvania. The room is beautiful, decorated for the season, dimly lit, warm and inviting.

That place, on the evening of December 23 each year, continues to be a sacred place for us. As always, we order something to drink and toast, "Merry Christmas!"

We sit back, soothed by the fire in front of us, grateful for the season. We are relaxed and comfortable. We exchange gifts. We have no agenda except to enjoy a relaxing holiday evening together. We both feel very open tonight. Reflective. Willing to explore.

It doesn't take long. Tom asks the first question.

"I want to learn how I can love you better, how I can be the best friend, brother and partner I can be for you. So, what is the most demanding thing to love about me?"

I gulped. No one had ever asked a question of such intensity of me before. The risks for both of us were high. If I answer too quickly it might seem as if I've been holding onto some resentments or grudges for too long; having a ready reply might imply some deeper work needs to be done between us. Not answering at all would seem evasive, lacking in the openness we say we model. I could hurt him deeply or I could be dismissive with his honest desire to know how to help our relationship grow even stronger. I didn't want to ruin the night nor did I want to cast an awkward cloud between us over the holidays.

"After you answer me, I'd like to turn the question back on myself, if that's okay. I want to let you know how you can love me even better."

I gulped again. "Oh no," I thought to myself. "Did he have something he had been waiting to communicate to me? Something that would be dreadful for me to hear? Was his answer going to wound? Would it be unpleasant for me to hear?"

I took this moment seriously. I wanted to offer a thoughtful, sensitive, helpful answer. I replied, "I need to go to the bathroom. I do want to answer your question. I want to answer it well. Just give me a minute or two and I'll be right back. I'll weigh in then."

It bought me a few moments of time to reflect on the type of answer I wanted to give. When I returned, I was ready.

"First, I want you to know I have absolutely no interest in fixing you or pointing out your faults and flaws. I don't. I want you to know that the only thing I want to do is to love you unconditionally, the best I can. There are enough others who like to offer their fixes and their critiques and their suggestions about how you—or any of us—can be better. I just want to simply celebrate you for who you are and to show you that you are beloved."

"I know you do and I am very grateful for that," Tom quietly and softly responded.

"But, since you want me to answer your question—and it's Christmas—I'll respect your request.

"Sometimes your insecurity is distressing for me. Sometimes you put yourself down and think you don't know what you are doing. Sometimes I feel lumped in and think you believe neither of us knows what we're doing here.

"In my mind, I see in you someone who does know what you're doing. You are smarter than you give yourself credit for. Your ideas and your vision are tremendous. I am awed by what you do in our work together, in how you manage the harrowing, delicate balance of being a husband and a dad to four young kids. We've made it this far because of your commitment and drive, because of your faith and compassion, because of your abilities to rise to every occasion and do what needs to be done.

"When I see you doubting your abilities and questioning your goodness, it wounds me for you. I want you to know how gifted you are and how much your vision has brought us to this place and how I believe it will carry us to even greater places. I believe in you, even when you don't believe in yourself. Every day you impress me and give me confidence to believe in what we are doing.

"I have a tough time when you doubt God has gifted you with something special. I see a much better, stronger, more capable, generous, compassionate person in you than you do in yourself. I know most of the time each of us is our own harshest critic, we know our darkest places much more intimately than anyone else does. But . . . you don't recognize how much you offer and how vital you are . . . which worries me and causes me to question if you think we don't have the gifts and faith to continue our mission."

I stopped. Tom was silent for a moment before he responded.

"Your answer wasn't the answer I expected. There were other things I was sure you'd say. I'm going to have to think about what you said for a while. Hmmm . . ."

He chuckled and then said, "I thought you would have brought up about my driven nature and how I can sometimes focus so much on the end goal, forgetting to stop and celebrate along the way. Or, I thought you'd mention my tendency to see the glass as half empty and how I forget to recognize and receive the gifts before me. I actually wrote down your words and I will have to ponder on them for a long time. Thank you! What an incredible gift to me."

"Now I'm the one who needs to use the restroom," Tom stated.

"Sure, but then it's your turn!" I responded.

Tom returned to his seat next to the fire. It took him a few moments before he began.

"First off, I want you to know, I hadn't thought much about the question before we arrived here tonight. Maybe it's the drink that made me ask it?!"

We both laughed.

"I treasured all that you revealed a few moments ago. Much of what I have to say dovetails nicely. Like you mentioned, I have no desire to try and fix you or turn you into someone other than the remarkable person you are. You are an absolute gift to me! This is all about knowing and being known more intimately and fully; all about loving one another the way Christ loves us. I want to know how to love you the best way I can and to have the best friendship and partnership in ministry we can have together.

"As you know, our greatest gift can also be our greatest vulnerability. I've mentioned hundreds of times before about how much I appreciate your consistency, your positivity and your gratitude. Your ability to see the glass half full in every situation stretches me like no one ever has. You know all my areas of brokenness and how I often labor with wanting things to be flawless.

"Sometimes your positivity can actually foster disconnection between the two of us. Here is what I mean. People in distress don't need clichés. Life is unyielding for most of us and clichés only create more discomfort. Only you and Sarah know about all I am facing physically, emotionally, and spiritually on any given day.

"Sometimes your positivity can almost come across as a cliché . . . and I know that isn't what you are intending. But when it happens I don't feel safe to be myself, to express my suffering, to express my disappointment, to express frustration. This may seem a bit strong but it almost seems like you are living in a dream world, out of touch with the realities I am experiencing? Make sense?"

"It does make sense," I told him. "And I appreciate you expressing it. Kathy has said the same thing to me before, about seeing the good in everything. She is also irritated at times."

I went on. "I want to love you in the best way possible, so how can I best do that for you?"

Tom thought for a moment and then answered. "There are days, when what I need from you, is the same thing we try to offer to everyone else who is angry, depressed, lonely or hurting in some way. We don't stand outside the rain cloud, pointing at the rain cloud, but we walk under the rain cloud with them. We don't say much, other than maybe, 'I'm sorry. This sucks. I don't have anything to say. I'm here with you.' You don't need to point out the positive for me. Just walk with me through the rain."

We left the lounge and walked outside. It was surprisingly mild for late December. Tom had another gift for me, something we could enjoy together. He handed me a bag. Inside were two cigars. Our conversation continued out on the terrace of the hotel and as we walked around the moonlit grounds with cigars. It turned out to be one of the most meaningful discussions we have ever had.

We all want and need someone in our lives with whom we can have those kinds of discussions—open, intimate, of great depth, the kind of conversation permitting us to know and be known in vital, authentic ways. Those kinds of relationships don't just happen. They take intentionality and investment.

We have to start with the things we have in common, especially cherished values. We have to extend grace and gratitude for one another's unique gifts and for the contrasting perspectives we will surely bring to the relationship. Any close relationship requires perseverance and continual commitment not to give up or walk away when there are differences in thinking and reaction.

We have to be safe havens for one another, offering sanctuary and a haven from the harsher, more critical ways of the world. We have to develop and live in trust, holding one another's best interest as our own. We have to be willing to enter into crucial conversations and to be willing to listen with great patience.

We need to be willing to ask questions helping reveal the true sentiment of every situation, no matter how emotionally and spiritually intimate the topic may be, which requires listening intentionally and well, listening closely to the nuances and inflections of another's voice and body language, to go beyond the surface and into another's heart.

But with the right people, all of it is worth it.

We create sacred spaces in our daily routines in ministry and friendship together in order to do this, to have a relationship of meaning and of depth. Neither of us like to remain at surface-level discussions. "What do you think of this weather?" "How about those Yankees?" "Can you believe how the Phillies played last night?"

By our nearly daily walks in parks and other natural settings, by committing to our ritual of celebrating Christmas and the year gone by at the same time, in the same place, in the same way, by asking penetrating questions and being willing to listen to and to explore together the answers, we foster a bond celebrating our common values and gifts. We strengthen a bond carrying us through times of hesitation and opposition, and connecting us spiritually in friendship, as well as in partnership. There is always more to learn and more to reveal to nurture a deeper respect and love.

We want everyone to have similar unions with other people in their lives—with their spouses and partners, with their closest friends and family members, with at least some other person who can echo (though pale in comparison) in some healing way the grace, unconditional love and devotion of God. We have been profoundly blessed to have those kinds of relationships with our wives, with whom we have these same kinds of discussions and emotionally intimate connections, as well as with one another.

Asking one another how we can love each other better prompted us to ask the same of our wives a few days later. And, we encourage you to ask the same of those you love, too.

We always make time to nurture a deeper, fuller, more sacred love. Tom and I do our best to model what a relationship of grace and love means between us. We try to exhibit depth. We try to model trust. We try to nurture forgiveness and greater understanding. We hope and pray you can do the same.

It's what's success means to us.

Home Tonight? (Tom)

"Be kind, for everyone you meet is fighting a hard battle."
-PLATO

"You have made us for yourself, O Lord,
and our hearts are restless until they rest in you."
-SAINT AUGUSTINE

". . . The real trap, however, is self-rejection. As soon as someone accuses
me or criticizes me, as soon as I am rejected, left alone, or abandoned, I
find myself thinking, "Well, that proves once again that I am a nobody."
. . . [My dark side says,] I am no good . . . I deserve to be pushed aside,
forgotten, rejected, and abandoned. Self-rejection is the greatest enemy
of the spiritual life because it contradicts the sacred voice that calls us the
"Beloved." Being the Beloved constitutes the core truth of our existence."
-HENRI NOUWEN

I ROLL OVER and grab my phone to see what time it is. I sigh. The clock reads 2:50.

It is the middle of the night and I am unable to sleep. I am in distress. Sometimes the pain comes and it goes, like a gust of wind on a cold winter's night. Sometimes it comes and stays—like tonight—a most unwelcome guest in my life.

In addition to many broken bones, chronic headaches, concussions, and surgeries I've experienced throughout my life, I live with a chronic condition called Fibromyalgia, and it can bring severe discomfort.

Earlier in the evening, my discomfort level reached, on a scale of one to 10, an unmanageable 10. It wouldn't go away. It has been an especially bad night. There just isn't much, other than pain medicine with the side effect of dulling my mind to ease my burden. Five hours later my pain level has decreased to a three out of 10. Thank God! Physically, I am feeling better; emotionally, it's a very different story. It's not the physical issue keeping me awake now, but the thoughts and insecurities gripping me.

My mind goes, as it so often does, to the late Henri Nouwen, prominent writer, speaker, and spiritual director. In one of his books, he relates a story of a man he worked with at L'Arche, a facility in Toronto, Canada, for individuals with special needs. The co-worker, a middle-aged man, would often ask Henri two questions— questions Henri would meditate on almost daily.

"Henri, so where's your home?"

Knowing the emotional needs of those around him, the man would then ask a second, more poignant question:

"Are you home tonight?"

Throughout Henri's life and ministry he openly spoke and wrote about the emotional distress he faced internally. In many of his writings, he relates about his personal experiences with depression, loneliness, sadness and a general lack of intimacy with God and others. On the outside, Henri would appear to be someone who had it all together. On the inside, it was a very different story.

Henri's writings and insights strongly resonate with me because I often feel as if he is writing my story. I'm someone who, on any given day, is battling emotional—and even mental—pain, along with the physical.

I recently spoke with an older man, who, having read our first book, said to me, "You are someone who seems to have it together. You have a beautiful family; you have a beautiful wife; you are in shape. I have heard you speak before and you are a gifted communicator. I've read your book, which truly spoke to me. And yet, you have far more going on below the surface than I had any idea was ever going on."

I close my eyes and hope to capture some elusive sleep.

The next morning, I arrive at Michael's son's house where we plan to work for the day. And what a day it is! It's a spectacular summer day and the Internet connection is strong enough for us to work outside. We are sitting on a deck overlooking the refreshing, calming waters of a swimming pool.

We have several Skype, Facebook, and email conversations scheduled with people from across the country, as well as around the world. We will listen as they share their struggles with self-worth, self-doubt, sadness, disappointment, sickness, and matters of faith. Blog writing and a board meeting in the evening are also on our agenda for today.

There is almost nothing I enjoy more than being able to enter into the chaos of someone else's' life and story by offering, with God's help and strength, ease and support. To help other people know they aren't alone. To show I empathize their brokenness, pain, and hurt. Doing so gives me—and Michael, too—energy, fulfillment, and enthusiasm for life.

But, last night took its toll on me. Externally, it seems like I have it all together.

I have a beautiful family of six. I have a wife and four children who love me. I co-founded a non-profit making a difference, we pray, in the lives of those who need "someone to tell it to" and I get to work with my best friend.

And yet, thoughts from the previous night continue to occupy my mind. Like a wrestler who has been pinned, I don't have the strength to get up. Internally, I feel vulnerable, weak, and worthless. And, although it doesn't happen often, today I also feel unlovable.

We begin our day, as we do most days together, offering prayers and quieting our hearts and minds to receive the love of God. We share how we are doing and also how we can pray for each other.

I turn to Michael on this picture perfect summer day and I share as freely and candidly as a child with no inhibitions. I tell him what I'm feeling so acutely:

"Many days I feel grossly insecure." "I know you do." "Today is one of those days." Michael then asks in his calming, caring, and sensitive voice: "What is making you feel so insecure today?"

I explain. "Yesterday I had a difficult conversation. Without even knowing he was doing it, a friend said something making me feel like I'm not measuring up. It was something simple. But for whatever reason it hit a nerve. It's like a scab on my knee that doesn't seem to go away; it keeps getting jarred and bloodied from time to time. And if it's not a disquieting conversation, well, then it's an inauspicious email message, and if it's not about a message I've received, then it's about the insecurity I harbor about my abilities as a dad. And if it isn't insecurity about my abilities as a dad, it's my insecurity about not providing enough financially for my family. And if it's not my financial insecurities, then it's my need to feel like I am making a difference in others' lives, for my life to have resonance and merit. And if it's not for my life to have resonance and merit, it's my insecurity about leaving a legacy . . . and the list goes on and on and on."

"What can I do for you, besides pray, this morning?" Michael asked.

I affirmed the value of prayer and then told him that talking, asking questions about how I was feeling and why, and listening is most helpful. Since our conversations with others weren't scheduled until later in the morning, we had time to explore the darkness together and shed some light in it.

So, for the next two hours, we did. One of things most helpful for me was when Michael confessed: "I still feel as if I'm a child. I feel as if I'm a little boy in a grown-up man's body. I don't know if I've ever felt as if I'm an adult, someone who has the answers, who has it all together. Instead, I often feel as if I'm an imposter, a boy pretending to be a man. I'm still waiting for the time when I'll feel as if I've reached adulthood, whatever that means. I wonder if almost all of us feel as if we're imposters. The more we hear the stories of others, the more it sounds as if so many of us are feeling a similar way. We're all insecure about some things, many things, actually."

Michael then asked,

"Are there any areas of your life where or when you actually feel secure? If there are, let's talk about them."

What seemed like a simple question with an easy answer took some time to process.

"Yes! Yes, there are actually many areas where I feel comfortable in my own skin. I feel 'at home' and at peace when I am hearing God say good things about me, coming through studying or meditating on a passage of the Bible. Other times, as Nouwen says, I need to be silent and listen to God's voice calling me 'A Beloved Son.' Yet, often, it comes through my connection with others—with Sarah, with my kids, and certainly, with you, too."

In moments and conversations such as these, I am drawn to the humanness of Jesus: those moments when he had a righteous anger at how people were treating one another; the tiredness he experienced when the weight of ministry was so great; the utter sadness over his friend's death, moving him to tears; his desperate and fearful anxiety the night before he died; his abandonment when one of his closest friends turned him over to those who would crucify him; or the excruciating loneliness he felt on the cross when he felt like God turned away from him.

Being a "follower of Jesus" doesn't free us from feelings of self-doubt, worthlessness and insecurity. In fact, it's just the opposite; it makes us totally aware of our humanness and our need for God and to receive God's love.

Who among us has ever been free of feelings of anxiety, fear, anger, pain, loneliness, abandonment, betrayal or insecurity?

All of the emotions we feel as human beings, Jesus felt, as a human being too. The emotions I was expressing that day were emotions God felt, in the form of Jesus, giving me comfort then, and still doing so now. Michael and I believe in a God who knows what it's like to hurt, who knows what it's like to be afraid, and who knows what it's like to feel alone. God felt and experienced all aspects of the human condition. We believe in a God who is present with us in our emotions and our feelings, because God knows intimately what they feel like.

On a hot, summer day, we talked about our humanness, finding strength God's presence, knowing we aren't—ever—alone in any of it.

But, what can you do in between those times of confessing with someone you trust? What can you do each day to be reminded of your belovedness in your humanness, as a child of God? For me, it's simply this: I pray, I journal, I focus on being grateful, and I meditate on certain passages of scripture (Psalm 139 is a favorite of mine—"I am fearfully and wonderfully made").

And, how do we relate to others who reveal and express their insecurities? What do we do to support them? This is what Michael does for me. He reminds me regularly of the things I do well. He listens intentionally and allows me to say whatever I need to say without judging it or me. He will reveal his own insecurities, reminding me I'm not alone in mine. He doesn't try to fix me and he never trivializes how I am feeling.

It's exactly what we try to do for everyone else we engage with, too. Everyone has insecurities and we all need someone to allow us to be open about them. Michael allowed me to be open on that hot, sunny day on the deck.

My mind goes back to that day and how I felt. Tough night. Better morning. That's what it's like to be home. Safe. Knowing I am loved. Secure.

"Home is the center of my being where I can hear the voice that says 'You are my beloved, upon you my favor rests'." Henri Nouwen

Wounds

*"People have scars. In all sorts of unexpected places. Like secret roadmaps
of their personal histories. Diagrams of all their old wounds.
Most of our wounds heal, leaving nothing behind but a scar.
But some of them don't. Some wounds we carry with us everywhere
and though the cut's long gone, the pain still lingers."*
- MEREDITH GREY

*"When we're looking for compassion, we need someone who is
deeply rooted, is able to bend and, most of all,
embraces us for our strengths and struggles."*
-BRENÉ BROWN

SHIVERING, we stood in the rapidly falling snow—freezing, disturbed, and
awkwardly silent. Our wounds had gotten the best of us. The tension between
us was as strong as we'd ever felt it. The question before us was:

How are we going to deal with this?

Wounds. We all have them. The bruised knee of rejection. The bloodied lip of
perfectionism. The stubbed toe of a lack of self-worth. The black eye of regret.

Yet, for many of us, those wounds remain hidden to the rest of the world,
only to be opened up when they are causing distress to someone else—often times
without us even knowing it. Often those old wounds lie sleeping until something
triggers an awakening. When that happens those wounds cause us to lash out or
hurt others and we may have no understanding or awareness of what is going on at
a deeper level.

People often ask us, "How do you guys spend so much time together and not
get on each other's nerves?" After one of our speaking engagements, one business-
person even adamantly declared, "It's only a matter of time; something is going to
split you guys up!"

The person was serious.

Our relationship, like all relationships, is sometimes messy, fractured, broken
and in need of healing, restoration, and grace—and a lot of super glue too! It's

35

important to be open about that. No relationship, especially a very close one, is perfect. Though rare, we have moments of misunderstanding, miscommunication and misinterpretation. At times we are insecure, impatient, and insensitive. Often, those moments come unexpectedly.

The day we stood in the cold followed an incredibly demanding and nerve-racking few weeks for us. The appointments, speaking engagements, and general administrative responsibilities had been piling up for some time and we were worn-out and short-tempered. One brutally cold day in the middle of January, our souls were brutally cold, too. The tension could be cut with a switchblade.

HOW TOM WAS FEELING

I began the day feeling resentful. Our non-profit ministry was in transition and I was unable to deal with the confusion happening all around us. It felt as if I was walking into a messy house loaded with boxes and boxes of junk in every corner of every room. I thrive when I can express my creativity and vision openly and freely. However, I also need and appreciate some sense of stability and rootedness along the way. I need at least one "clutter-free," protected and sheltered room in the house. You can ask my wife!

The deeper issue for me was timidity about the future of our organization. I was worried I had made some bad decisions, keeping us from moving toward sustainability. Like many men, one of my greatest wounds in life, is feeling as if I am not measuring up in some way, and on this particular day I was feeling exposed. I didn't even know it at the time.

HOW MICHAEL WAS FEELING

I was feeling vulnerable and afraid too—on the surface it seemed as if it was for different reasons. But, when I dug deeply into what I was feeling, I realized I feared I wasn't measuring up, as well. When I'm tired and feeling particularly overworked, I can descend into a place of feeling as if I'm inadequate to the task. I can focus like a laser on what needs to be done, but I take it all too seriously, as if everything falls on my shoulders. I have to constantly work internally to keep myself from taking on the mantle of a martyr.

EVERYTHING "HIT THE FAN"

The snow continued to fall outside, increasing the murkiness of the day. It was rush hour; our respective drives home were not going to be easy. The rapidly falling snow was creating increasingly treacherous conditions, symbolic for how we were feeling toward one another—cold, halting, apprehensive.

We were standing in the parking lot of a Panera Bread, ready to say goodbye for the day when everything seemed to "hit the fan" between us. The tension we were both feeling began to erupt.

How would we respond to one another? It's part of human nature in moments like these for our minds to go to dark and extreme places:

Will our friendship make it through this tension?

Will our working relationship be fractured forever?

What will the future hold for us personally and professionally?

We each had those thoughts, which caused more fear, more stress, more anxiety, more inadequacies, more shame, and more confusion.

While we are supposed to be a "model" for how to have healthy relationships and how to treat each other with respect, grace, compassion, and unconditional love—we were anything but "models" then. We didn't treat each other well as the snow continued to fall all around us.

Tom: "So things obviously aren't 'right' between us."

Michael: "Yeah it's been a bad day."

Tom, defiantly: "We should just call it a day and go home."

Walking toward our cars, almost ready to leave, we both stopped, knowing we didn't want to leave like this. Although, both of us handle conflict differently.

MICHAEL'S APPROACH

I am slower to respond because I need time to process what I want to say before speaking. And when we communicate with one another, especially in tense moments, I want the timing to be right. I want very much not to say things in the heat of the moment I might regret.

TOM'S APPROACH

I process outwardly. I like to talk things out quickly with the hope of finding answers as we unwrap what we are feeling. Those differences in reaction presented a problem. There was awkward silence as the snow began covering us both. I broke the ice: "You seem stressed out today. Is there something I'm not doing?"

Michael: "No, it's nothing about you." Tom: "What is it then?" Michael: "I don't know." Tom: "Well, I can sense you are mad and it seems directed at me." Michael: "I'm sorry. It's not directed at you."

Tom: "What is it about? Because we are at a standstill as an organization until we can get this crap figured out!"

More silence. More shivering. More snow piling up on top of us. More awkward silence.

MICHAEL OPENS UP

Even though I knew the conversation needed to happen, I didn't want the conversation to happen. I was embarrassed about my real feelings. But, I also knew I would piss Tom off more if I kept stonewalling.

My real feelings came from an email we received earlier in the day. When I read it, I felt like I was being excluded from decisions about the future of the organization; I felt as if my voice didn't matter and I didn't belong. The email was sent by someone associated with the non-profit and, without realizing it, the sender put Tom in the middle.

Unaware how Tom was likewise feeling incredulous and weighed down, I told him: "It was the email!"

Tom: "What email?"

Michael: "The one we got earlier today. This is not the first time we have gotten this message (encouraging Tom to join a certain group, but not me) and it has bothered me every time. I feel like I'm being left out."

Tom: "Left out of what?"

Michael: "I feel like I'm being left out because when it comes to future planning, maybe people think I'm too old and my thoughts don't matter."

Tom: "Well, I'm sorry about the email, I had no idea. Why didn't you voice your feelings earlier when it happened?"

Michael: "I guess I was embarrassed. I also needed time to figure out how I was feeling."

Tom: "I'll be honest with you; I'm frustrated because this has turned into a much larger issue than it needs to be! I'm already feeling like our ministry is going nowhere and this has put us at even more of a standstill."

Michael said nothing more. The silence was deafening. We could hear the snow falling all around us. I ended the conversation quickly by saying, "I'm freezing and it's time to go."

We got in our cars and departed.

THE DRIVE HOME

On the drive home, both of us fixated on the conversation; we thought about what we should have said or could have said or knew we shouldn't have said. We started placing more shame on ourselves and more blame on each other; our wounds were bleeding all over the place.

"Is this it?" we each thought. "I wonder if we can overcome this roadblock in our relationship. What a sad way for this to end."

We both felt sick to our stomachs and broken in our hearts, trying to figure out what to do next.

MICHAEL SENDS AN EMAIL

In the evening, I responded to the voice inside my heart, the voice both of us was hearing, *"Don't let it go on like this. Our relationship is too important to throw your hands up in the air and say the hell with it."*

So I sat down and wrote Tom an email:

I will sleep better tonight (a relative thing lately) if I write this out. Maybe it can help you too.

It's happened before. We're both tired, pressured, overwhelmed, scared, and uncertain about how all this can come together and we desperately want more light to shine ahead of us to show us it will all be okay. And so, when it builds to a boiling point, it doesn't take much to unwind us.

I'm sorry about what happened today. I apologize for any way I rubbed raw your wounds and made you feel less than the wonderfully created person you are. I'm appalled I hurt you and created an atmosphere of tension and disagreement. That was never—is never—my intention. I regret my wounds collided with you.

We can talk about why everything happened if you want. I would like that. In short, as is typical, my greatest gift is also, on the flip side, my greatest insecurity. My sensitivity works remarkably well when it's focused on others, but painfully so when it's focused on me. I wish it could be different—and with your help and forbearance—I will make sure it is so.

My deepest wounds—feeling left out, feeling as if I don't measure up— got the best of me today. I'd love to talk more.

Add the underlying trepidation of the impending results of Kathy's CT scan today, I was surely even more sensitive than usual. Again, I'm sorry it created strain and made today what it was.

I feel as if I let you down.

I pray you will accept my apology and tomorrow—and all our tomor- rows—can be better.

TOM RESPONDS

My phone vibrated. I received a new email. It was late at night and I was al- ready in bed, but I too, was planning to reach out to him. I read the message twice and then quickly responded with a long text message.

You beat me to the punch. I was going to send you a quick message expressing my apologies over how things went down today. I'm sorry for the way I responded and how my 'wound' affected your wound, causing more heartache and pain. We can talk this through tomorrow. Maybe we can meet early for breakfast before our first meeting? I hope you can get the rest you need.

Even though we know each other's core wounds, we are constantly learning more about each other. We continually learn what to do and what not to do, what to say and what not to say in tense situations. We intentionally try not to push on those sore spots, knowing if we do, we will cause even greater harm; but inevitably, as human beings in relationships, we sometimes hurt each other. It's expected we will cause one another heartbreak and even just flat out annoy one another based on our individualism at times. The important thing is not to leave the wound hanging between us.

THE NEXT DAY

The next day we met at a diner.

Before the conversation began, we took a few moments to pray together, expressing sorrow to God, and to each other, for how we had treated one another intentionally and unintentionally the previous day. We asked for God's mercy and mercy from one another. We thanked God for the model of unconditional, unending, perfect love to have for one another.

We then talked very openly about our wounds and how those wounds don't define who we are.

Tom: "Even though our wounds have healed, the scars always remain. And sometimes they get bumped into or scraped unexpectedly, causing more pain, blame, and shame."

Michael: "Exactly. Our wounds don't define us, but they do make us who we are as individuals. We can't avoid them, but we can examine them with each other and bind them up together."

The conversation was intense. It quickly became very vulnerable and emotionally intimate. Through it, we learned much more about one another and ourselves. During such times, we have learned to focus on the tremendous good we see in each other. In a world in which we're conditioned to critique others for who they aren't, or could be, or should be, we have to consciously make the decision to see light and goodness in each other. When things have "hit the fan" and bitterness, resentment, jealousy, anger and vindictiveness try to trump unconditional love, grace, forgiveness, and kindness, we have to take a deep breath and trust in the perfect love God has first shown us. Then we can respond to God's love with love for one another.

So we spent time, as we have many other days before, focusing on the qualities we possess in our nature as beloved sons of God.

WOUNDS

Wounds are not evil, although sometimes our culture makes us think they are. Wounds actually make us who we are. They are unexpected injuries, giving us a limp, but not incapacitating us permanently; when treated well, wounds can actually draw us closer together than further apart. We have to choose to focus on the good and talking about our wounds openly and honestly helps us do so. Too many marriages and relationships end because we don't admit our broken places and dialog about them before they get in the way and cause problems.

Henri Nouwen has insightfully written about wounds:

Some of us tend to do away with things that are slightly damaged. Instead of repairing them we say: "Well, I don't have time to fix it, I might as well throw it in the garbage can and buy a new one." Often we also treat people this way. We say: "Well, he has a problem with drinking; well, she is quite depressed; well, they have mismanaged their business. . .When we dismiss people out of hand because of their apparent woundedness, we stunt their lives by ignoring their gifts, which are often buried in their wounds.

We all are bruised reeds, whether our bruises are visible or not. The compassionate life is the life in which we believe that strength is hidden in weakness and that true community is a fellowship of the weak.

Without the love of our parents, sisters, brothers, spouses, lovers, and friends, we cannot live. Without love we die. Still, for many people this love comes in a very broken and limited way. It can be tainted by power plays, jealousy, resentment, vindictiveness, and even abuse. No human love is the perfect love our hearts desire, and sometimes human love is so imperfect that we can hardly recognize it as love.

In order not to be destroyed by the wounds inflicted by that imperfect human love, we must trust that the source of all love is God's unlimited, unconditional, perfect love, and that this love is not far away from us but is the gift of God's Spirit dwelling within us.

FOCUS ON THE WHOLE PERSON

We've learned over and over again, the best way to have healthy, strong, satisfying relationships is to remember the whole person. When someone is spiraling into a negative path or not exactly who we want or expect the person to be, it's easy to lose sight of all his or her positive qualities. In those moments, especially, it is vital to make it a point to remind us, *at that moment*, of the specific strengths she or he possesses. It is being purposeful about remembering those qualities empowering us to save and to savor our relationships.

We were intentional at the diner when we shed light on our hurts and our feelings. And we were deliberate later in the evening when we sent each other affirming follow-up emails:

Michael,

I especially wanted to thank God for the attributes making you, you, even if my words are insufficient. Here are several qualities, which make you so special:

Your grace. *You are always showing God's grace (despite instances where others (myself included) may not show you the grace you deserve).*

Your love. *You love God with all your heart, soul, mind and strength and you love others as yourself. This draws me closer to God's love every day and enables me to love others the way Christ loves me.*

Your compassion. *The way you express compassion toward everyone, regardless of opinions, religious or cultural views, etc. is a gift to witness. You see others the way God sees them, as beloved sons and daughters.*

Your consistency. *As I've said to you before, you, along with Sarah and a few others in my life, show me consistency every day. Consistency is one of your strongest qualities, especially in a world tending to ride the waves of our emotions. I am one of those people—so someone like you helps me stay connected to "The Vine" every day.*

Your patience. *You are one of the most patient people I know. You are always patient with others, even when they have a tendency to "push buttons." Thank you for showing me patience every day—even when I "push buttons."*

Your sense of humor. *Thank you for helping me to make light of things when life is hard. Your laughter and your light-heartedness keep me from getting bogged down with disappointment or frustration.*

Your gratitude. *I have a way of seeing what's wrong or what can be fixed or what is disappointing in this life, rather than seeing goodness and joy. You help me see God's goodness and joy every day, which is a gift. You keep me grounded as a child. Because of you, I'm able to see God's faithfulness.*

Tom,

In every way, my words will not even remotely or adequately express the depth of my feelings and, even more importantly, express who you are. But I want to share these humble thoughts about you. These are seven gifts, in particular, I see God has given to this world through you—

Grace. *I am constantly amazed by the grace you exhibit and model. It is so easy not to show Grace in many of our daily interactions. But you work so hard at it. I am humbled, every day, by your capacity to be the very essence of Grace.*

Compassion. *In you, it goes hand in hand with your Grace. Your Compassion is sometimes astounding, as you see in others inherent gifts and worth many do not.*

Generosity. *You are always thinking of ways to help others out; you see something significant they need and you offer your heart, your time, your resources and your self to them. It's remarkably impressive, your Generosity.*

Open-mindedness. *In a world of judgment and condemnation, you display an incredible capacity to consider and accept the value of other ways, other ideas and other people. Your Open-mindedness is extraordinarily refreshing.*

Humanness. *You embrace your Humanness—your vulnerability and your tests—in a way, which I've expressed so many times before, moves me only to love you more.*

Vision. *You astound me daily with your Vision and the ideas you have for our mission. You have incredible instincts and embrace a way of dreaming globally which is exceptionally exciting.*

Connection. *The ability to connect intimately and deeply with others is rare. But you possess that ability. There is something intangibly tangible about you making it so easy to form an uncommon Connection with you and feel uncommonly safe.*

Writing and receiving each of those messages to one another touched us both. Unavoidably, when we have close, intimate and treasured relationships, we will rub open wounds and we will upset each other at times. But when we are sensitive to the wounds we all carry with us, we can forgive and have grace. We can celebrate our common humanness and love one another even more deeply because of it. We find it to be true every day.

Naked and Unashamed

"To whom can any man say—Here I am! Behold me in my nakedness,
my wounds, my secret grief, my despair, my betrayal, my pain, my tongue
which cannot express my sorrow, my terror, my abandonment. Listen to
me for a day—an hour!—a moment! - lest I expire in my terrible wilder-
ness, my lonely silence! O God, is there no one to listen? Is there no one
to listen? you ask. Ah yes, there is one who listens, who will always listen.
Hasten to him, my friend! He waits on the hill for you. For you, alone."

-SENECA

GENESIS 2:25, as the story of creation unfolds, declares that Adam and Eve in the perfection of the Garden of Eden, were "naked and unashamed." (NKJV)

We understand this description to be not just about one couple, but a symbol of the way God created us all to be with one another. In a world as God intended it, God's desire and intention for us is to be vulnerable, authentic, and unashamed. He wants us to be unafraid to communicate our very human, very common, anxieties, moods and nuisances with those who are part of our lives.

Between us, we use this phrase, "naked and unashamed" often. It serves as a metaphor for a way of relating to one another. It serves as a model for what deep, intimate, healthy relationships look like. We know we need to strive for this kind of relationship with each other if we have any chance of helping—with integrity—others to create those kinds of relationships. It is truly freeing to trust one another implicitly and to not be afraid of who we are.

We were in the midst of writing our first book, and exploring some of the more distressing times in our lives, when the following email exchange took place. It was another cold January day, which was symbolic of how each of us was feeling inside. It serves as an example of how we nurture our friendship and how we honor God's desire to be naked and unashamed with those who are in our lives.

MICHAEL'S EMAIL

Tom,

This short message from (Henri) Nouwen felt very appropriate to me today:
Vulnerable, Like a Bird
"Life is precious. Not because it is unchangeable, like a diamond, but because it is vulnerable, like a little bird. To love life means to love its vulnerability, asking for care, attention, guidance, and support. Life and death are connected by vulnerability. The newborn child and the dying elder both remind us of the preciousness of our lives. Let's not forget the preciousness and vulnerability of life during the times we are powerful, successful, and popular."

To be truly naked and unashamed with you, I have to admit that I have been feeling very fragile the last few days. I can't pinpoint exactly why, necessarily (but you'll see, maybe, as I continue writing this message I may actually grow in greater understanding of much of it!!). I just know I've been feeling that way. Writing to you last night and talking together was helpful and alleviated a lot of those feelings. So, thanks so much. Especially because I know you weren't feeling great at all, I want you to know how much your unexpected call meant to me. Yet I woke up at 3:45 this morning to the howling wind and the frigid darkness and felt vulnerable all over again. I lay there exasperated, got up and walked around the house for a while and checked some emails to maybe get my mind off the cacophony of thoughts invading it. I also prayed, haphazardly at best, incapable to focus or concentrate. But I knew reaching out to God, who already knew my thoughts (better than I), could help to calm and reassure me. It did help. The light of day has brought a better feeling and it's actually been pretty good so far since then.

Working on some of these stories, several of which I had forgotten the details of until I reread them again, has in large part conjured up these feelings of insecurity, I think. Recalling times in both of our lives in which we have felt diminished, not good enough, debilitated, has kind of placed a heavier weight on me the last couple of days. But that's okay, actually. I know shedding more light on some dark, shadowy corners will ultimately bring clarity, comfort and healing. So, as hard at times as it is to dig into these stories I know very well it will be a good thing for both of us.

On my first Sunday at First Church, 20 years ago, I shared a story about Charlie Chaplin in his prime. In short, he was so popular in the 1920's that there would be Charlie Chaplin look-a-like contests all around the U.S at county fairs and carnivals and bazaars. One day Charlie Chaplin himself quietly entered one of the contests. The real guy, the real thing. And he came in 12th! The real guy lost, big time. The people didn't know the real thing even when it was right in front of them. My point in telling the story then was to encourage us all to be the real thing in our faith—loving, compassionate, gracious, generous, forgiving, kind. Not a facade of the real thing, but the real thing indeed, throughout. One that would be recognized as real and good and true so that the world would know what was real and good and true. I shared the same story 10 years ago on my last Sunday in the church, saying I hoped I had been the real thing for them helping to see more clearly who the real thing—the real Christ, the real God—was.

I share this with you because I have realized for much of my life I have not felt as if I was the real thing—a real pastor, a real man, a real friend, a real husband, a real father, a real . . .. fill in the blanks. I can speculate as to why this is, but I am not sure I can understand it absolutely. It's confounding. In so many ways I am secure, confident, strong, self-assured and self-aware. Even as a pastor, a man, a friend, a husband, a father, a real . . . In so many ways I am content, grateful and aware of God's (and others') favor. Yet, there exist these moments in which I feel as if I am not enough—good enough, caring enough, gracious enough, worthy enough—to enter the stage and share what I believe is the real thing.

Yesterday's comment by (someone we had been meeting with)—"Not that you guys aren't real counselors"—somehow hit a raw nerve in me, massaged a vulnerable place which is still reverberating within my deepest soul. On the surface her comment, while inelegantly stated, wasn't harsh or probably meant as a slam. But it just happened to be the wrong phrase at the wrong time for me and coupled with the writing of the essays and some sadness at the cultural winding down of the holidays (as well as the underlying anxiety of Adam and Kate's challenges (with the scarily premature birth of their son Emmett) and Kathy's medical concerns—she stopped by the doctor's office yesterday to learn if they could tell her anything and they promised to get the doctor to get in touch, but he still hasn't) it struck me harder than it normally would have.

I'm actually glad it didn't hit you as profoundly. You helped me to move toward a more accepting place because of that. That's where we can help each other. What I felt yesterday was "left out."

I have come to realize that feeling "left out" is most likely my most susceptible wound. When something is said or done rubbing open the wound again, it is where I am most insecure.

This specific insight has just truly been a very recent understanding, just within the last week or so as some routines have slowed down and I've had time and space to reflect and pray. Even as I write this I am gaining a deeper understanding, which is greatly helpful to me.

As I reflect on all this I need to and certainly want to express how much I am incredibly grateful to God and to you, for reminding me I am enough, I am worthy, I am loved. In those moments when I forget it or question it, I am grateful for the reminders and the reassurance, which inevitably always comes. Just because I was often chosen last for basketball, for one example, as a kid, doesn't mean I am not the real thing in all the places where it matters, where it truly counts.

I pray from the bottom of my heart with these insights and this growing clarity I can not only understand and know myself better, but I can also be a more gracious, loving, supportive, knowing, encouraging, generous best friend and partner to you. In re-reading your stories—of your wounds and the brokenness you are healing—I continue to grow in deeper and more grateful appreciation of the beloved, gifted, insightful, sensitive, caring, gracious and generous person you are. I pray to be enough to honor all that you are.

Thank you for allowing me to be so naked and unashamed today. It really, truly helps.

TOM'S EMAIL

Michael,

Wow. I'm moved you took the time to write out your thoughts in this way—and I'm very pleased you can relate them to me. There is nothing, absolutely NOTHING, in my mind, which brings more reassurance of God's abiding presence than having someone else who can be in the middle of our circumstances, thoughts, and feelings WITH US. I hope and pray I can always be that person for you, despite my own wounds, insecurities, and shortcomings. Together, we bring healing to each other's wounds. . .

Thank you for your sincerity. Vulnerable like a bird, Nouwen says. So simple, yet so profound. In his words, I was reminded of Jesus' words about caring for the birds of the air. He cares for us, and makes us feel special, even when others (intentionally and unintentionally) communicate a different message.

In addition, thank you for sharing Charlie Chaplin's story. Very emotional. I can't imagine how exposed he must have felt.

To be naked and unashamed with you. I'm feeling kind of vulnerable, like a bird, myself. This morning when I woke up, I found out Lilly would be off of school. You would think I would be able to celebrate such wonderful news with her. Sadly, I didn't. For most of the morning, I was simply trying to survive. While the babies were sleeping, I took Lilly and Luke outside to shovel our neighbor's driveway. But instead of savoring the beauty of the day and the special moments I could have been savoring with my children, I focused too much on accomplishing tasks. Now, the kids (Lilly and Luke) are gone for the evening. Sarah's parents took them to their place for a sleepover. Once again, you would think I would be grateful for this opportunity. Sadly, I'm struggling with it. I'm sad the kids are gone. I didn't savor the morning as much as I should have—with them. I'm feeling as if I don't take advantage of the time God gives me with them as I should.

Anyways, I will enjoy the quiet. The babies should be sleeping for a few more minutes so I will start reading your stories. Thanks, always, for the time, energy, and investment you make in me (and so many others). You are an absolute gift to me.

Naked and Unashamed

"How Do You Create and Foster *Healthy* Relationships of Depth and Intimacy?"

An Abundant Life

*"We must learn to regard people less in the light of what they do or omit
to do, and more in the light of what they suffer.*
-DIETRICH BONHOEFFER

"I don't like that man. I must get to know him better."
-ABRAHAM LINCOLN

TOM

"*L*IFE SUCKS *and then you die. This world is going to hell in a hand basket." "Did you hear the news last night? Another bombing, another suicide,
another murder, another. . ..." "If it bleeds it leads!"*

Every day, every freaking day, I would hear the same disapproval, the same
demoralized outlook on life, and the same dissatisfaction in his life. And although
I may have agreed with him about the nature of the world's news and how it is
presented each day, I was especially downcast by the lack of joy this man felt. He
hated getting out of bed. He hated the work we did together. And dare I say it, he
hated his life.

It was the summer between my freshman and sophomore years of college and
I needed a job to help pay my way through school. A local contractor needed help
doing odd jobs and asked if I would be interested. Needing to save a significant
amount of money, I quickly said "yes," knowing it would be a physically demanding
position. What I didn't realize is how emotionally demanding it would become too,
because of the attitudes of one of my co-workers.

I can't remember much from the summer; in fact, I've tried to forget most of
it. I can't remember how many trenches I dug, how many asbestos ridden walls I
tore down, or the number of bathroom tiles I cut. But what I do remember is what
happened one sweltering Thursday morning in the middle of July.

Recognizing the emotional toll my co-worker was having on my life, I would
get up extra early to read, to pray, to meditate, whatever (yoga wasn't as big back
then or I may have given it a try). I tried anything to give me a sense of harmony in
my heart amidst such cynicism.

51

I opened a book I was reading at the time, which quoted one of my favorite verses in the Bible:

"I have come so that you would have life and have it abundantly."

John 10:10 I remember praying that morning, and almost every other morning for the rest of the summer:

"God, I have no idea what an abundant life looks like for this guy. But I pray you would work through me to possibly open his eyes to the joy, the hope, the peace you came to offer all of us."

But every day by about, oh, five minutes after being around the man, my prayer would change to:

"God, I'm about to punch this guy in the face if he has one more negative comment about his life, my life, and the current and future state of the world. If you don't give me patience, I may start acting on some of these violent thoughts running through my head, including taking this hammer and...."

The crazy thing about my co-worker is that he was successful by the world's standards. He helped to build houses for a living - massive, astonishing, glorious works of art. He built houses so people could "build a home." He made money and lots of it. Yet, on the inside, he was wretched.

I wish this could be one of those stories about an awe-inspiring conversation I had with the man where the heavens opened and he met Jesus face to face. But none of those wonders ever happened. There weren't any flashing lights, no angels, no choirs. He didn't fall on his knees and pray a prayer, none of it. I guess I could theorize there was no real change in him.

But there was a change. There was a change in me. I can think of several pivotal moments in my life when God showed me a vital lesson about myself through someone else. I, for example, think about the time when I worked with a woman on Wall Street in New York City and how she encouraged me to pursue my dreams instead of working some life-sucking job the rest of my life. Working for this builder was another one of those instances.

One scorching summer I learned, as I am continuing to learn, about an "abundant life." The "abundant life" isn't about choirs, angels, and worldly success. It's not about fame and fortune, although cachet would be nice some days. It's about relishing the journey despite the perplexing days or perplexing seasons (where I literally feel as if I've been beaten with a hammer).

But the difference for this man was that gratification for him seemed almost impossible to unearth. Even saying, "enjoy the journey" would have been totally offensive and probably would lead him to even more acrimony and uneasiness. He may have been the one grabbing the hammer and . . .

If there is one thing about the summer I wish had been different it's this: I wish I had been more intentional about asking him, attentively and considerately asking him, "what caused him to be so despondent" (although I probably wouldn't have phrased it that way). I let his emotional baggage weigh heavily on me each day. I wasn't able to look at him with anything other than pure rage, and possibly even hate.

I don't live with regrets. But what if I had been able to look deeply into this man's life and into his story and genuinely taken an interest in it? What if I had started off every day asking him:

"So, tell me about your relationship with your wife, your kids, your upbringing? Tell me about how you became a builder and what was it about the job which sparked such an interest in you."

What if I affirmed him for the amazing abilities he had and how he offered those gifts to the world? What if, every day, I said,

"You know what, I sincerely appreciate the way you created this living room, there is a family who will absolutely love this some day! You know what—the house you built around the corner—it's the best-looking house on the block. I'm sure the family living there is creating all kinds of wonderful memories together."

Most of us, actually no—all of us—go through suffering in our lives which causes us to be who we are today. Maybe it's the loss of a loved one far earlier than she should have passed away?

Maybe it's an abusive upbringing forcing you to lose your innocence far sooner than you should have had to? Maybe it's a lack of connection with your father or mother emotionally? Maybe your parents never told you how proud they were of you or loved you for who you are? It could be any number of things which turned the man into the jaded, conflicted, distraught, aggravated old man he was. There had to be something.

But what if we could look at a person, like I could have looked at this man, and said to myself,

"You know what? I bet he has had a lot of brokenness in his own life. A person just doesn't become a warped, frustrated old man unless he has dealt with some immense distress."

We don't help people experience the abundant life by telling them they should be experiencing the abundant life. We show people how to experience this life by modeling it first. We help others experience the abundant life by taking a genuine interest in them and reminding them that someone else thinks their life is special, that their life is consequential, that the world wouldn't be the same without them.

There is a quote we love to share from the Broadway musical *Mame,* in which the play's namesake pronounces: "Life is a banquet and most of you poor sons of bitches are starving to death!"

Life is a banquet, an abundant one. And yes, woefully, far, far too many people are starving to death. But our response shouldn't be, "Let's tell people that they should be having an abundant life" because if they knew how to be experiencing such a life they would be experiencing it, right? Our response should be, "Tell me about your life. Let's talk this out together. Let's see why the abundant life is so elusive for you to find and what we can do about it—together." And maybe, just maybe, it means doing nothing more than being a listening ear and a good friend to people, especially those people who have been kicked around their whole lives.

MICHAEL

Everything about her was big—her height (6'2"), her intellect, her voice, her artistry, her laugh, her life. She simply lived large. She embraced with joy her bigness and her life. She was supremely outgoing. When she entered a room, the very force of her personality took over. She had a way of instantly drawing attention to herself, not in a "look at me; I want all the attention" kind of way. But her charisma, inquisitiveness and love of people automatically drew people in. She made instant friends wherever she went, winning them over because of her genuine interest in their stories and lives. She loved to travel and had the ability to connect with people around the world, no matter where, no matter the culture, no matter the language.

She taught drama to children—writing, producing and sometimes taking supporting roles in plays and musicals starring her students. She would always sing at a party; the blues and Janis Joplin were among her standards. She had her own cabaret act and videos to further showcase her creativity and talent. Her inventiveness and vision exceeded anyone's we knew.

When she died, far too young, far too suddenly and unexpectedly, from a heart infection, at age 63, one of the brightest, most effervescent lights in our lives was extinguished. Her name was Susan. Big Sue, to many of her friends.

She was one of Kathy's older sisters. When Sue's four sisters traveled to San Francisco to hold her hands and be by her side as she clung to life in the final two weeks of her life and then to care for her belongings and close out her apartment after her passing, they were confronted with a reality only exacerbating their grief: Sue lived in physical and financial poverty. We all knew she lived very frugally and was impressively resourceful. Yet none of us fully knew the intensity of the scarcity she experienced. The exorbitant cost of living in San Francisco and the small income she received as a dramatic arts educator for children, supplemented by a few singing gigs and income from her play productions, made it extremely difficult for Sue to survive economically. Her very meager living conditions made life a daily financial juggling act. While each of her sisters, as well as I, had visited her in San Francisco over the years, none of us saw the depths of her poverty as starkly as we did after she was gone.

She had never complained or allowed her economic circumstances to get in the way of living an abundant life. Her life was about the many and varied friendships she could foster and the creative gifts she could share with children and the rest of the world. She was a wealthy woman, indeed. But it wasn't found in money or investments. It didn't come through prestige or fame. But it came in the music she loved to play and sing, in the plays she wrote and the children she molded into confident and accomplished performers, in the places she visited and the people she connected with along the way—and kept in generous touch with throughout many decades. It came in her delight in loving her growing number of grand nieces and nephews and in the bond she maintained with all four of her sisters and their families. It came in her diplomatic and sensitive way of relating to people with whom she differed politically, philosophically and religiously. It came in her unending generosity of heart, in her infectious spirit of joy and in her passionate love of life.

When I picture an abundant life, Sue's big laugh, voice, talent and life are what I see and will remember. I miss those gifts of hers very much. So few others possess them as wonderfully as she did. I miss her and the abundant life of joy, gratitude and just plain fun she brought into mine—into all of ours who knew her—through her big, contagious love.

Sue's abundance was infectious. Being around her rubbed off. It was impossible not to laugh, not to rise above everyday annoyances and trials, not to celebrate life's wonder and beauty. The simple joys—her love of Christmas lights, her tendency to break out into song for no apparent reason at all, her love of a good beer and her tender tears when holding our day-old first granddaughter, the first newborn baby she'd ever held. When we were with her, we never "starved to death" at the banquet of life. Hers was the kind of wonder I wish all of us could possess. She exuded an eternal beauty I believe God desires all of us to know. I wish all of us could live with more of her kind of abundance every day.

Abundance is so much more than having "things." Abundance is as Epicurus writes: "Not what we have but what we enjoy, constitutes our abundance."

Compassion (Michael)

"Peace I leave with you; my peace I give to you.
I do not give to you as the world gives.
Do not let your hearts be troubled and do not let them be afraid."
-JESUS

TODAY IS PASSOVER. It makes me think of my dear friend and that Monday morning call.

When the phone rang, the caller ID told me the story before I even answered it.

The number indicated the caller was from Florida. I knew what I was going to hear—Nathan had died.

I was expecting it. When we talked just a few days before, he was so weak his wife Rachel had to hold the phone for him. His voice was soft. I had to listen carefully. But characteristically, his wonderful sense of humor was intact. He was a lawyer and he made a crack about lawyers and lawsuits, and I laughed.

Rachel said the words I expected. "Our Nathan passed away just a little while ago." She went on. "Here's my credit card number. The service will be on Wednesday and I'd like you to come tomorrow and stay through Thursday. Use my card to book a flight and a hotel. Here's the name of a nice hotel nearby where you can stay. We'll have someone meet you at the airport with a car."

Even though I was expecting it, it was moving too fast. I didn't want him to be gone. He had been a warm and comforting light to me, even though he was the one who was sick and dying. He was wise and insightful. He fought to overcome his cancer. He traveled to South America and Germany, he read everything he could about traditional, complementary, and alternative treatments. He had a powerful spirit, which wouldn't yield until he tried everything he could. For four years we spoke on the phone nearly every week and we visited in person twice when I traveled from Pennsylvania to Florida to meet him.

He and his wife wanted me to speak at his service. There was so much I *could* say. I just didn't want to say it because I wasn't ready for him to go. But, whether I was ready or not, he was gone.

What could I say to best convey my relationship with such a wonderful friend? After four years of listening to him—and Rachel as well—I came to know him (Rachel, too) very fondly. I listened to Nathan as he detailed his experiences and the lack of dignity a person living with cancer often endures. I listened as he dispensed his feelings about all of it. I knew him intimately. I loved him deeply.

As these thoughts swirled in my mind on the flight to south Florida I began to think about what I would say. As I wrote my thoughts down, they flowed quickly.

His three sons were sharing too, as well as five more of his friends, and his rabbi. For the moments I would be sharing, I decided to focus not on his decline and pain, but rather on his spirit and touching kindness.

I would tell the story behind a package Nathan sent me a year earlier, at Thanksgiving, and the letter accompanying it.

It was the previous summer when I received an email from him. "What's your favorite word? Think very seriously about this. After you do, let me know what it is."

My favorite word? I took the request seriously because Nathan asked me to do so. But it didn't take much thought. The answer was simple.

"Compassion."

So I sent him my response. A few days later, another email.

"Can you give me some examples in songs, in hymns, where the word 'compassion' is used? Scriptures? Stories? Poems?"

I did some research and sent him the examples.

Months went by. Honestly, I forgot about Nathan's request. The leaves changed color and fell from the trees. Summer turned into autumn and the week of Thanksgiving arrived. And so did the package from him. Curiously, I ripped open the box.

Inside the box, carefully, tightly swaddled in bubble wrap, was a beautiful wooden frame. Inside the frame was a print of the word "compassion" with more than a dozen uses of the word in most of the songs, hymns, and verses I had sent to Nathan those many months before, along with the word written in 10 languages. Expressions such as these . . .

. . . "You may call God love, you may call God goodness. But the best name for God is compassion." –Eckhart

. . . "Lord is good to all, and his compassion is over all that he has made." –Psalm 145:9

. . . "Be kind, for everyone you meet is fighting a hard battle." –Plato

. . . "I feel the capacity to care is the thing which gives life its deepest significance." –Casals

. . . "Mitleid, חמלה, сострадание."

And with it, a letter. Heartfelt. Touching. It brought tears to my eyes.

Dear Reverend Michael,

The support you have given to me cannot be put into words. Thank you so much for helping me through this journey . . .

. . . I have such gratitude for your continued personal support for my journey, especially in light of your own personal burdens. The amazing thing is how many people you support on such a personal basis. Truly exceptional . . .

. . . I looked up the meaning of compassion in the dictionary and traced its roots. I then came up with the idea of using compassion in a bunch of different languages as it is a universal concept . . .

. . . Michael, words are inadequate to express my appreciation for all the compassion you have shown me personally each and every week and in between. Thank you my friend . . .

. . . I am a member of three temples with various levels of orthodoxy. One of the temples Rachel and I were founding members. Each has something to offer as does all religions. Notwithstanding, it was a Christian Reverend who jumped into the pit with me during this cancer journey . . . The word thank you is just not enough.

From my heart to yours,

NH

I shared the story of Nathan's gift at his funeral as I stood before all the people who knew and loved him. Wearing the yarmulke all men at the service were given to wear, I shared the story, which captured the essence of Nathan for me—his grace, his sensitivity, his compassion.

I treasure the framed print. It hangs on my office wall and reminds me of what "compassion" means—in Latin, to "suffer with."

For four years I "suffered with" Nathan. I listened to him detail many of the harsh realities of his disease. The severe weight loss. The months and months when he couldn't eat solid food. The indignities he endured. The constant search for a way to hold cancer's advancement at bay.

When its advancement was too much and it took him from this life, I stood in line by his grave, and in the Jewish tradition, took my turn with a shovel full of dirt. I poured the soil onto his casket, an act of final reality and respect. He was gone.

I sat Shiva in his home with his family and friends for two days, reciting the ancient prayers, recalling God's mercy and deliverance from the painfulness of life.

I remembered his laughter, his jokes, the brave front, and the dignity he exhibited especially when dignity was unknown.

I remember his compassionate, caring life. And I remember the words of his youngest son, who told me, "He loved you so much."

There was nothing I could do for Nathan except the most important thing of all—to love him. To love him when he was funny and to love him when he was in pain. To love him when the latest word from the doctor was good and to love him when there was nothing more a doctor could do. To love him when hope was real, strong, and to love him when hope was absent, gone.

It wasn't always easy to be present with Nathan on his journey as his health and his strength declined. I wanted him to grow stronger and feel good and live—abundantly and for a much longer time. I didn't want him to grow weaker or live in pain or die. I wanted Rachel and their sons to be able to enjoy his laughter and his love for years and years to come. But, increasingly, as his body grew weaker, the reality became clearer; his life would soon end. It's heartrending, very heartrending, to watch someone you respect and treasure decline and die. It would have been easier to pretend it wasn't happening and deny his cancer's course. It would have been easier for me if he or Rachel hadn't written to keep me informed of what was happening to him. It would have been easier if neither of them called to talk.

But they needed to write. They needed to call. They needed to tell the story and to know they were not alone. They needed to feel others cared and were with them along the way. They needed to be loved in their darkest hours. They needed to be connected in their deepest pain. No matter how rough it may have been for me to hear and to learn the realities they were living, it was infinitely harder on them and their sons. I needed to keep everything in perspective in order to support them and love them.

The compassionate way isn't always easy. In fact, often, it's exceedingly arduous. But it is the way bringing help and comfort to the people we encounter and those whom we love.

One of the greatest gifts we have been given is the gift of each other.

The compassionate way announces to others that we are not alone. It helps us all be much less afraid.

It is the way that leads us through the bleakest, deepest valleys to bring us consolation and peace.

Security (Tom)

"Security is mostly a superstition. It does not exist in nature,
nor do the children of men as a whole experience it.
Avoiding danger is no safer in the long run than outright exposure.
Life is either a daring adventure, or nothing."
-HELEN KELLER

I T IS PASSOVER.
The day when our Jewish brothers and sisters celebrate God's deliverance from bondage in Egypt; this year it is also Good Friday for Christian brothers and sisters, the day when we commemorate the crucifixion of Jesus Christ, a truly special and important day for all of us.

On the inside, I wasn't feeling so special; focusing on the meaning of the day was impossible.

Our last appointment was with a woman who had lost a child in a car crash.

"He was here one moment, and the next moment he was gone!" she said with tears flooding down her cheeks like tributaries.

On the drive home, I was feeling an overpowering sensitivity to the weightiness of her loss. I can't imagine anything worse than a death of a child.

"Poor, poor soul," I said out loud in the quiet of our station wagon.

The stoplight in front of me must have turned green, but I was in too much of a fog to notice. The car behind me started agitatedly honking, quickly pulling me back to my present position. The traffic was heavy two days before Easter.

Rush hour had come to a standstill. I actually couldn't move. While I waited, I turned on my phone to see if any emails had come in. I hadn't had an opportunity to do so for most of the day. The first email jumped out at me as if it was the only one in my inbox. It was the email we had been waiting for since the beginning of the week. The message came from the agent of a prominent speaker we invited to speak at our fourth annual fundraising banquet. We had extremely high hopes because our missions paralleled very nicely. The email read something like this: "We are very sorry to inform you, blah, blah, blah but we won't be able to serve your organization next year. We appreciate the work you do but due to time restraints in her schedule, blah, blah, blah."

I started gasping for air. The row of cars started crawling again, but I couldn't move. I rolled down the window and took a deep breath. For a few brief moments I wondered if this is what it feels like when a high-end executive has a huge business deal fall through.

The slowness of traffic was a good thing because it gave me some time to "get it together" and "lick my wounds" before greeting my wife and four young children. I try intently not to take my work home with me, but some days it's nearly impossible, especially days such as this one.

I walked through the door and was welcomed by one of our twins crashing into my leg in her motor scooter.

"Da Home, Da Home!" she cried out. Thank God for moments like those. Thank God for children. Sarah, could sense my uneasiness, as she always does.

"Are you okay? What happened today?"

I started off with the surface level answer: "We had a few tough conversations."

She knew better, so she asked, "Anything else?"

I can't hide from her for too long, so I started explaining: "We heard back from the agent and she can't come. I'm not at all happy about this."

The night before Michael and I had bought a copy of her book in preparation for next year's event. Sarah jokingly asked, "Are you guys still going to read her book?"

I chuckled, "I don't know, I kinda want to boycott by not reading it."

We both laughed. We finish eating dinner and the kids rushed off to the living room to build a fort with pillows. I put on a pot of coffee knowing it was going to be a late night of writing and emails after the kids went to bed. Sarah looked at me and said, "You just need trust. It's going to be fine. Look at the speakers God has provided the last three years."

I look at her and grin. She knows her word of surety is the last thing I want to hear. We laugh out loud again which was therapeutic, at least for a few moments.

Two weeks earlier, on a Friday afternoon, Michael and I ended the workweek as we so often do together, walking and praying and voicing appreciation for all the ways God had shown up in our lives. That day we walked on a trail with a flowing stream on our left and a thick forest on our right. I said to Michael, "You know, we have about four or five important opportunities on the table right now which could affect the future of our ministry. If all five of those opportunities come through, we could be at a much better place a year from now."

"I know," Michael acknowledged. We continued walking and praying. We prayed about how grateful we were for the prospects and how exciting they were, but we also asked God to keep us grounded—remembering this whole journey is God's deal and God's will, will be done. "The good stuff happens when you are the One who initiates, not us, and when we align ourselves with what you are already doing in the world" we prayed.

We ended our walk by reminding each other, out loud, the mantra we have articulated since day one of our journey together: "This isn't about working harder to make things happen, it's about trusting more."

By Saturday morning, the day before Easter, I've had some time to process the previous 24 hours, including, and especially, the email from the speaker's agent.

What I am continuing to learn about myself is that I like to try and control things; I'm guessing most of us do. Sorrowfully, anything I try to control doesn't seem to ever go the way I would have expected it to—and this is one of those situations.

It was almost inevitable at least a few of those opportunities would fall through, but for whatever reason I had "put all my eggs in one basket" with this speaker, dreaming of what it would be like to have her speak about our mission and her mission and how they parallel so perfectly.

Why do I do that? Why do I give my heart away so fully and place my identity on something or someone other than the One who gave me a new identity?!

I was reminded of the time during my senior year of college when I went on two dates with a girl down the hall. Immediately, I started having these outrageous, illogical thoughts she would someday be my wife. We never made it to a third date; I was crushed emotionally.

I think of several instances over the previous four years when I have done the exact same thing. There was one time about a year before when I was utterly crushed after learning we didn't get a $25,000 grant to support our ministry, taking me several days to recover from the low blow.

Easter Sunday arrived. It is the day when Christians are reminded God reinforces, remakes, and remedies those things, which we think have been ruined. One of my spiritual mentors sends me a message on Facebook a few minutes before we leave for church.

It said, "What am amazingly full week Jesus experienced! Praised, death and resurrection. My week is calm by comparison!"

His words really spoke to me. My week had been disconcerting; in fact, it was a roller coaster ride emotionally. But my week wasn't anything like the week

Jesus experienced 2,000 years ago: the betrayal from his best friends, the fear of his impending fate, the physical pain and abuse he experienced, and even the silent response from God during the most vulnerable moment of his earthly existence. It all left him questioning.

Later, in the middle of his sermon, the pastor of our church shared a quote from theologian Frederick Beuchner: "Resurrection means that the worst thing is never the last thing."

At the end of the day, I get into bed and gave "thanks" for the aching and agony I faced during the week; most importantly, my aching and agony isn't the last thing.

I wish the spiritual hangover in my soul went away, it didn't. I so badly wanted resurrection in my heart and for gladness and harmony to return.

Easter, with all its fun and festivities came and went. Early Monday morning, Michael and I met at a park to start our workweek.

We're not sure how many times we walked around the park's perimeter path, but we know it was plenty because our feet started throbbing. We love to walk together and often times our walks have brought about some of the most essential and transformative conversations and moments of our lives.

Round and round and round we went, in the very same park where, in the words of one of our board members, "this beautiful notion of Someone To Tell It To" first began. The first several laps, we didn't say much, which is atypical for us. The only sounds we heard were our steps on the pavement, the geese and airplanes flying overhead, the flowing stream next to the path on which we were treading, and the occasional joyful exclamation from a young child playing on the jungle gym nearby.

On most of our walks and most of our journeys together we are very open with one another about all of it: the high points; the low points; the burdens associated with having four young children and a 29-year-old son living at home with profound developmental disabilities and autism; the intense physical pain I live with; the hopes and dreams we have for the future; the God-given blessings all around us; and so much more.

This walk would become another pivotal moment on our "journey" together. It was a conversation we were dreading and one we had been praying wouldn't bear fruit.

"I'm not sure if this is going to work," I said to Michael.

A long silence occurred. This time the only sound we heard were the sounds of our hearts beating, rapidly.

"I know. I'm not sure either," Michael quietly uttered. Then our feelings and fears emptied out like water.

"This is just so incredibly complicated. I never thought it was going to be this complicated. We have worked and worked and worked and so much good has happened."

"The article about our mission written in Sunday's (Harrisburg, PA) newspaper about 'miracles happening every day when people have someone to tell it to' was such a beautiful article! But none of it means anything if we can't make it financially, if we can't support our families."

"We've had so many amazing things happen, even in the last few months. Connections with people such as business leader and author Ken Blanchard, an inspirational fundraiser with best selling author Wm. Paul Young, larger financial commitments, and the list goes on and on, but for whatever reason, our situation doesn't seem to be changing."

"I'm scared. I'm discouraged. I'm depressed. I don't know what to do."

There was another long silence. But not an awkward one. A moment of true empathy where both of us were feeling and thinking and experiencing the same things.

"We've come so far. And now this? What the hell? I just don't understand why God would lead us this far only to stop us, right here and right now. This mission is so important. It has changed lives. It is changing lives. It has changed us and is changing us."

Neither of us had answers; we didn't try suggesting any because there weren't any.

We did what we always do, with each other, and Lord willing, most everyone we speak with each day:

We remained calm. We shed a tear or two (or three). We listened.

We went through it. Together.

I wish I could say the distress went away after our conversation. It didn't, at least not for several days. But it did go away—for now. Because we acknowledged it, together. But, it will inevitably come back; it always does, in other ways and in other situations. That is why we believe, as author Miles Franklin so eloquently puts it:

Someone to tell it to is one of the fundamental needs of human beings.

Can you imagine a world in which all of us had this kind of comfort and support? A world in which we didn't rush in and offer platitudes, clichés, or short-term solutions.

Sometimes, actually, much of the time, saying nothing is the best gift we can give, particularly to those who are suffering or in pain. Saying nothing is saying something, something important. Instead of trying to have the right answers, listen with intention and simply be with someone.

We offer one another what we believe all of us need, simply someone to tell it to.

We all need a safe place where we can get out the worst about ourselves and they don't run us off, a safe place where we can get out all of our fears, our doubts, and brokenness and pain, and not be loved less because of it, but more. We believe the way we can alleviate so much of the sadness, discomfort, and sorrow we feel, is by embracing it, all of it, together.

Unashamedly. Completely. Vulnerably.

Touch

"I JUST MISS GETTING A HUG."

Softly, hesitantly, in the middle of the conversation, he voiced it. It wasn't easy for him to say. It took a new level of intimacy he wasn't used to. He was lonely. It was a new, and unwelcome, feeling for him.

It had been several months since he had lost his wife. Her illness had been lingering. Caring for her had taken a lot out of him. His new life was more uncomfortable than he ever imagined it could be. As we sat together in the park that afternoon, the warmth of the sun and the splendor of the day were barely noticed by him. He could not enjoy any of it; the loneliness was tremendous.

"I've never been this alone. We did everything together. Sure, I have some great buddies who'll go out to breakfast with me. They and their wives invite me to dinner sometimes. I've had a few days on the golf course. But much of the time I feel hollow. Maybe even pitied."

He lowered his eyes and his voice.

"No one thinks about actually touching me, that maybe one of things I miss the most is some physical contact. Holding hands when we took a walk. The kiss in the morning. The kiss good night. Her hand on my shoulder when we were talking to our grandkids together on the phone. When I crawl into bed at night and she's not there beside me. It's cold without her warmth there next to me.

"I miss getting a hug. The interesting thing is I've never been a big physical touch person, it was never very important to me. But I never realized how reassuring those small gestures are. Since I don't receive them I miss them terribly. No one ever talks about that. Trust me; as a man I do not express that easily. But what've I got to lose? I've lost it all already."

We listened a lot that day. He needed to tell us his story. But even more, he needed a hug. So a hug is what we gave him when it was time to leave. The embrace he needed.

"Thank you, guys. I needed that more than anything else today." It's the least we could do. Show him we would listen. Show him we heard what he was feeling.

We trust it helped him to feel a little of the warmth of that day's sun. Maybe its brilliance could bring him a few moments of consolation. Maybe in that instance he wouldn't feel as if there was nothing more to lose.

Jesus healed people with a variety of sicknesses and disabilities, different ages, socioeconomic statuses, races and religious affiliations. It didn't matter to him; he simply reached out and touched them. In the Gospels, the Greek word for "touch" is ά πτομαι, meaning, "to modify or change someone by touching."

In so many instances, we find Jesus displaying the power of touch to change someone's life and someone's story. For example, from *The Message* version of the Bible:

> *Just then a woman who had hemorrhaged for twelve years slipped in from behind and lightly touched his robe. She was thinking to herself, "If I can just put a finger on his robe, I'll get well." Jesus turned—caught her at it. Then he reassured her: "Courage, daughter. You took a risk of faith, and now you're well." The woman was well from then on. Matthew 9:20 – 22*
>
> *They beached the boat at Gennesaret and tied up at the landing. As soon as they got out of the boat, word got around fast. People ran this way and that, bringing their sick on stretchers to where they heard he was. Wherever he went, village or town or country crossroads, they brought their sick to the marketplace and begged him to let them touch the edge of his coat—that's all. And whoever touched him became well. Mark 6:53-56*

> *Everyone was trying to touch him—so much energy surging from him, so many people healed! Luke 6:19*

> *They arrived at Bethsaida. Some people brought a sightless man and begged Jesus to give him a healing touch. Mark 8:22*

> *People brought babies to Jesus, hoping he might touch them. Luke 18:15*

Moved with compassion, Jesus reached out and touched him. "I am willing," he said. "Be healed!" Mark 1:41 Deeply moved, Jesus touched their eyes. They had their sight back that very instant, and joined the procession. Matthew 20:34

One of the things that we do to end our day together—every day together—as we're saying goodbye, is give each other a hug. Both of our wives would honestly tell you that physical touch is one of the least important ways of showing us love. And not only that, it's a bit uncharacteristic for two grown men to give each other hugs, especially every day. However, giving each other a hug is bigger, much bigger, than simply giving each other a hug. It's our way of saying to each other, that we are loved, unconditionally, by each other, and most importantly, by God. There hasn't been a day that we can remember, since we first met eight years ago, when we didn't end our time together in this way. Even after days of stress, days when we are physically, emotionally or spiritually tired, we do it.

Every Monday night, a group of men gets together to unashamedly express all they are living with—the good and the bad, the beautiful and the ugly. They laugh together, as well as cry. They stand with each other through addictions and walk with each other through the darkness of doubt that, if we're honest and admit it, we all experience. They make it a point, as well, to make certain that every one of them hugs every member of the group before they say goodbye each week. They do it for two reasons, one of the men told us. First, because those hugs represent the unconditional grace, acceptance and love of God. They want to offer those gifts and remind each other every week that they are freely and generously given. Second, because they never know when they may not have the opportunity to share those gifts again. Life is fragile and changeable. The men never want to carry the regret if they failed to express their own love and respect for one another.

We feel the same way, too. On days when our world feels as if as the Psalmist said in Psalm 46: *(that) the earth (is) giv(ing) way and the mountains (are) fall(ing) into the heart of the sea, though its waters roar and foam and the mountains quake with their surging,* we give each other a hug. Those hugs remind one another of God's intimate touch and of our own respect and love for one another's presence in our lives.

Hanging on the wall at our office is a picture of Rembrandt's famous painting, *The Prodigal Son.* In the painting, the younger son—the "prodigal"—after owning his mistakes and recognizing his shortcomings, returns home to his father. His father, of course, is a symbol of God the Creator, and of God's relationship with each of us—we are God's beloved sons and daughters. The father in the picture is eagerly embracing his son, warmly, forgivingly, graciously, and compassionately. He loves his son so much—and by holding his kneeling son close to his chest, he is saying, "You are my beloved son. You will always be my beloved son."

Whether the wayward son in the story was big on physical touch or not, it didn't matter. In such a moment, he needed the warm embrace of his father to know he is loved and will always be loved. He needed it to know that all the hurtful, disappointing, irresponsible things he had done, all the important things he left undone, couldn't keep him from his father's loving touch.

When she received the diagnosis, it wasn't hopeful. Metastatic breast cancer. It left her with little hope. Her life was going to end in a short amount of time. So, she went about the business of saying "goodbye." There were people she wanted to see, things she wanted to do, and conversations she wanted to have. She embraced her reality. It certainly wasn't what she wanted, at all. But she felt it left her with only this choice – despair about what was happening and live the remainder of her days in bitterness and anger or embrace what was real and live those days with fullness and joy.

She chose to embrace what was, a decision that lifted her to a place of peace; she greeted her days with a deep passion for the life remaining. Yet as she lived, she prepared each day to die. She left her job. She prepared meals for her husband and stocked the chest freezer in the basement with enough food for months. She spent as much time in their vacation home at the beach as she could, a restorative place that she loved dearly. She lunched with her friends and spent as much time as she could with her mom. She savored her children and never let them forget her deep affection for them. She wanted to take every opportunity she could to share with the people she loved, as she prepared to die.

And then, she didn't die.

Against the odds, it didn't happen when they expected it would. In fact, she continued to live. Her health improved. Her diagnosis appeared to be wrong. Her prognosis was definitely wrong, too. She looked healthy. She was active in her community. She kept on going and did all the things she wanted to do.

And, she grew angry. It's not that she didn't want to live. She loved her life and those who were in it. But after all the preparations, after leaving her job, filling the freezer, traveling to the beach, saying goodbye to her friends and lovingly caring for her mother, husband and children, she had gotten to a place where she was genuinely ready to go. She had made peace with her mortality and, in fact, found comfort in it. And after making all the plans, she didn't know what to do when what they told her would happen, didn't. She had done everything she needed to be able to go and then she couldn't.

There was a ceramic miniature palm of a hand that she loved to touch for reassurance during that time. The palm was very smooth and it was comforting for her to rub her thumbs on it whenever she felt anxious, uncertain or dispirited. Something about that tactile touch quieted and reassured her. It represented the hand of God to her, a hand that she could hold onto, take with her wherever she went or simply stroke to provide a reminder of the divine presence. She gave the hands as gifts to those who were close to her. They too were blessed to receive her gift.

And when she did go, more than a year after she was told she would, those symbolic gifts reassured so many of those who loved her how they too were held in God's comforting hands.

When he received his diagnosis—told he had less than a year to live with pancreatic cancer—he had a choice too. It was the same as hers. Resent it or embrace it. Hold a hostile grudge or find a way to create the best life he could with the time he had left.

He told his friends that there was something to be thankful for. It was the gift of time. Not unlimited time. But finite time. "How could that be good," they wondered? How could he be thankful? For him, knowing there was a determined amount of time left has helped him to establish his priorities. If there are people he wants to see, things he wants to do and conversations he wants to have, he has them. He also finishes each conversation and visit with an embrace because he doesn't ever want to leave a meeting without his friends knowing their lives are important and deserving of love.

It's been said that our most important conversations happen when we are in doorways, when we're leaving some place, someone. It's true. It's usually when the "I'm sorry's" are expressed, when the "I love you's" are said, when the most important words needing to be expressed now or maybe not at all, are offered. It's when we prepare to take our leave from any thing or anyone—including our leave from this life—when we can be compelled to prioritize and make certain what is important to us is met. So vital things are not left undone. So we love people are not left out. So essential words are not left unspoken.

It is a gift to learn this vital, transforming lesson. The fortunate people among us learn it standing in the doorways. The most fortunate, though, learn it before the doorways loom, embracing our lives and all life offers when there is even more time left.

So, we hug each other every day.

We imagine the prodigal son kneeled in the loving embrace of his father, and of God, for a long, long time. He needed to. For as long as it took for him to feel utterly, wholly, safe as a child of God, again.

At various times in all of our lives we need a reassuring embrace and the comforting gift of touch. We need people in our lives with whom we can ask for a hug, those rare, safe people who will hold us in their embrace or in the palm of their hands as long as we need holding, reminding us of how we are precious and close to their hearts.

Using Our Brokenness as a Source of Strength

*"I am struck by how sharing our weakness and difficulties is more
nourishing to others than sharing our qualities and successes."*
-Jean Vanier

*"Though you have made me see troubles, many and bitter,
you will restore my life again; from the depths of the earth
you will again bring me up."*
-Psalm 71: 20

ASK JUST ABOUT ANYONE what she would most like to do with her life
and many would respond by saying she would like to do something she en-
joys, something about which she is passionate, or something with great meaning to
her. Still others would take it a step further by saying something such as: ***I would
like to live out my passion in a way that blesses the world and leaves a legacy.***

We arrived at her scrapbooking shop early on a Saturday morning for a book
signing. The shop, though not easy to spot from the road, is what one of her customers described as "a hidden gem." Inside, we could see row after row and shelf after shelf of scrapbooking supplies—albums, kits, stamps, stickers, organizers, quotes
and sayings, layouts, die cuts, scrapbooking paper and so much more. On the front
desk is a banner reading:

**"Cre · ate: {kre-at'} tr. V. To produce through artistic or imagina-
tive effort. Create and inspire. To make your own."**

On the wall closest to the counter, we spotted a beautiful picture frame with a
photo of her and her mom, arm in arm, this poetry decorating the frame:

*"There is a time for everything, and a season for every activity under
heaven: a time to be born and a time to die, a time to plant and a time to
uproot, a time to kill and a time to heal, a time to tear down and a time to
build up." Ecclesiastes 3:1-3*

Scrapbooking, as she describes it, is a way to preserve some of the best and worst moments of a person's personal and family history. Here is her story, the defining piece of her personal and family history:

> *In December 2003, my father shot himself in his apartment. He left a note for the family that his sadness was too much and his failing medical health was continuing to spiral him downward. He was severely diabetic and had another ulcer on his foot that he didn't tell us about. This would have kept him off work and he had no disability insurance or any way to provide for himself if this happened. He never let us know, nor did he ask for help. His kidneys were also failing and he had watched his own father suffer through a horrible three years before dying with diabetes.*
>
> *His father had both legs amputated and had most of his stomach removed. He went blind in both eyes and was just a shell of a man who lived in a nursing home until the day he died. My father didn't want that for himself or for us, so he chose what he thought was the easiest way out of his pain and something that would save us from experiencing what he did.*
>
> *No one can understand the grief and feelings that go along with a suicide of a friend or family member unless you have been there yourself. Grief in and of itself is erratic; it's horrible and it doesn't behave the same way in all people or situations.*
>
> *When my father died, I was numb. While I don't believe I could have loved him more, or done anything to make the outcome different, I still always wonder, could I have done anything else?*
>
> *While I missed him greatly, I don't believe I grieved his death when it happened. I felt like he made a conscious decision and if his pain was too much to bear—then, I got it. I understood. I could think over my own life, about the times when it would have been so much easier to end it than to cry out to God as I did. I also remember what it did to our family watching my grandfather die. Every single night of the week Dad would go sit at the nursing home watching his own father die of diabetes. I believe that each of those visits destroyed part of who my dad was. And as he suffered his own illness, I believe those memories probably haunted him.*
>
> *But the one thing I remember vividly, is that I was just so open and raw during the time after Dad died. I was vulnerable to anything that happened to me.*
>
> *Mom was very wounded through this. She struggled with her own guilt and demons. My husband, Scott, and I convinced Mom to move in with us. We*

have so many happy memories from that first year: canning, baking Christmas cookies and just having fun together. I loved having her with us for breakfast and dinners and I appreciated all the help she gave us too.

I watched as she got some release from her grief during a retreat weekend. She told me she felt the touch of God releasing her from the guilt and she began to finally heal from Dad's death. But, she continued to struggle with her own inner feelings and her depression worsened.

My health was beginning to deteriorate and Mom's anxiety over losing me because of my health problems continued to grow. She feared I would end up sick like my father or dead.

My health began to improve but Mom's depression continued to get worse. February was coming around again, and so was Dad's birthday, a time for her that was almost as hard as the day of his death. My father was her best friend and the emotions and the loss she continued to feel consumed her. Her doctor continued to tweak her medications and the side effects continued to get worse. We could see Mom's depression worsening, but we couldn't do anything. I remember many nights when she came home sad, went to her room, and turned off everyone. She slept as much as she could (by heavy doses of medication) and just ignored the world. She wasn't eating right and she got defensive and agitated as I tried to help her. We now know those behaviors were side effects of the medication.

As Dad's birthday passed on the 19th, Mom had reached her final breaking point of suffering. I know God was with her when she took her own life on February 22nd, 2007; I know he was with her when she came home and took all the medication she had just refilled three days before.

As the final drop of water was poured into her glass of life, and she felt she could no longer go on—I know God was there, carrying her into His presence. We knew on the night of her death, that her mind was no longer her own. She knew how much my father's suicide had ripped our family apart and we knew she would have never consciously made the choice to leave us.

All I can do to even survive is surrender. From the moment I found Mom, I knew God's presence with me. I felt Him holding me up as I called 911. I immediately knew He had strengthened me my whole life to be able to handle just this situation—losing my true best friend. As the ugly word of suicide gripped my family again, I could do nothing except say to God, "Now what am I supposed to do with this? Let's see how this will work together for good."

The way to recover is to surrender to the grief while you embrace the in-filling love of God.

As it turned out, God opened the door for me to become an owner in a scrapbook store and I now have my own business. I am teaching Faith Scrapbooking classes regularly and bringing a different atmosphere to the company. He is using me to build deeper relationships with our customers and I now have customers who come in and ask for prayer. If I had been too scared to follow God in this job change, I would have lost out on the ministry opportunity he was opening for me.

As we visited her shop that Saturday morning we were touched, personally, intensely, by the spirit of compassion evident everywhere in it. She is very modest about what she has built there. But we were very impressed.

We sat with a group of six women around a big table in a tucked away upper room of the store. Stickers, markers, glitter, magazines, paper, paints, glue, scissors, stamps and stamp pads, along with all kinds of scrapbooking supplies we didn't recognize, filled the open spaces. The women chatted with each other, familiarly, as they worked on their respective scrapbooks.

We were the first men invited into the group.

The young woman sitting closest to us asked if we'd like to see what she was working on. We were eager to see. Her scrapbook was about her mother, who had passed away months before. The book was filled with photos of her mother, with page after page of handwritten thoughts and feelings about her mother's life and death, a myriad of symbols illustrating life and death's meaning to her. We viewed her labor of reflective love in a sacred light. It was a holy book. Expressing longing. Sharing gratitude. Showing anger. Chronicling life. Conveying death. It was real and raw, beautiful and blessed by warm memories and visceral emotions.

Each of the women expressed how meaningful this time together in the shop was for them. Healing. Draining at times, yet helpful.

Some lost parents, one a sister, another a son. For some it had been mere months. For others more than a dozen years. The wounds were still there, but scrapbooking's artistry and expression washed over them like a fragrant perfume.

She has created a sanctuary for women, especially, who need to find relief and care from the oppresion they feel, often because of death and its attending grief. They can come to her scrapbooking shop to give meaning to their feelings through creative expression. She wasn't with us the in upper room that day. She was working with others downstairs. She wanted to give us private space with the women. But her presence was felt in the way the women supported and encouraged each other to offer their stories for us. Each of them, hurting and brokenhearted, was enabling the others to find reassurance. Some were reluctant to open up at first, the details of their stories too uncomfortable to talk about. But one by one they rendered their reminiscences and enabled some of the pain to flow forth. As they did the healing continued. The wounds were a little less open and sore. We experienced a powerful time together.

She is a wounded healer, someone who is showing others the way to healing. Someone who knows the devastation of wrenching loss, and who still feels it every day. But, someone who uses her losses to allow others to find succor in theirs. She is picking up the pieces of her broken heart and helping others to mend theirs too. She allows God to work through her in a ministry of restoration to new life.

When I found this location, and began working to get the store ready, I was talking to my sister on the phone and I was trying to describe where the place was located. As I stood at the front door, describing landmarks, I looked across the street and began to weep. I told her what I just realized. I was standing across the street from where we used to live when our parents got back together after years of being divorced. That home was full of happy memories of our parents preparing to remarry. It was a safe place as we rebuilt our family.

She was "back home" again, creating another safe place for other families to rebuild their lives too.

Transformation (Tom)

"Just when the caterpillar thought the world was over,
it became a butterfly."
-Anonymous

"Pruning . . . not only speaks of cutting back but also of the
ultimate blossoming that takes place when it is done properly."
-Henri Nouwen

"Confronting our feelings and giving them appropriate expression always
takes strength, not weakness. It takes strength to acknowledge our anger,
and sometimes more strength yet to curb the aggressive urges anger may
bring and to channel them into nonviolent outlets. It takes strength to
face our sadness and to grieve and to let our grief and our anger flow in
tears when they need to. It takes strength to talk about our feelings and to
reach out for help and comfort when we need it."
-Fred Rogers

I REMEMBER SITTING in eighth grade science class learning about the wondrous process by which a caterpillar morphs into a butterfly. Without comprehending it at the time, I too was undergoing a transformation, a transformation from adolescence into impending young adulthood.

And now, many years later, what my teacher didn't teach me then, I am learning (not through a textbook or lecture, but from real life experience), the gruesome transformation occurring inside the chrysalis. In short, for a caterpillar to turn into a butterfly it has to digest itself before cells grow into the body parts of the future butterfly. It's quite a rigorous process.

Following the teacher's lecture that day, I remember asking the question: **Why do caterpillars turn into butterflies?**

Her response, from what I can remember, was a good one. Essentially, she said, "Caterpillars are the growing stage for the butterfly, they eat as a way of preparing for the transformation about to occur. What they can't do during this phase is reproduce, whereas adult butterflies can. In addition, adult butterflies can separate by flight, sometimes long distances, to either colonize new areas with fresh plants for the caterpillars or even migrate long distances to escape freezing winters . . . something they obviously can't do when they are caterpillars."

I stagger out of bed and head downstairs to the kitchen to make coffee. I grab my journal. Most days I start my day with a pen in my right hand and a devotional book in my left. That's if Madelyn, one of our twin girls, doesn't beat me out of bed—she tends to be an early riser like her Daddy.

As I write this I am reading through the Gospel of John. John's Gospel has always been a formidable one—not that the words are demanding to read—but challenging to comprehend. Ever since I was in the fourth grade, reading comprehension has been something I have had to be diligent at. I remember Ms. Madison, a retired schoolteacher, meeting with me several times a week to practice reading the same short story over and over again as if I were studying for a final exam. Undoubtedly, my skills have improved over the years—at least I hope they have—but there is always room for improvement.

I wipe the sleep from my eyes and open to John 15. I hurriedly read through the chapter. "There is no prize for speed-reading," Ms. Madison would declare, so more slowly and purposely, I re-read the chapter. I'm always astounded at how the Bible can speak to each of us in new ways at various times and in various seasons throughout our lives, and I'm hoping on this day, it does the same. I've read the Gospel of John many times before; I've even led studies on it, and yet, there is still so much to soak in and receive. The writer of the Gospel tends to be more philosophical and theological—and I tend to be more practical and hands on—which also makes the book arduous to comprehend. I think deeply about a lot of things, but I often take a longer time grasping things with deep meaning.

I start writing in my journal:

> *I need to hear something special from you, God. I woke up with this overwhelming sense of fear and anxiousness, which has been happening so much lately, and I don't know what to do with it. Everything is turmoil; even sitting here with a pen in my hand is taking every ounce of energy I have left. You know me better than I know myself so you know that I can't control what is happening inside of me. But it does make me wonder, why aren't you controlling it?*

I re-read the passage because Jesus' words aren't "sticking." I sense there is something special God is trying to say to me, but nothing seems to be connecting. The coffee is ready. I fill my cup. I take a sip, savoring the warmth it gives, the same warmth I long to have in my heart and in my soul.

I've written previously about the severe pain issues I live with on any given day. What I haven't written about as much are some of the emotional burdens I carry too. I have friends who battle depression, and most of their battles are far more intense than mine are (and I pray ever will be). But nevertheless, it is a particular hardship for me. There are some days when I have overwhelming feelings of sadness and anxiousness, such as today. Other days I am totally numb emotionally, experiencing neither highs nor lows. And then there are those especially trying days, when doing anything, literally anything, seems such an impossible hill to climb.

"Wouldn't it be nice if depression was like an on/off switch hanging on the wall—I could just turn it off when I need to focus my energy on the tasks at hand—and turn it back on if and when there is meaning in it?" I think to myself.

I continue reading.

Jesus says:

> *I am the true grapevine, and my Father is the gardener. He cuts off every branch of mine that doesn't produce fruit, and he prunes the branches that do bear fruit so they will produce even more. You have already been pruned and purified by the message I have given you. Remain in me, and I will remain in you. For a branch cannot produce fruit if it is severed from the vine, and you cannot be fruitful unless you remain in me. Yes, I am the vine; you are the branches. Those who remain in me, and I in them, will produce much fruit. For apart from me you can do nothing.*

I read it again, even more slowly and deliberately:

> *I am the true vine, and my Father is the vinedresser. Every branch in me that does not bear fruit he takes away, . . .*

I read it again, sounding out every word, emphatically.

> *I am the true vine, and my Father is the vinedresser . . .*

I read it again, and again, and again.

"What are you trying to say to me today? I'm here to receive from You."

I take a break and pour a second cup of coffee.

My mind starts wandering to the many responsibilities I have for the day.

I get comfortable in my chair again.

"Be here," I pray.

I read the passage again.

In that moment it's as if the sun has just appeared from behind a cloud on a summer afternoon and I am blinded by its glow: *Every branch in me that does not bear fruit he takes away, and every branch that does bear fruit he prunes.*

"Wait! Hold on. It doesn't make sense? Who is Jesus talking to in this passage? Isn't he talking to the disciples?!!!"

I pull out a few commentaries to study up on the passage. The passage seems to leave many ambiguities and even some of the best religious scholars at a loss. Sixteenth century theologian Martin Luther has written: *When the angels want a good laugh they read the commentaries.*

I'm not laughing, but I am perplexed. The commentators all suggest that Jesus identifies with the nation of Israel. In the 80th Psalm, the nation of Israel was symbolically referred to as a vine.

I'm not a vine keeper, nor have I ever the privilege of being introduced to one, but I am a gardener. In my garden, pruning helps all of the plants become the healthiest plant that it can and should become. With that thought in mind, it seems logical to me that Jesus would be saying to his disciples that the pruning process is an important part of their individual and corporate growth. But why would he reference himself as undergoing the pruning process? If Jesus is the Perfect One, why is **he** saying that **every branch in him that does not bear fruit, it is taken away**? And why would **he** say that **every branch not bearing fruit in him is pruned**?

Most of us have this picture of Jesus as being this flawless, faultless, perfectly compassionate individual—which he was. But we forget the fact that he was born by an unwed teenage mom in a farmer's stable. His birth was messy and happened in utter isolation. He was public enemy #1 from the moment of his birth to the point of his death. He was a wrongfully convicted criminal. He was tortured. He was abandoned by his best friends in his time of deepest need. And as the Apostle Paul writes,

He died the worst form of death any human being could possibly undergo, death on a cross. (Philippians 2)

So even Jesus underwent a pruning process in his lifetime? I record in my journal.

I rest in thought for a few moments.

Madelyn wakes up. I groggily climb the steps and head to her bedroom. She greets me in joyous exhilaration, the same greeting I receive every day of the year, "Hi Daddy!"

I try my best to transition back to reality; I don't have a choice. All of the depressed feelings welling up inside of me need to be kept at bay. I have four mouths to feed, diapers to change, bags to pack, as well as other obligations to fulfill. I dress all four kids in their "Sunday best," which actually means anything that passes the "smell test" (if it doesn't smell bad you are good to go!).

We leave for church; the depression hasn't left.

The church service has already started. We unobtrusively take our seats in the back of the room. I smile and whisper "hellos," but on the inside I'm not smiling. Fortunately, I don't have any responsibilities during the worship service.

Two weeks have passed since my last round with depression, which happened to be another Sunday morning. I drove part way to the church and I literally couldn't finish the trip. We made it one block away and I turned the vehicle around and went home. I couldn't put on a happy face and act as if I was well. So I didn't try to.

But here I am, two weeks later, in a very similar situation. On this day, I have help from Sarah. She knows I'm not well.

After the announcements are completed, we are invited to greet our neighbors sitting around us and to grab some coffee at the coffee bar. One of my closest friends stops me and asks how I am doing. He is also a professional "listener" and a pastor.

Do I hide the fact that I am hurting on the inside OR do I express what I am feeling and experiencing? Do I practice what I preach about openness, vulnerability, and authenticity?

"I'm okay."

He could sense otherwise.

"You aren't okay, are you?"

"No, no I'm not."

He invites me into a private space at the far side of building. We help ourselves to another cup of coffee.

"So, what's going on?" Knowing that my friend is one of the "safest people on earth," I open up,

"I think I've mentioned to you before that I live with depression. I just don't understand it? I don't understand why things have to be so relentless?"

We go on to have a lengthy conversation about depression and the effect that it can have on us as individuals. He indicates that it can also can play a crucial role in our lives.

"What kind of a crucial role?" I ask.

He is a little older than I am and he goes on to disclose how depression has made him into the kind of pastor he is. He talks about how depression has made him become someone who is sincere, someone who understands, and someone who is filled with grace for others.

He says, "Our pain is what forms connection. It gives us sensitivity, empathy, compassion, patience and an ability to see beyond the surface with people. Empathy means we see a bit of ourselves in everyone we meet.

We all have our own hardships—it might not be depression—though for a lot of people it is. We are all connected because of it. Jesus experienced pain to form connection. God didn't just create us to go through hardship without experiencing it too. Jesus wanted that bond; he wanted us to know there isn't anything in this life he is unaware of. So whether it's mental illness, loss, grief, loneliness, poverty, abuse or fear, Jesus wants us to know that we aren't alone in it. God fully understands the condition of being human. We can choose to be bitter about it OR we can use it as a form of connection to help others to face their own."

Our conversation continues. I weigh in about what was revealed to me in the Gospel of John earlier that morning and how Jesus underwent "pruning" in his own life. We talk about how important it is for us to remember that God doesn't force pain upon us. God doesn't enjoy being the vine keeper in that illustration, eager and ready like "Edward Scissorhands" to cut off branches that are fruitless or need updating. It's not the way God works. God is about the business of redeeming the whole plant. God wants all of us to bear fruit. We see evidence in Jesus' own life. All the suffering he experienced has been redeemed because we are now able to enter, fully, into relationship with him. God can fully relate to our human condition.

"Thanks so much for allowing me explore all of this today. There is so much baggage around depression and mental illness and other human vulnerabilities. So many people, it seems, have this idea about individuals who have a mental illness— or any illness for that matter—that they need to either prove how sick they are OR they try to fix us of ours. Neither response is helpful. I know for both of us, what we need more than anything else, is to do exactly what we are doing right now, creating a safe environment to express it. Can you imagine if all of us did for one another what you just did for me? Churches, really, could be the safest places on earth, right? Recently I read a book by Rachel Held Evans where she said something like—we long for churches to be safe places to doubt, to ask questions, and to tell the truth, even when it's uncomfortable . . . we might just create sanctuary."

We chuckle.

"Tom," he said, "you know you can call me anytime, day or night if it is an especially rough day. I will come and sit with you because I know what it's like. And I know you would do the same for me. We will continue to create sanctuaries for one another."

It's so uncomfortable to be vulnerable, isn't it? Its uncomfortable for me, and even embarrassing at times, to talk about all of these issues—my depression, my fibro, my pain, my loneliness, my sadness. I don't like feeling weak, especially as a man, so the easier route seems to be to keep it all inside. But that causes more problems in the long run. We believe it is in the telling when we find light in the darkness, a belief offering us hope. Pruning, whatever kind of pruning, emotional, physical, spiritual, is painful in the short-term. But in the long run, the pruning process leads to blossoming beyond our wildest imagination.

Another one of my close friends, who is also an author, reminds me to think of 10 things in life I love. Every one of those 10 things, although joyful, also brings a great deal heartache. For example, we love our home. After moving seven or eight times in seven years, we love being in the same place for more than a year. But on the flip side, the house brings about a lot of stress (dripping faucets, leaky roofs, no insulation in winter and summer months, and so on). The same is true with our own individual journeys. Pruning, which inevitably happens along the way, can also be a special thing. Life is complex for everyone; we all deal with tests, obstacles and fragmented days. But those tests, obstacles and fragmented days are what can bring about the most good.

My soul is overwhelmed with sorrow to the point of death.

Several weeks later, Michael and I were on a yearly retreat, sitting next to several monks in the sanctuary of a Benedictine monastery. Each of the monks, dressed in their black robes and with their long gray beards, were chanting psalms and songs, trying to give voice to the emotions running through their hearts and minds. It was Maundy Thursday (also known as Holy Thursday, in the Christian tradition), the day commemorating the final night of Jesus' life and the last supper he ate with his friends and disciples.

At first, we didn't pay much attention to the words because they are words we had read and heard hundreds of times before. But for some reason, on this special evening, we were drawn to them: *My soul is overwhelmed with sorrow to the point of death.*

Words expressed by Jesus on the acute knowledge that within hours he was going to die, violently, humiliatingly, utterly painfully.

"Wait! Jesus was "overwhelmed with sorrow"?! It can't be! Jesus shouldn't be expressing how he felt overwhelmed with sorrow by his circumstances. Or should he?"

So much of our human experience has taught us that Jesus was some sort of superhuman, extraordinary, miraculous being. All that would be true. But what is so often taught ignores the very real fact that he was human. There is virtually nothing said about that humanness. How often do we hear about him expressing raw human emotion? How about him laughing or grieving or crying or tired or being hungry?

"After all, he is God, right?" But that's not what the texts (Matthew 26:38 and Mark 14:34) say. They say that he was *OVERWHELMED WITH SORROW!*

It is now two weeks later and it's still complicated to comprehend what we read and heard that night. Both of us have a book of quotes by Fred (Mr.) Rogers— *The World According to Mr. Rogers: Important Things to Remember.* In the introduction, Fred's wife Joanne wrote this about him:

> *It was not all fun and games for Fred—he had his struggles, too, as we all did. I remember his moaning and groaning to us, "I just know I'm going to fail this course!" Of course, we'd all get worried for him. Then he'd get an A—and we'd all get mad at him. . .It took courage and a lot of support when he faced the cameras for the first Neighborhood programs. Someone once asked which one of his puppets resembled him the most. It was, of course, Daniel Striped Tiger—an uncharacteristically shy tiger. Despite Fred's tendency to shyness, that trait never got in the way of his capacity to make many friends, to whom he readily lent an empathetic ear. Fred was always a good listener for as long as I knew him. . .When we were together, he was able to show his lighter side—perhaps I even enabled it sometimes, as did several of his friends who had "the gift of whimsy." He could laugh heartily and with much pleasure at pure silliness, and was, at times, the funniest person I have known. . . . When I think of the entire persona of Fred Rogers, my inclination is to put him on a very high pedestal, despite the fragilities that are part of being human.*

In the last few years, we have been even more drawn to the humanity of Jesus and so many others who express the fullness of human emotion—with its rawness— not despite their humanness, but because of it. We are continuing to learn that our humanness is what makes us unique, it's what makes us free, it's what makes us as Fred Rogers, who studied to be a pastor and whose ministry was his long-running TV show, always said—'special'.

Expressing human emotion is what makes us normal, it is not weak to say we are scared, to indicate we are uncertain, to be open about our insecurities. We remind others we have been created to open to one another—our triumphs and our defeats, our laughter and our tears, our "fragilities." When we are only willing to open up about what is "right" with our lives, what is going well, and not able to disclose when we feel sad or lonely or "less than good enough," we deny ourselves the healing we need.

We believe, very strongly, in looking more closely at the times and situations in which Jesus was portrayed as being fully human. Those times when he wept, when he was tired and needed to rest or be alone, when he was afraid, when he despaired, when he cried out in agony, when he expressed the need for friends and when he hurt as his friends abandoned him. It is essential to recognize them. We believe it is essential because in seeing him in his humanness, we can understand better our humanness. And in understanding our humanness, we can begin to have more grace and understanding about one another and ourselves. It enables us to see one another as less alone, as having so much more in common than we have previously known, as being on life's journey—with all its wonder, with all its demands—together.

Jesus' vulnerability is a model for us. His humanity serves as a guide for ours, to embrace humanness. And as we spend time with so many others who open up to us about their own humanity, we learn increasingly more about how vital it is to be vulnerable with those who provide a haven of grace for us in our own.

... With You I Am Well-Pleased

"I'm going to make fathering very simple: answer your child's question.
Answer, 'Yes, you have what it takes,' or 'Yes, you are lovely.'
Answer it a thousand times in a thousand ways over the course of
your son or daughter's life, and you will have done your job,
you will have offered the best gift a father can give."
JOHN ELDRIDGE

"I'm proud of you for the times you came in second, or third, or fourth,
but what you did was the best you have ever done."
FRED ROGERS

MICHAEL

"GO, MICHAEL! GO!"
He yelled out to encourage me as I ran past him that late October afternoon,

"Come on. Keep it up. You can do it!"

Today, his is the one voice I remember more than 40 years later. The one that matters the most. The one I wanted—and needed —most to hear.

Yes. I wanted to impress the large crowd gathered for the school's soccer match that was being played simultaneously with our cross-country meet. Our starting and finishing line was within full view of everyone at the soccer field. I wanted to impress my classmates – especially the female ones. I wanted to impress my teammates. I wanted to be good for them. To win the race as some thought I could. For all of them. For me, too.

But mostly, I wanted to impress my dad. I wanted him to be proud of me. At age 16 and at the start of my senior year in high school, it was important to me. It remained important to me until the day my father died. Even since he's been gone I still want to make him proud.

Rarely did more than a small handful of people come to our meets. The fact was we were a lousy team. In my first two years as a runner on the team, we never won a single event. Never even came close. Before then, the team had not won a meet in years and years as far as I knew. Soccer was the premier fall sport in our school. All the "best" athletes were on that team, or at least it seemed as if they were. But on that afternoon, the cross-country team actually had a chance to win. We were running against a neighboring district in its first year fielding a team of runners. They were inexperienced and in this exhibition, our team was actually, improbably, unprecedentedly expected to win. Expectations were such; it would have been humiliating to lose.

The pressure was on *me*, in particular. In my senior year I entered as the team's best runner. What an unexpected and unbelievable position for me, after years of believing my small stature wasn't conducive to me being a decent athlete. I always had to take many more steps than all the taller runners, as my legs just weren't as long as theirs. When we walked the courses at away meets (to familiarize ourselves with them) I always needed to half-run just to keep up. Invariably, I was putting out almost twice as much effort even before the meets began. But the mix of my competitive spirit, my desire to be known as a good athlete and the near constant presence of my dad at the races, propelled me into a zone in which I was actually notably good at long distance running.

If I was going to be the first runner to break the tape at the finish line, I had to set the pace and keep it going. Enough of the rest of my teammates also had to beat enough of the other school's guys, obviously, if we were to win the entire meet. But it was on me to set the stage and the speed.

I was nervous. Petrified, actually. The expectation weighed on me for weeks, building to an internal fever pitch on the day of the meet. The adrenaline coursing through me was palpable, unsettling, actually. I hadn't ever recalled such an intense feeling and pressure to succeed, especially athletically. It was both a blessing and a curse: a massive crowd would be assembled for that afternoon's school soccer match – in full view of a significant portion of our race and the finish line. If we won, everyone would see our victory. If we lost, well, everyone would see that too, which would have been humiliating.

I desperately wanted to break the tape, to win. This was out team's best shot. My best shot.

After an excruciating wait throughout the day to just get it over with, finally it was time. My teammates and I exited the locker room in our uniforms; cheers and well wishes went up from the crowd assembled for the soccer match right outside the locker room door. We walked around the edge of the field toward the far side to our starting line. We shook hands with the opposing team and lined up in the traditional manner, with me, the seeded front-runner, in the number one position. My heart was pounding, my stomach queasy, my nerves pulsing, my mouth desert dry.

"Runners ready. On your mark, get set, …"

The starting gun's shot pierced the air. We shot across the line. The 2.2-mile race was on.

I needed to pace myself. I couldn't let those who leapt out too quickly in front intimidate me. Inevitably they would falter and slow down considerably before too long. But I also couldn't get too far behind anyone. Psychologically, it can be daunting and self-defeating to constantly be racing to catch up. Our team knew that fact all too well. We were in a similar position all too often. I tried to settle into a manageable and sustainable pace.

By the time we approached the first inner loop around the soccer field, the crowd noticed – I was in first place, leading all contenders. They cheered me, encouraged me, motivated me. Let it be said, in my experience, at least, such encouragement really *does* make a difference. I want to do better when others have high expectations of me. On that day it made me run faster, harder. I was in the zone.

I heard my father's voice above all the others in the crowd,

"Michael, come on. Keep it up. You can do it!"

I caught a momentary glimpse of him as I ran by. I really wanted to make him proud.

I was still in the lead, a wider one (at least in my memory!) by the time we made the second broader loop around the soccer field. Sooner than I expected, I found myself to be in the home stretch, the long passage down the far side of the soccer field, and the fans at the soccer match noticed. The crowd began yelling – cheering me on when I came into their view. It felt incredible. I wasn't used to the attention. I had no idea how fast I was going; I turned my head slightly to see how close anyone was to me. I was stunned to see no one in sight.

"What?" I questioned. "How could this be? Did I miss part of the course? Did I take a shortcut without knowing it? Was I actually that far ahead?"

The cheering fans, the realization of my lead and with the finish line in sight, I picked up the pace even more. Something beyond myself was propelling me. I don't remember any pain, any shortness of breath, anything else but my eyes on the coveted prize.

For the first time in my life, I broke the tape. I was first. I won the race!

But it got even better than that.

My coach ran up to me.

"Do you know what you just did?" he roared.

I thought I was in trouble. My elation diminished. But that wasn't it.

"You just broke the school course record! 11 minutes, 18 seconds! You set a new record!"

"What?" I couldn't believe it. "I broke and then set a school record? Me?" I thought to myself, incredulously.

As I let the news wash over me I simultaneously turned to cheer on my teammates as they began crossing the finish line. As one by one they came down the stretch it became increasingly clear we were going to win the meet, the first elusive win for our school's cross country team in "who knew how many" years. And a new course record in the process. I still couldn't quite believe what had happened. Especially since I led it.

Our team was jubilant. It was hard to leave the locker room that afternoon. I wanted to stay and enjoy the incredible (and unparalleled) celebratory moment with my teammates. But I couldn't linger too long. My dad was waiting in the parking lot to drive me home. I showered quickly, got dressed, congratulated my teammates one more time and met my dad in his pickup truck.

He came to virtually every cross-country and track meet, Little League game, band concert, play, Sunday school program and other event I participated in while I was growing up. He was always there. As an adult, he would still come when I asked, to hear me preach or present a talk or to other special programs in which I had a significant part. He came to many of our sons' athletic events and band concerts when they were growing up and in college, when the competitions were close enough to attend. He was always there when we asked and when he was needed. His loyalty and faithfulness was evident and real – to me and to my sons, as well as with my sisters and brother and to his other grandchildren too. I know now, looking back, how his presence was a tangible expression of his love for us and his pride in us, his offspring.

But I'm not certain I always knew it at the time.

I grew up in a region of south central Pennsylvania that is predominantly, historically comprised of German/Swiss immigrants – stoic, undemonstrative, non-effusive people.

While some family outliers are more emotive and expressive, I was surrounded by a large family and by neighbors, friends and classmates with their large extended families, who are not outwardly affectionate, easy communicators of vulnerability or comfortably openly affirming.

There's the conundrum for me.

I am wired to need affirmation. "Affirmation" is one of my favorite words, one I realize I use a lot. If anyone speaks words affirming me in any way, I am more motivated, more confident, more apt to take valuable risks. I thrive on hearing or reading words encouraging something I've done, written or spoken. I am simply inspired to do more, to be better, when I am affirmed.

Growing up, the culture didn't often provide me with the affirmation I needed. I didn't often hear how I was good enough, smart enough, significant enough. I now know I was loved and valued for who I am. But I didn't really know it then. I often had to dig deeply to find the evidence, because it was predominately an unspoken love. While presence—attending games, plays and special events—is absolutely huge when it comes to showing approval and support, for me, and I think for nearly all of us, words are necessary too.

The conundrum in not hearing it as much as I needed often left me wanting more.

But on that day when I ran the race of my young life, I don't remember my dad saying "congratulations" or that he was proud of me, even though he was there to see it. Yes, his presence meant the world to me that day. Yet truth be told I had often wished he wasn't there on all the other days when we lost, usually miserably. I didn't want him to see the disappointment and defeat.

But the culture he grew up in, I grew up in and continue to live in, isn't one in which verbal affirmation comes easily for many people, most especially for men.

On that record-setting, victorious day, I needed and wanted to hear, from my dad, how I made him proud; I never heard those words.

Around the same time I got a vital insight into why I rarely heard the affirmation I needed. At a moment of frustration, in which I did expressed a sentiment I very rarely ever did with my dad, I questioned him about why he "never told me that he thought I did anything right, that he only seemed to let me know when I did something wrong."

"It's not my job to tell you what you've done right. It's my job to let you know when you haven't."

I was yearning for words I was not likely to ever hear. I learned a lot with his answer that day. And you know, it was an answer so utterly similar to many other friends' experiences with their dads, too. Part of it was generational. Our larger culture isn't always very affirming either. We're much quicker at pointing out what's wrong with something or someone more often than we are to affirm someone for what is right or to point out something, which is good.

Many other dads I knew growing up seemed to believe that same mantra—affirmation wasn't necessarily part of the job description for many fathers.

Actually, part of it's a theological concept as well. There's a huge strain in the faith espousing a belief in a God who is out to judge our failings and faults, who is quick to punish us for our wrongdoings, who focuses more on listing our sins, rather than acknowledging our belovedness and giftedness. The church often focuses on our sinful nature and our need to repent, rather than on what Tom and I believe is the biblical message throughout—of God's great graciousness and compassion for our human condition. The climb toward affirmation is arduous when competing against such long-held tenets as this one.

Throughout my career I've been privy to many people's admissions about how they've never felt truly appreciated or considered or good enough. I've heard from so many others that they feel as if they don't measure up or they are a disappointment or they haven't lived up to others' expectations. There is a pervasive anguish among women and men alike who are still trying to feel their parents' approval and, ultimately, love. Deep down – and maybe not so deep down – we all need to know we are loved and good enough, how others, especially our parents, are proud of us. Even after they're gone.

It seems to us as if it is time – well past time – to break the cycle of stoicism, emotional invulnerability and lack of expressed verbal affirmation pervading too much of our culture at large. Tom and I both try to break that cycle with our children. And we remind each other regularly how we are proud of one another and how we are beloved sons of a God who is well pleased with us. We aim to remind everyone we possibly can in the work we do together that they are beloved daughters and sons of a God who is well pleased with them. God knows that far too few of the people we meet hear such good news. Few believe the good news about themselves.

We want to change this cultural – and spiritual – deficit. We know how very much we need to hear we are beloved; to hear simply because we are born into this world, our essence, our presence, amounts to something good.

A few years ago, I had the privilege of being invited to preach at the three services in the church where Kathy and I attend. The day corresponded with a visit home from my brother Steve and his family, who lived in Hawaii. My sons, parents, sisters and brother and their families were all coming to our home after the last service for a cookout. I invited them to come to the late service to hear me speak, since it was near our home. Everyone accepted the invitation. I was thrilled.

Following the service, as I stood at the door shaking hands and greeting worshippers, the pastor of the church stood next to me. As my father approached the door, I introduced him to the pastor, who exclaimed to my dad,

"You must be very proud of him!"

My sisters, standing behind our father, looked at me and then at each other with quizzical expressions, wondering how he'd respond. Having grown up in the same culture as I did, they weren't used to hearing "I'm proud of you," either.

But without hesitation, our dad replied,

"Yes, I am!"

My sisters immediately burst into laughter, a nervous, spontaneous response to something so unprecedented—and coveted. The three of us looked at one another as if to silently ask,

"Who is this man? Is he *our* father?"

I let out a quiet breath of relief. That moment negated all the other times I never heard those words. It superseded any previous longing I had to be told that he was proud. The moment was enough. Considering how our cultural environment didn't foster a lot of affirmation, I was grateful for the pastor who asked my dad the question and for the response my dad gave that day.

I'm especially grateful for the question and for the response today, as I write this five months after my father passed away. Those words will always remain in my hearing and in my heart, even more than the words,

"Go, Michael! Go! Come on. Keep it up. You can do it!"

TOM

I was sitting in the bleachers, watching my six-year-old Luke's T-ball game, when one of the coaches on the opposing team started berating his son for not swinging the bat properly. It may have only been for a few seconds, but it seemed as if it was forever. Naturally, his son started crying.

The father yelled, noisily, echoing throughout the sports complex,

"Boys don't cry. Pull it together. There is no crying in baseball!"

Almost humorously, I remember thinking to myself,

"I thought those were only lines from the movie *A League of Their Own*. It can't be real life, can it?"

Growing up, my dad attended every soccer, basketball, and baseball game I ever played in, every Boy Scout meeting, every award ceremony, and every significant event I was part of. He was present to pat me on the back and tell me of a job well done. He was there when I scored three goals and two assists in an important soccer match. He was there when I helped our team make it to the state playoff game. He was there when I became the Boy Scouts district Pinewood Derby champ with a perfect 27-0 record. He was the first person to hand me the local newspaper with articles mentioning my name in them. He was the first to retrieve my home run balls after they sailed over the fence. He always affirmed me when I succeeded.

My freshmen year of high school, I remember jogging off the baseball field, feeling especially good about myself. I had finally made it off the disabled list, recovering from a broken ankle I had suffered six weeks prior, and was excited to be back on the field again.

In my last game, I had hit the game winning home run, along with several diving catches, helping our team get a much-needed victory. In the current game,

I had already hit a single and a double in my first two at bats, with two runs batted in.

The field we were playing on that day reminded me of the sandlot fields my friends and I played on during warm summer afternoons growing up. The grass in the outfield was dense, with divots every few feet, resembling a giant game of whack-a-mole. The infield felt like a concrete playground with a patch of crabgrass every few feet, resembling a giant checkerboard.

I had just made the final out of the second inning with a catch in centerfield and was due up to bat. Approaching our team's dugout, I noticed, as I always did, my dad looking in my direction. I could see he was happy for me, knowing how patiently I had waited for my ankle to heal the previous six weeks. He was also especially cheerful, because I was playing well that day ...

Growing up, I had amazing parents. They worked very hard to train up their four boys so they would become responsible young men ... I think they succeeded ! They did their best to provide for our family and they made HUGE sacrifices to make this happen. Nevertheless, as parents, there are always areas in which we inevitably fall short. We are humans, raised by humans. Humans who have insecurities, humans who are fearful, humans who have brokenness of all shapes and sizes.

While my dad was always affirming when I did something well, he became intimidatingly quiet when I "messed up." It has frequently been an internal conflict for me to work through.

One beautiful summer evening last year, my dad and I sat outside on the patio talking very openly and candidly about our lives. Never before had we had such an intimate and vulnerable conversation. At one point in the conversation I remember asking him about his dad and more about his own upbringing. I didn't know much about my grandfather other than the brief time we spent together on family vacations. My dad told me about some of the things his father was not able to give to him. He expressed how he is still picking up the broken pieces from his dad's own wounds. He offered how, beginning at age 12, he was forced to move from young adolescence to adulthood far quicker than any child should. He discussed his dad's dad and the relationship his father and grandfather had together; it was not warm. The conversation was an insightful one for me, and I'm forever grateful we had it.

Day by day, as I grow older, I'm learning to extend even more grace for my dad. I focus on the many character values he exhibited and taught me – especially his own sense of compassion, generosity and mercy. I realize that sometimes my temperament clashes with my dad's. My need for affirmation wasn't always something he could inherently fulfill. As my own children grow older and I can see their various temperaments, I already know that I'm not perfectly equipped to satisfy every need they have. It's inevitable with every parent and every child. This is where compassion for each person's unique qualities is most evident; none of us can perfectly satisfy anyone else's needs.

In our family there is an ongoing problem, which started several generations ago. We show appreciation and approval when we *succeed in life*. But when we make mistakes or aren't perfect or don't quite measure up, we haven't always been able to express a helpful measure of grace. My dad never, ever, berated me like the father did to his son at my son's T-ball game. But what I didn't receive has always been hardest for me to work through now that I am an adult.

... *"Ahh!!!!"* I yelled out, falling to the ground, writhing in pain.

I had just stepped into one of the field's potholes. With tears streaming down my face, I knew my season was over. I was embarrassed not only because I had fallen down, but also because I was crying in front of the whole team.

My dad rushed over to me.

I wanted my dad to say that he was dreadfully sorry for what had happened. But he said nothing. Nothing at all. It felt as if he was mad at me for playing so soon after my injury. I was devastated.

One of my best friend's dads, also sitting in the stands, saw the commotion. He ran out on the field. He was a former weight lifting champion. He bent down, picked me up, and carried me off the field and across the parking lot to my dad's car.

"Hang in there, Tommy. You will be back on the field soon," he stated compassionately, knowing it had been a hard-hitting road for me. His response was the one I wanted—and needed—from my dad.

We rode to Dr. Snyder's office, the same office we had visited many times before. My dad didn't say much, if anything at all, along the way.

I cried the whole trip.

As a father of four small children, I'm realizing more and more, there are a lot of things in this life we can give to our children. But inevitably, there will be areas where we fall short as parents, based on our own humanness; areas in which we need an extra special amount of grace, trusting our children are God's children, and we simply can only do the best we can.

And so what resulted for me, and for my own dad, (and probably his dad too), is a son who is constantly trying to earn approval. The impact of this relationship affected me for years, even to this day, and I think a lot of those emotions transferred to my relationship with God. I tried hard not to annoy God or upset God with my little problems. I had no aspiration of being wanted by God; I was just happy not to be loathed or hurt by God. Some of the pain as a result has come out in unhealthy ways—not expressing my anger in healthy ways, trying too much to be perfect or wanting to please everyone.

Here is an example how this has played out in my life:

I was at a park with Lillian and Luke. I brought a bag of leftover bread to feed the ducks. At one point, I turned to my right and handed Lillian, who was six (at the time), a hunk of bread. When I turned back around to do the same with three-year-old Luke, he had fallen into the water and was bobbing down the creek. I immediately jumped into the water to rescue him. He was unharmed, thankfully. It was an honest mistake, or so I thought. I called my dad expecting to receive his empathy or maybe even a laugh or two. Instead, the first words out of his mouth were the words:

"Not good Thomas, not good!"

For a long time, this is how I viewed God ... God saying:

"Don't screw up Tom. You'd better put forth lots of effort if you expect to please me. You'd better succeed. You'd better be perfect. I won't be satisfied with you if you fail."

Fortunately, my relationship with God took a major turn when I became a father myself. After Lillian was born, I began to see how wrong I was in my thinking about God, and to give my own dad far more grace than I ever had before. My dad and I are actively working through the issues of imperfection and different temperaments, knowing we will be healthier and stronger for it as we do.

For the first time I got a taste of what I believe God feels towards us. I thought about my daughter all the time. I prayed for her while she slept at night. I showed her picture to anyone who wanted to see it. I wanted to give her the world—and I still do. But I'm still a parent and I will unavoidably fall short—and do so on a daily basis.

Most days when I arrived home from work, my little girl would greet me by running out to the driveway and jumping into my arms before I could even get out of the car. As you can imagine, arriving home became one of my favorite moments of the day.

My own love and desire for my kids' love is so strong that it opened my eyes to how much God desires and loves us. My daughter's expression of love for me and her desire to be with me is the most wonderful thing. Nothing compares to being truly, exuberantly wanted by your children.

Through this experience, I came to understand that my desire for my children is only a faint echo of God's great love for me and for every person God made. I am just an earthly, imperfect father, like my own father, and I love my kids so much it hurts. As parents we try to give our all. My dad gave his all. I'm thankful for him. We can only give out of what we've been given and there are certain things my dad wasn't given. It's as if the toolbox he was handed didn't have all of the tools he needed. None of us have been handed the perfect set of tools to be the perfect parent our children hope us to be.

How could I not trust a heavenly, perfect God, who loves me infinitely more than I will ever love my kids?

In Mark 1: 9-11, we find one of the most defining moments of Jesus' earthly ministry:

> In those days Jesus came from Nazareth of Galilee and was baptized by John in the Jordan. And when he came up out of the water, immediately he saw the heavens being torn open and the Spirit descending on him like a dove. And a voice came from heaven, "You are my beloved Son; **with you I am well pleased.**" (ESV)

We believe this story to be of absolute importance for what God wants us all to know unequivocally – God loves us infinitely and perfectly and is unabashedly proud of each one of us!

In the original text, the Greek word for "pleased" is εὐδοκέω, meaning: *I take great delight in… I am overwhelmed with joy… I am truly happy. In* **you.**

God favors each of us that much too!! God sees us as God's own beloved ones. God wants us to wake up every day knowing we are unconditionally loved and wholly approved. We are made to be beloved; we are designed to feel beloved, yet most of us live our lives never celebrating and reveling in it. We have a part to play in experiencing belovedness because fathers and mothers aren't perfect, no human is. We are humans, raised by humans; humans who are fearfully and wonderfully made, yet greatly broken at the same time.

But it certainly does help when we hear it from others, and especially from those whose affirmations matter the most.

We all need to hear the words: *"I am pleased with you! I am proud of you!"*

We need to hear them a thousand times in a thousand ways. Our human nature causes us to need to hear those words over and over and over again.

One of the biggest graces we can give to our kids is to have them know we unequivocally celebrate and revel in their humanness, the same way God does with each of us.

This is what creates closer relationships.

SECTION 3

"What Makes a *Good* Listener?"

A Safe Place

"The most amazing thing happens when the door of shame is opened.
Light comes in! It's no longer a dark secret; it's actually the secret
of your life that is first your breaking and then your making."
-BR. CURTIS ALMQUIST

"Vulnerability is courageous. Life keeps asking us to show up and
be ourselves, with all the varying emotions and all the messiness.
Being vulnerable is being human. Leaning into it,
embracing vulnerability is life-giving."
-BR. LUKE DITEWIG

H ELP! *That is what I've wanted to shout for most of my life. But I didn't. I continued to suppress all my negativity, hurt and ill-will toward self. All this suppression re- sulted in bubbling to the surface self-destruction in the most in-opportune times. I believed that I didn't deserve the happiness and successes that I did achieve. I never received guid- ance on how to deal with the positive things in life; I only learned anger, only to focus on the negatives. Yes, I grew up in era where you suffered your pain in silence. You were never encouraged to say what you were feeling or missing. My soul is full. . .of all the wrong things. I needed help in digging through my fractured soul; to come to terms with the fact that "I am a good person and I'm allowed to feel good about myself and my life."*

A lot of years have passed in my life. A lot of years wasted suppressing my feelings.

To meet with us, he needed the place to be very private, not in a coffee shop or public place. He wanted to talk at night, because after revealing what he needed to express he just wanted the day to be over. What he had to say could not be rushed; he was going to need a lot of time to bring it all out.

He needed to set the time and place, the circumstances and conditions to talk. Feeling so out of control, he needed—desperately—to have some control over the way his confidences would be revealed. So we let him have the control he needed. He required its safety, its consolation.

Setting those parameters, it was important for us to recognize what he needed. We had to listen beyond the trepidations, to hear what he was actually saying.

All the years of holding it in, his default position, created a barrier for him to divulge. It took him more than an hour just to feel relaxed and trusting of us before he could get to the heart of the affair. And when, like a volcano, his emotions erupted to the surface and he realized he had to begin to dialogue about what was going on inside, he was reluctant to do so, notably irresolute. But he knew that with this eruption, the time had finally come; he couldn't hide his past any longer.

A week before our meeting, in a very public way, he embarrassed himself in an evening of excess, in front of friends and peers. Both his body and his self-esteem were bruised in the process. He was taken to the ER where he remained for observation overnight. He was utterly humiliated by the shame he caused himself and his family. But the incident served as a wake-up call where he realized something had to change—and the something needing to change were the secrets he had been holding inside for over 50 years. He grew up being taught to hold in his emotions and "either buck up or shut up." And he did both.

But on the night of our meeting he was determined to keep the invisibles, invisible no longer.

The following day he wrote us a message. He detailed what aided him in making the unseen, seen:

Our openness—to hearing all he had to say and not prescribing how and where we had to meet, but allowing him to be met in the way that would be most comfortable.

Our truthfulness—not allowing him to continue buying into the lie that he is no good, but instead reminding him that no matter what, he is deserving of being heard.

Our patience—giving him the time he needed to come to reveal the essence of his secrets, being sensitive and not pushing him to go faster than he could.

Our understanding—reminding him that we are human too, expressing how we know what it's like to be scared, to feel shame, to disclose something to which others may react unkindly.

Our non-judgmental response—we didn't point out his flaws and weaknesses or shame him for the mistake he made or for the secret truths he revealed to us.

He concluded by writing:

Thank you so much for meeting with me last night. You made the intimidating opening of my soul a calm process that I believe I can trust.

As I'm sure you've heard many times before, to embark on such a journey of laying bare your pain is a very private and difficult decision.

When I arrived home last night, my wife asked how I felt. I responded that I felt more at peace than I ever have in my life.

What a moment to realize that all I needed was someone I could tell it to. Thank you both for being that someone.

––––––––––––––

The author and physician Rachel Naomi Remen writes in her book, *Kitchen Table Wisdom: Stories that Heal:*

> *I suspect that the most basic and powerful way to connect to another person is to listen. Perhaps the most important thing we can ever give each other is our attention . . . when people are talking, there's no need to do anything but receive them. Just take them in. Listen to what they're saying. Care about it . . .*
> *. . . One of my patients told me that when she tried to tell her story people often interrupted to tell her that they once had something just like that happen to them. Subtly her pain became a story about themselves. Eventually she stopped talking to most people. It was just too lonely. We connect through listening . . . When we listen they know we care. (pp. 143–144).*

––––––––––––––

"I used to go to church high."

That was our introduction to him.

"It wasn't a high that came from the Holy Spirit," he explained. "The reality is, my life has been filled with darkness, deep, dark mental darkness."

He worried others in the pew would know he was high. "Frankly, I'd sweat with anxiety, as I'd wonder if anyone sitting near me noticed I was high. What would they think of me? How many people are looking at me? You kind of get a little paranoid when you're in that state. And then I'd wonder if anyone was even concerned with what I was doing? At the same time it didn't matter to me what anyone thought. I didn't matter to me much, either.

"I spent a lot of my time in college making poor choices. Although I attended a Christian school I discovered that drugs and alcohol were available to anyone who wanted them if you found the right people. That's when I quickly realized I could dull my mental anguish quite nicely with a bag of weed and a six-pack. I liked that."

What followed was a 20-year downward spiral into a world of substance abuse.

He was raised in a home perceived as Christian, but what happened behind closed doors was anything but Christian. A mother whose will and spirit were broken when her father abused her growing up, verbally, emotionally and spiritually abused him and his siblings, and their father.

"She was also very physically abusive to me. While not every day, she managed to hit me often enough to make me want to fight back. I vividly remember going after her with a knife one day when I had been pushed too far. But, fortunately, I came to my senses before I ever attacked her back."

Even after graduating from college, getting married to the love of his life and having two daughters, the horrible memories and ongoing interactions with his mother continued to plague him. And, so did his drug and alcohol use. He thought of himself as a high-functioning addict who could handle life, family and career in spite of his internal torment and self-medication.

Holding his adult life together for 13 years took its toll. After his mother found fault with his parenting and made threats to take his daughters away from him and his wife, they had their most searing altercation. The words they exchanged were "beyond heated." The anger spewed was toxic and venomous and they stopped talking for months.

"I slipped into a deep, dark depression that affected me profoundly. I hated myself and the life I was living. Thoughts of desperation and suicide became commonplace. My worst day came when I broke down in front of my wife.

She held me while I sobbed like a little child. I will never forget when she held my face, looked me in the eyes, and told me I needed to seek professional help."

Therapy slowly helped him begin to heal. Though he was working toward improving his life, he recognized his addictive personality was continuing to dominate and torment him. He told us he knew he couldn't give up drugs and alcohol on his own.

He tried to re-engage with his church and he became close friends with one of the pastors. But his drug use continued and he continued to go to church high.

"I joined a men's group there. Yet, I kept my substance struggles from the guys in the group. I didn't trust enough to be vulnerable with them about what I was doing.

"I prayed to God that day to do whatever it would take to change me and take my addictions away."

He believes God answered his prayer.

"On my way to buy a bag of weed I stopped to do an errand. When I did, something totally uncharacteristic of me happened. I argued with two young men and it quickly became physical. I was charged with assault.

"I was shaken to my core; my desire to continue abusing substances was taken from me. My life was turned upside down. I began to meet with a group of guys who had agreed to hold each other accountable and the change they helped make in my life was undeniable.

"I finally began to let God in."

Though the change was moving him in the right direction, he admitted that his struggles didn't end. As the drugs left his system, he no longer had a way to deal with his anger. He started to take out his anger on his wife, and arguments turned rapidly into fights. Forgiveness became tiring. Nearly 20 years of marriage began to unravel and the possibility of a breakup became more and more realistic. His friend and pastor stepped into his life in a way that no one else had ever done and with compassion, he helped him see how he needed to allow God in more than he ever had before. His marriage strengthened slowly and he and his wife's love for each other was revived.

All that he went through – as the son of an abusive mother, as a person with addictions who tried to free himself from the stranglehold of weed and alcohol, as someone who for 20 years tried to run from the demons he carried within him – he realizes, has brought him to where he is today. He recognizes how he gained from every attempt, every relapse to overcome his addictions. He grew from the estrangements and broken relationships. He learned something valuable and lasting every time he grappled to break free and start a new way of living.

His journey through brokenness and his search to find and receive grace and compassion continues today. He learned he couldn't do it alone. What he knows now is that he needs God's love and guidance in order to find and maintain a life in which he doesn't simply "self medicate" to numb his sadness and anxiousness away.

He's also learned he needs others to embody God's love and guidance every day and to remind him of the healthy, grateful, and free life he wants to live. And if those others couldn't be everyone from his family of origin, then he's learned he could invite others in to be part of a larger family who could walk through it with him. Jesus re-defined who family is, broadening people's understanding of what constitutes a familial structure. He reminded us that family isn't just those whose blood runs through our veins. But he tells us family also includes whomever we are with who can love us well.

"Someone who has experienced trauma also has gifts to offer all of us—in their depth, their knowledge of our universal vulnerability, and their experience of the power of compassion." Sharon Salzburg

---

Safety. We need it, all of us. If we are to open our souls, if we are to allow others into our hurts and insecurities, if we are to acknowledge honestly our vulnerabilities, we need safety. We need others to listen who will not condemn us for the perplexities we reveal. We need others to meet us where we are not condemned or criticized.

Without safety, most of us won't reveal our true selves. Without safety, few of us will allow the light to penetrate our darkness. Without safety, it is nearly impossible to heal.

We need others who will help make us feel at ease in conversing with them about what is piercing . . . what is tormenting . . . what is causing internal conflict. We need others to help us understand that we are not solitary, that restoration can be had in being with safe people in safe places.

"You hide them in the secret place of your presence from those who scheme against them. You keep them in a secret shelter, safe from quarrelsome tongues." Psalm 31:20 (New Simplified Bible)

I Never Felt I Was Worth It

*"I learned that people may forget what you said, they may forget what
you did, but they will never forget how you made them feel."*
-MAYA ANGELOU

*"The greatest disease in the West today is not TB or leprosy; it is being
unwanted, unloved, and uncared for. We can cure physical diseases with
medicine, but the only cure for loneliness, despair, and hopelessness is
love. There are many in the world who are dying for a piece of bread but
there are many more dying for a little love. The poverty in the West is a
different kind of poverty -- it is not only a poverty of loneliness but also of
spirituality. There's a hunger for love, as there is a hunger for God."*
-SAINT MOTHER TERESA

THE ROSES were just starting to bloom. She bent down several times to take
in their scent, commenting on each one that was particularly fragrant. Row
after row she observed, excitedly, their diverse colors and particular beauty. At every
turn she glowed with the magnificence and splendor.

We followed her into the butterfly house, as she pointed out the dozens and
dozens of types flying around us and the varied colors and patterns on their wings.
She laughed as she watched them, in child-like wonder, at how many different
shapes and kinds there were.

The Japanese garden brought welcome relief from the draining heat of the
mid-afternoon sun. Its thick shade and flowing stream cooled us down and we savored the interlude as we slowly ambled through the garden.

Throughout the grounds we noted, as we walked along, so many other colors,
blooms and species—the unusual soft needles of a particular evergreen tree, the
uniqueness of the climbing hydrangea, the orange zinnia petals that caught her
eye.

Before that day, when we got together to visit each month we had met in her
small living room. Several times over the course of many months she'd expressed her
phobia of going out in public. This was our first visit with her outside her home. We
hadn't heard from her in a while and we wondered if she'd reach out to us. When

she hadn't, we got in touch with her and suggested we could walk and talk in the gardens, a place near her home where she said she'd actually like to go.

Sitting on a bench under a big, shady tree in a far corner of the gardens, the conversation unquestionably got started in depth, as it moved from her delight of the flowers and gardens to her admission that she never felt as if she had much worth as a person.

She was apprehensive to meet with us that day. We wondered why. She said she was reluctant to "bother" us. She felt as if there were so many others who deserved our time more than she did, that she wasn't important enough. This was a mantra throughout her life. She's never put her interests and needs first, always doing what someone else wanted her to do before she'd imagine doing something for herself. She's forever buried her own interests and desires for others.

We asked if she considered cancelling the visit to the gardens with us. She admitted she had. We had suspected she might. This was a huge deal for her, going out with us, propelling out of the cocoon of her house like a butterfly discovering for the first time it has a set of wings.

She never felt she was worth it.

Fulfilling her own needs was not second nature. It wasn't part of her nature at all.

Her two divorces, the recent dissolution of a third relationship, her children who are distant from her and who have all but cut her out of their lives. Her years of profound weight issues, the chronic fatigue syndrome she endures, intense social phobias and a house overflowing with far more paraphernalia than she can possibly use, all have contributed to, and are symptoms of, her feelings of unworthiness.

But we reminded her she is worth it. She is worth our time. She is worth us enjoying together an afternoon in a beautiful garden. She is worthy of being known and cared for and loved.

Our good friend Tim Madigan, author of *I'm Proud of You: My Friendship with Fred Rogers,* told us how during a low moment in his life, he questioned why well-known Fred Rogers would make the time to talk with him. After all, wasn't Fred a very busy man, with more important people to talk with than Tim?

But this was Mr. Rogers' reply:

> *Do you know the most important thing in my life right now? Speaking to Tim Madigan on the telephone.*

We recited Fred's words with her in the garden as we rested on the bench. At that moment, she was the most important person in our lives. She needed to know this reality, this truth.

One afternoon together in the gardens was meant to show her goodness, dignity, and naturally, love.

During one of our visits to her home many months later, as we sat with her, tears welled up in her eyes. It was shortly after the holidays. The emotional strain of the season had been too much for her to bear—alone. In the safety of our presence, she finally let it all out, like an enormous gale: "I need to be honest with you. In the last few days I've had serious thoughts, more strongly than ever before, about ending my life."

She showed us the doctor's review, a summary listing all of her health problems:

Abrasion . . . amblyopia . . . anxiety . . . arthritis . . . back pain . . . meta-typical basil cell carcinoma . . . chronic depression . . . chronic fatigue syndrome . . . chronic pain . . . excess skin of thigh . . . fibromyalgia . . . gastric bypass clinical pathway . . . Gilbert's syndrome . . . hypertension. . .insomnia. . .joint pain. . .lumbar radiculopathy . . . lumbar spondylosis . . . Mersa carrier . . . numbness . . . overuse of medication . . . renal mass . . . Serotonin syndrome

For most of us any one or two or three of those outcomes would be paralyzing enough; but for her, on top of each of those conditions, the emotional damages may be most daunting.

Her life-long dreams of having a happy and mutually loving marriage, of being a stay-at-home mom, cooking and nurturing her two sons, celebrating the joy and excitement of holidays with them, is nothing but a dream and a distant reality. In recent years, she has become more and more isolated. She feels profoundly lonely every day. It isn't that people haven't tried to reach out to her, inviting her to their own family dinners and gatherings. She knows those gestures are thoughtful and well intentioned, and she is very grateful for them. But they are all far from the ideal she wants. She longs for memories past. She remembers holiday gatherings when life was as our culture tells us it should be—family dinners, gift exchanging, enjoyment, child-like-wonder, no pain, just pleasure. As a mom, she yearns to be needed again, providing the special love for her own family as only a mom can do—as she once did. The disappointments of her life have taken her longed-for childlike wonder away.

"Every morning I take my pain pills, and for the first time, I've had serious thoughts of taking the whole bottle, ending it all. I don't know why I'm here anymore, the despair is so deep. Life is so excruciating, every day seems worse than the last. I'm scared to get out of bed every morning because I'm waiting for the other shoe to drop one more time, and I don't know if I can handle it anymore."

We keep listening, too—and we celebrate and confirm her decision when she voluntarily checks herself into a psychiatric program to confront the deeper demons in her life. As a result of such attention, she's gotten to the place where, in her words,

"I no longer need to ask why. Why has all this happened to me? That just keeps me in the past and I simply can't change the past. I have to move on. I can't keep living there."

"I believe God is real," our friend tells us one day. "But sometimes I just need a physical presence here to remind me of that. You do. You help to remind me."

Isn't that what friends are for?

There is a cure for many of the problems in our lives, but it doesn't come from medicines in a bottle, it comes from love presented, it comes from love's presence.

Since the holiday season had just ended, we recalled lines from the classic holiday movie, *It's A Wonderful Life*:

Strange isn't it, each man's life touches so many others. When he isn't around, he leaves an awful hole, doesn't he?
Remember no man is a failure who has friends.

George Bailey, the main character, is a man who has given up his dreams in order to help others. As fate would have it, his dreams are shattered. In utter despair, he contemplates suicide on Christmas Eve. His contemplation brings about the intervention of his "guardian angel," Clarence. In order to show George his life has purpose, Clarence shows George all the lives he has touched and how different life in his community of Bedford Falls would be had he never been born. That revelation keeps George from taking his life. George came to see how his life did mean something to his community.

There isn't a day going by during which we don't hear from someone about how lonely he is. Loneliness pervades like nothing else. Staggering numbers of people are not connected to others in ways which bring them gladness or contentment. The number of people who feel as if no one cares about them is heart-rending and taking one's own life often seems like a worthwhile option.

When any of us are in especially fragile places in our lives, we can forget how our lives do have a purpose, how they do touch other peoples' lives as well—many times without us ever knowing it. During these times we need other people to remind us.

The most powerful message of *It's a Wonderful Life*, is that the protagonist, George Bailey, needed to be stripped down to his essence again—to be reminded of how his life impacted others. He needed to receive others' encouragement, respect and consideration again. We believe *It's a Wonderful Life* has been widely popular because all of us can relate in some way. All of us have had moments in our lives when there has been too much to bear, alone.

In the most dramatic scene in the movie, George Bailey, in profound despair, takes out his aching despair on his family. In the midst of his ranting, proclaiming his rage and regret over his life's circumstances, his wife stands by him through it all, promising, *I'll love you to the day I die.*

Even though she was afraid in the face of his impassioned anger, she could see through it, looking beyond it and understanding how he was in inner-turmoil and he needed to be bolstered.

She stood by him through his agony, alongside him as he worked through it.

We are moved acutely by that scene, by its rawness, by George's vulnerability and by the pathos it conveys. The scenario speaks to the human condition, all too strongly—of the disenchantment and hopelessness too many of us feel at some point (or many points) in our lives. We are moved by the climactic scene in which all of George Bailey's friends, neighbors and associates crowd into his living room to tell him what a positive difference he has made in their lives. Those friends give him new life, new hope, and a new outlook again. They save him from himself.

Chapters (Tom)

"A father is a man who expects his son to be
as good a man as he meant to be."
-FRANK A. CLARK

THE DAY WAS "SUPPOSED" to be one of the more memorable days of my life—and it was—but for very different reasons than I expected.

June 3, 2006. Our wedding day. It was a day filled with meaning, beauty, joy, and love; it was a Hallmark card type of event.

June 4, 2006. We arise early in the morning and head to my in-laws to pack for our honeymoon and open the many wedding gifts we had received. We were knee deep in boxes and suitcases like children next to the tree on Christmas morning. Later, in the evening, we would leave for the airport to fly to the breathtaking mountaintop vistas of the Grand Tetons, in Wyoming—one of the most extraordinary places on earth.

With anticipation, one by one we carefully open each gift. First a blender, then a toaster, then a crockpot. We savor each gift and each moment. We know this will likely be the only time in our lives when we would be graced with so many blessings all at once. My in-laws pass the last box in the corner to my new bride; it is another Hallmark card moment.

Even today it seems unreasonable to put into words the gratitude and thanksgiving I experienced in that moment; I had married the woman I loved and so many people had showered us with their support and love.

After all the gifts were opened, Sarah leaves the living room and enters the kitchen. I remain seated in the rocking chair. Rocking back and forth, back and forth, I reflect on the day and the new chapter of my life beginning yesterday as if I were an older man pondering the ripples of his life. I pull out my journal to record some of what I am feeling. Not knowing exactly how to describe the emotions running through me, I start writing. The thoughts stream effortlessly.

As I turn a page in my journal, I find an envelope with my full name "Thomas" written across the front. There is only one person in my life who calls me by my full name, "Pops," as my brothers and I call him. My dad.

An envelope from my dad? Beside my name on the front of the envelope is the stamp of The Community Church of Harrington Park, the church where my dad pastors, the place where he has used his gifts in ministry so faithfully for the past 20 years.

I open the envelope, not knowing what I would find inside. My dad performed our wedding ceremony the preceding day and I knew it was an emotional day for him, even though he held his emotions in check.

Throughout my dad's career as a pastor it has always impressed me how he stays strong, offering comfort and encouragement to those who need it during the most intimate, sincere, and even uncertain times.

Inside the envelope is a letter. I open it:

My dear son Thomas, I wanted to write you this note because as I get older, as one day quickly passes to the next, and as you make ready for your wedding, I feel that there is much unsaid that should be said.

When we were out fishing the other day, (a day I was looking forward to and now, a day already gone) I was hoping we would engage is some deep conversation about life and our relationship together. Of course, I probably shouldn't have expected this. We were together enjoying what we both take pleasure in—fishing with one another. You seemed a bit quiet and being quiet isn't bad. You have a lot on your mind; no doubt your thoughts drifted toward your new wife, wedding day, honeymoon and life ahead. And so it should be.

Forgive the foolish reflections of an aging man but I want to tell you I will miss our days together. You and I have always enjoyed many common interests: fishing, baseball, and sports in general. We've shared many special occasions together and I want you to know how much I'm really going to miss them. Oh, I know we will spend similar moments together in the future. Sarah will so neatly fit into our shared and common interests but our relationship will certainly change.

Son, I have always treasured our moments together. I vividly recall, and thoroughly enjoyed, watching you compete in sports, sitting with you watching other sporting events, and having you home living under our roof. I'll miss all of it. I'll miss you.

Please know and never forget how much I love you, know that I would do anything for you, and know how proud I am of you and how wonderfully delighted I am that God is leading you into ministry and has provided Sarah for your life. She's a wonderfully special woman—a real gem who will bring you life-long happiness. You're richly blessed and so am I. But, also know the way in which our lives have been linked and shared over the years is something I will truly miss.

My intention is not to be a downer. How can we be down when God has so graciously blessed us? Yet I know how much our friendship has meant to me, how valuable your life has been in mine and I will always treasure our memories. You've been a blessing to my heart.

May the good Lord continue to guide you and prepare you to do His will—I will always look forward to your visits and anticipate God will use you to accomplish His purpose. Enjoy to the fullest your life with God, Sarah and in ministry. God bless you son.

I love you!

Pops

I stop rocking. My tears start running, flooding, overflowing, and I don't understand why. Belly aching, gut wrenching, uncontrollable sobbing. For what seemed like an eternity, I remain perfectly still in the rocking chair and I allowed my feelings to run their course.

I've done a lot of reflecting on the genuinely heartfelt moment. Why did I cry so intensely? What was it about the note that caused or awakened in me such raw human emotion? It has been 11 years since that day and I have come to believe the answer is a simple one. A new life chapter had begun and a new day had dawned for Sarah and me. But my previous life chapter had ended never again to be experienced or revisited in the same way.

For 20+ years I had lived under the same roof as my parents. We were together in most mealtimes, every holiday, every family vacation, every peak and valley of our lives. We experienced it all—together. A new chapter in my life had begun, and while the new chapter has been a wonderful, miraculous, fruitful chapter, it meant the end of something precious as well.

Sarah walks back into the room. She hears the sobs and sees my tears. She knows, even though I don't, why I am crying. She sits next to me. She holds me. She comforts me. She genuinely cares.

She was with me.

She listens.

God knows, even though I didn't, why I was crying. God sits next to me. God holds me. God comforts me. God genuinely cares. God was with me.

God listens.

She was with me toward the end of my previous chapter. She is with me as the page turns. She will be with me through the next chapter too.

God was with me in the previous chapter. God is with me as the page turns. God will be with me through the next chapter too.

Transitions can be quite uncomfortable to undergo. Whether it's a returning veteran, a new baby, a marriage, a death, a job loss, a job change, an empty nest, a divorce or a major illness, it's often not seamless releasing what we cherish and accepting what is ending. Often, it's not seamless receiving the changes and the new life ahead.

I was sad that day because a wonderful phase of my life was ending. And even though a new one was commencing, one I knew would be especially pleasant; I was speechless by an unbelievable sadness. I think my dad felt it too. An important life chapter was ending for him as well.

I am so grateful for Sarah, who understood what this transition meant for me. She allowed me to feel the sadness amidst the joyfulness. She didn't take the sadness personally. She didn't laugh at me or tell me I was senseless. She didn't discredit me or think any less of me for my feelings. She let me express them and knew in doing so this new chapter could begin with gratitude for what had been. It would begin in grateful appreciation for the promise our life together could bring.

She, along with God, will listen.

Cure Without Care

"Our tendency is to run away from the painful realities or to try to change them as soon as possible. But cure without care makes us into rulers, controllers, manipulators, and prevents a real community from taking shape. Cure without care makes us preoccupied with quick changes, impatient and unwilling to share each other's burden. And so cure can often become offending instead of liberating. "
-HENRI J.M. NOUWEN

"A hurting person is in a storm. They are cold, wet, shivering, and scared. Preaching, platitudes, and advice will not get them out of the storm. Don't tell a person in a storm that it's a sunny day. There will likely come a day when the clouds part, but it is not today. It's not your job to pull them out of the storm. It's your job to get wet with them."
-ADAM S. MCHUGH

AUTHOR AND SOCIOLOGIST Dr. Tony Campolo, tells a story about being in a church in Oregon when he was asked to pray for a man who had cancer. Campolo prayed boldly for the man's healing. A few weeks later the man's wife called him.

"You prayed for my husband. He had cancer."

Campolo was elated. When he heard her use the past tense verb, he thought his cancer had been eradicated! Before he could say anything, she continued, "He died."

Campolo felt terrible. But she reassured him.

"Don't feel bad," she said. "When he came into that church that Sunday he was filled with anger. He knew he was going to be dead in a short period of time, and he hated God. He was 58 years old, and he wanted to see his children and grandchildren grow up. He was angry this all-powerful God didn't take away his sickness and heal him.

"He would lie in bed and curse God. The more his anger grew toward God, the more miserable he was to everybody around him. It was an awful thing to be in his presence."

She paused and then went on.

"After you prayed for him, a peace came over him and a joy came into him. Tony, the last three days have been the best days of our lives! We've sung. We've laughed. We've read scripture. We've prayed. Oh, they've been wonderful days. And I called to thank you for laying your hands on him and praying for healing."

And then she said something incredibly profound. "He wasn't cured, but he was healed."

Sometimes we wonder if we are asking, praying, and pleading for the wrong things. Both of us can remember instances in our lives when someone asked us if it would be okay to pray for each of us in our unique situations, hoping to fix the realities we were living with at the time.

TOM

I remember talking with a close friend about my physical condition and its attendant pain. I opened up to him and he decided to lay his hands on my back and pray intensely for healing from the pain I suffer. For several weeks, every time I was with him, he prayed for God to heal me and perform a miracle. Every week, I would leave the prayer time, searching, wondering, and questioning whether God truly heard his prayers.

The pain never went away.

After several more weeks of the same monotonous routine, I found myself getting irritated when I was with my friend. I appreciated his initiative. I appreciated his desire to see me free from my chronic suffering. I appreciated his consistency. But nothing ever changed; I started to feel as if he was simply trying to cure my situation. I even told him my doctor said I'd never be fully healed, I would always feel discomfort, sometimes intensely. But my friend kept praying for me to be completely healed. My discouragement grew so much I began to avoid him whenever I could. It was less awkward.

My situation is incurable.

Doctors have told me the condition is something I was born with, but treatment may provide some relief to ease my burden. The doctors have told me the condition will likely be with me for the rest of my life. In other words, I would have to learn to live with it.

I used to wish my back pain would simply go away; and there are days I still do. The circumstances have gotten worse over the years and has required two spinal fusion surgeries, the second far more intensive than the first. In addition, broken bones, surgeries, fibromyalgia, concussions, and depression have caused my overall physical condition to decline as well.

It's been years since my friend's weekly prayers for healing. As I look back, it is clear to me God answered my friend's prayers. I have learned to accept and live with the physical handicaps confronting me every day—even if my prayers were not answered in the way I wanted them to be.

MICHAEL

Many years ago, a kind, older woman in the church told me nearly every time I saw her how she prayed every night for Matthew to be healed of his disabilities. It was her mantra. She was serious. She fervently believed his barriers could be taken away and he could live life just like his brothers.

She was a serious student of the Bible. She never missed a church service, and she was beloved in the congregation, a true saint of the church. She also mailed greeting cards to our home regularly, almost always with money inside, another sign of her care and concern for our family's well being. She showed us generously and faithfully how she loved us and wanted us to be well.

We loved her and appreciated her deep compassion and reinforcement. When she passed away, I was terribly sad. She was one of my favorite parishioners and I felt privileged to serve her. At her funeral service, I spoke gratefully and lovingly of her cards, her gifts of money, and her impassioned prayers.

But I never expected her prayers to work—at least not in the way she meant them to. She prayed for Matthew to talk, to not be incontinent, to not have to be in special education, to feed himself, to dress himself, to stop hitting and pulling hair, and to be "normal."

Kathy and I never thought any of those things would happen. Some of it might get better—and some of it has. There have been less severe moments of hitting and pulling hair, more times of properly using a toilet when he's placed there at regular intervals, and improved communication by pointing at pictures of things he wants. But the fact remains, intellectually he is younger than a two year old, his walking and hand coordination has worsened due to spinal cord compression, he still wets through his pajamas most nights, and he needs constant one-on-one watchfulness every minute of every day to protect himself—and our house—from harm.

None of it will ever change.

As much as we might desire it, we know it won't. In the natural order of the world God has created, we know that Matthew's disabilities will always be with him—and us.

We are perfectly fine with that. We love him just the way he is. Our prayer isn't for his disabilities to go away. But it is for us to have the stamina, the strength, the good humor, the patience, the serenity and the grace to embrace Matthew for who he is—a beloved child of God. We have not prayed for the physical and mental facts of Matthew's circumstances to change, but for our understandings and attitudes to change. We have prayed to know what can change and what cannot and for the wisdom to know the difference.

We both have experienced healing, but not in the ways our friends have prayed we might. In the decisions we have both made to embrace the pain, the challenges, the discomfort, limitations and the realities of our circumstances, we have been healed of lingering resentment. We both have learned to recognize the differences between what we can and cannot do and have accepted them. We have learned to live with greater gratitude and joy and to allow our challenges to help us have more sensitivity and empathy for others in theirs.

Dr. Kenneth Haugk, clinical psychologist, pastor and author, has written about "healing people," who they are, and how they respond to others' grief and discomfort. In an excerpt from his book *Finding Hope and Healing,* he writes:

> The key to walking through your grief is finding people who will let you talk and help you heal. I call these healing people. H-E-A-L stands for Here, Empathetic, Accepting, and Listening. Healing people are:
>
> Here for you when you need them. They're willing to be with you and make time for you. They know that their presence is one of the greatest gifts they can give.
>
> Empathetic. No one else can truly understand what you're feeling. But people with empathy will do their best to understand and to let some of your pain touch them.
>
> Accepting. They don't judge you, try to change you, or tell you what you should do or how you should think or feel.
>
> Listening. They really focus on what you have to say. They let you share your feelings and know how important it is for you to tell your story again and again.
>
> You can sometimes help a friend become a healing person. A woman told me about a friend who wanted to help but kept interrupting her with cheerful clichés. Finally, the woman told her friend, "Here's what I need from you. Let me be upset without trying to cheer me up or fix things. Let me talk—while you mostly remain quiet and listen. Let me cry. Give me a hug. You don't have to say or do a whole lot. Mostly just be there and care."

Her friend got the point and became a healing person from then on. The grieving woman offered a wonderful gift to her friend—the opportunity to care in a more helpful way, a gift the woman returned many times over.

For more than four years we've had an ongoing conversation with a woman from another state. Sometimes we talk over the phone or through Skype. Mostly, we connect via email.

Like so many, she and her family scramble, sometimes desperately, with their finances. There is never enough. Not even close. Every week is a master class in juggling payments, bills and overdue notices. She despairs most weeks at how little there is and how much is needed. Something is always sacrificed. The decisions at times are heart wrenching and she cries out—always in exasperation, often in rage, sometimes in misery—at how utterly grueling it all is to keep going, to keep it together.

Her mother, who lived with them, was in a wheelchair, completely dependent upon her for all of the essentials of daily life. Cutting her food. Feeding it to her. Administering her medications. Bathing her. Caring for her intimate toileting needs. A once active, capable woman now required her daughter's total assistance to help her through each day.

Her husband had cancer. He was weak, tired, worn. Trips to his medical specialists, 70 miles away, were an all-day affair and brutal on his fragile body. Finding reliable transportation and the brutality of the travel made it relentless to get to the appointments. At times they had to cancel them as a result. He spent nearly all his time closed in, unable to go out, and powerless to muster the might to do much of anything.

Responsible for the well being of both, she couldn't work outside the home. Teaching a few students piano lessons gave her a little spending money. But the students were sporadic; she couldn't depend on them for a steady income. The few dollars they received from the students, the disability payments her husband received, and her mother's Social Security checks certainly helped. Yet none of it was enough to make ends meet.

She emailed about her aggravations many times with us. We knew her situation was overwhelming. We'd ask her about options, answers, and about finding a way through her anxiety. We didn't know what to say, short of offering her money we didn't have, or how there might be a way to help.

She told us that she swallowed her pride one day and made an appointment with a priest. He was from the church she attended on the few Sundays she had a small break in her caregiving and was able to leave the house.

We wrote to ask her how the appointment went. It didn't take long for her to reply:

> To answer your questions . . . the discussion with Father was a total waste of time. He acted like he didn't want to know and made it clear that he was rather busy. His attitude was—and he actually said, "He (her husband, who was still a citizen of another country) should go back home where he can get National Health."
>
> I told my friend who encouraged me to talk to him and she said she'd talk with him. So? I have made a couple other calls and I am going to see a pastor at another church. I used to go there years back. I am thinking THEY might be more willing to help me/us. :(
>
> Today I am just exhausted with everything.

After seeing the next pastor she wrote again:

> Yet ANOTHER frustrating appointment. I saw the pastor of the other church here in town. I talked with him for an hour and a half. At least he listened. But basically he told me there wasn't any financial help they could give. He told me that God gives you peace and if I am not having that peace then I've moved away from him. He said I should be asking God what I should do to please Him blah blah. MY response was, "Isn't taking care of my mom and husband something that would 'please' God?" It certainly isn't the path I WOULD CHOOSE for myself. Even though he listened . . . I felt like I was being judged and coming up short. Honestly, this is one of the things that bugs me about religious people. . . I don't believe you have to say 'God' and 'Jesus' every other word for people to get the point. Helping and doing for others and loving others is what Jesus preached as well as loving God. Yes, my faith is on shaky ground right now, but look at everything I have been through, a marriage where I tried to do all the right things and it still ended in divorce, having to close down my studio which I loved because it wasn't economically feasible to keep it, falling in love with the most perfect man I have ever known and then he has cancer, watching my mom deteriorate to the point where I have to cut the food I put on her plate because she can't anymore, losing a tutoring job that I really liked doing . . . and financial hardships that you cannot believe. I am tired. Forget having peace, I need

an emotional rest. It is hard because there is only so much you can do to help
. . . my life still has a lot of anxiety.
. . . The last two days have been hell on earth. . . I am so frustrated I just
want to run away. I mean, I feel like I have this friggen curse on me, and
everywhere I turn I am being punished. . . . I mean I hate my life right now
and would give anything to just go somewhere else and start all over new.

There are little blessings every day and she acknowledged them, and is grateful. But, the daily slog of worrying how and when and if she would meet the week's bills is relentless. We wish so badly that somehow, in someway, we could change things with one swipe of a magic wand (we do not have) or a shot from a silver bullet (we don't own) to fix things the way we want them to be fixed. But we can't.

Some problems can't easily be resolved. They may continue for the rest of someone's life. Often, there are outcomes out of our control. It's easy to give up on someone when things don't work the way we hope and want them to. As Adam McHugh states, when a hurting person is in the midst of a storm:

It's not your job to pull them out of the storm. It's your job to get wet
with them.

Maybe our friend's storm will end. Maybe it won't. The outcome isn't ours to control. But at the very least we accompany her through the storm and be open to getting wet—to listen, to be a safe place for her, to remind her that she is cared for and loved. And maybe, as we show her this love, she will come one day to embrace what can be changed, along with what can't.

Friends

"Don't judge a book by its cover when you don't understand
what that person's been through."
-CORRIE LOUISE ROSE

I
F OTHERS SAW who we are on the inside, knowing our true vulnerabilities, our insecurities, our regrets, we wonder, wouldn't they have greater empathy for us? Wouldn't it be impossible to not have fuller love and mercy, deeper kindness and patience because we know the wounds and burdens someone else is living with? If, when we grow to know others more, wouldn't our insights compel most of us to empathize more, forgive more and respond with more compassion for them because we know what they are carrying with them every day? We believe such knowledge goes a long way toward enabling most of us to look at one another in a much more positive light.

Shortly after Christmas one year, we had a meeting with a prosperous businesswoman. We met her in her office and assumed the meeting would be a short one. She had a busy schedule; it was complicated to get on her calendar. We figured she would stick to "business pretty tightly." We prepared our discussion points about the mission of Someone To Tell It To and how her business might be able to collaborate with STTIT and help it to grow. By every outward appearance she was a success. Athletic. Articulate. Able. She is intelligent and well versed in her field. Her office is decorated comfortably and her clientele is impressive. When you look at her, it is easy to believe she has it all together.

Except she doesn't.

Our meeting started off smoothly. She asked how we were doing and how the non-profit had been progressing since our last meeting. We asked her how she was doing, how the holidays were and how her business was going. We expected short and positive answers before moving onto our intended "business" matters. But, the conversation quickly took an unexpected turn. We could sense something was going on below her polished exterior.

She confessed to us the holidays weren't so good. In fact, not good at all.

"We're very sorry. What in particular made them so horrible? What happened? Did you receive bad news? Did someone say something to hurt you?"

She opened more of her inner door. It seemed a comment from a friend triggered an intense, emotional reaction in her and clouded the entire holiday season. In fact, the reaction debilitated her. It dredged up long-buried memories and acutely powerful feelings. Those feelings upset her, frightened her and filled her with great uneasiness. They forced her to face issues, which she preferred not to face. They compelled her to give voice to experiences she had preferred not to remember.

But it was too late. Her memory had been blown open and there was no turning back. Since the long-buried memories had all come to the surface they couldn't be ignored. They had to be reconciled. And if they weren't? Well, she would agonize even more.

She confessed as past traumas were dredged up, and made painfully raw, her life nearly came to a standstill. The holidays were a terrible time for it to happen. The turmoil internally made them messy for her and her family. She confessed she was living a quiet, private hell—one she'd been carrying for most of her lifetime. But from the outside, no one knew.

Listening to her reminded us how we cannot know what someone else is living through, especially if we never take the right moment, or the time to ask deeper questions and actually listen to the answers. Without investing intentionally in someone else's life, we won't see or hear or experience the true essence of who she is. Without being interested in all of it—the positive accounts and the negative experiences, the blessings and the burdens—we will never truly know who she truly is. Yet, when we enter in, take the time, and make the investment in another's story, we grow more sensitive, supportive and encouraging—gifts all of us need from one another.

It would have been much easier to stick strictly to business in our meeting with her. It would have been much more comfortable to remain on the surface, to deal with the issues of finances and bottom line needs. It would have been much easier for her not to open up, not to offer the truth of what was on her heart, or to be vulnerable. But it wouldn't have been better.

We set aside business for a short time in our conversation with her and our relationships were deepened. And, we saw a glimmer of light and maybe some burdens begin to be lifted as the more important business—fostering true human connection—was approached.

———————————

Following an event we attended with several friends, one of our close friends sent us an email:

> *Dear Michael and Tom, I promised to send you something about what I was thinking at the restaurant. So here goes:*
>
> *I cannot enter the back room of that restaurant without thinking of my late friend Jack. He was my best friend. We had known each other since grade school. Our parents were best friends since they were in school together. I had lunch with him once a week for thirty years. He was a member of my wedding party and I was best man at his wedding. His rehearsal dinner was in that dining room.*
>
> *So when the speaker started talking about someone masking their true feelings and problems, and the need to remove that mask so that healing could begin, I was reminded of Jack, who never let his mask slip until it was too late, and he had killed himself.*
>
> *Actually, another of Jack's close friends, told me he also thought of Jack at that moment. It will always be a source of sadness and regret for all of us who knew him that there was something within Jack that he kept so carefully hidden until it took his life. Would we have been able to help him if he had let us in by letting us see behind his mask? I don't know; we will never know, because he never let on that anything was wrong.*

The business of truly knowing one another, means being willing to turn down the cover leading to a richer story, to a compelling narrative we all need to have someone else know. It strengthens the bonds between us and enables us to become a greater part of a supportive community. How terribly sad when we have no one before whom we can remove the cover and allow our truth to be known. Especially the most intimate truth which, if known by at least someone else who can accept it with grace, can be defanged in the revealing. It will not be so damaging and dangerous anymore.

The *New York Times* columnist David Brooks in a commentary entitled, "There are Social and Political Benefits to Having Friends," writes:

> *You can go without marriage, or justice, or honor, but friendship is indispensable to life. Each friendship . . . has positive social effects. Lovers face each other, but friends stand side-by-side, facing the world—often working on its behalf. . . friendship is a personal relationship that has radiating social and political benefits.*

In the first place, friendship helps people make better judgments. So much of deep friendship is thinking through problems together: what job to take; whom to marry. Friendship allows you to see your own life but with a second sympathetic self.

Second, friends usually bring out better versions of each other. People feel unguarded and fluid with their close friends. If you're hanging around with a friend, smarter and funnier thoughts tend to come burbling out.

Finally, people behave better if they know their friends are observing. Friendship is based, in part, on common tastes and interests, but it is also based on mutual admiration and reciprocity. People tend to want to live up to their friends' high regard. People don't have close friendships in any hope of selfish gain, but simply for the pleasure itself of feeling known and respected.

Here is a challenge for all of us. What if, when spending time with friends, or sitting around the table at our various clubs, and community and church groups, we started intentionally asking questions, which can foster greater depth and intimacy in our relationships?

Questions such as:

What is one area of your life where you cannot seem to trust?

When are you most proud of yourself?

When did you feel loved today?

When do you feel lonely, most appreciated or noticed?

What is one thing from your childhood—joyful or painful—that has helped to make you the person you are today?

How does your faith help you when you're feeling afraid? Where do you see God's activity in your life? When do you feel the freest? What brings you the most joy?

The right questions, those which, in gentle and in a non-threatening way, probe the deeper recesses of others' spirits and lives, can enable acquaintances to grow into friends and friends to bond even more closely together.

And perhaps, when we feel most alone and lost, we can be found and taken home again—or perhaps for the very first time.

"Have you ever felt like nobody was there? Have you ever felt forgotten in the middle of nowhere? Have you ever felt like you could disappear? Like you could fall, and no one would hear? Well, let that lonely feeling wash away. Maybe there's a reason to believe you'll be okay. 'Cause when you don't feel strong enough to stand you can reach, reach out your hand.' And oh, someone will coming running And I know, they'll take you home. . .

"Even when the dark comes crashing through When you need a friend to carry you And when you're broken on the ground You will be found."

Benj Pasek and Justin Paul, "You Will Be Found," from *Dear Evan Hanson*

The Old Man and The Sea (Tom)

*"Pain has a way of clipping our wings and keeping us f
rom being able to fly . . . and if left unresolved for very long,
you can almost forget that you were ever created to fly in the first place."*
-WM. PAUL YOUNG

SEAGULLS CIRCLED OVERHEAD waiting and watching for one of our four small children to throw them a donut hole from Dunkin Donuts. Airplanes buzzed overhead with the latest advertisement: "Eat at Gino's Pizzeria, $29.99 for a family of five." A school of dolphins bobbed in and out of the water in the distance. A spirit of delight and serenity was everywhere. It was a picture perfect summer afternoon, mid 80's, with low humidity. There wasn't a cloud in the sky to ruin the sun's tranquil glow.

Our family camped out in our familiar spot underneath the landmark fishing pier in Ocean Grove, New Jersey, the very same shady location my grandparents spent many summer mornings decades ago. Many photo albums had been filled because of this peaceful, sentimental setting.

My son Luke and I started building sand castles, imagining a world in which toy sea creatures ruled the day. Our eldest daughter Lillian tried desperately to pass the Frisbee into the gentle sea air, laughing hysterically as the breezes threw the disc in the opposite direction of her target. We smiled and laughed as if there wasn't a worry in the world.

A frail voice in a thick Italian accent called out: "You have a beautiful family."

I looked all around me but couldn't find the source of who had spoken.

"You have such a beautiful family! Do you come here often?"

I looked again and noticed a man, probably in his 80's, hunched on a bench as if he was camouflaged from everybody around him. He smiled, waved, and sat up to the best of his ability.

"Good afternoon!" I said. "Yes, we do come here often. Our family has been coming to this exact spot for decades!!!"

126

"That's great. This is such a special place, isn't it?!"

Now the old man had my attention. He obviously had been here before and so I felt it was important to take a moment and soak in, along with him, the beauty all around us.

"Do you live here?" I shouted as loudly as I could, sensing that he had some hearing issues. "I do live here. I live on Broadway St. I'm here all year round."

If he didn't have my fullest focus before then, he did now. Anyone who lives in the small community of Ocean Grove has a very special bond, one we all revel in together. Someone who lives there year round has an especially strong connection to the town, the people, and, of course, the beach. So many people come and go throughout the summer. Most folks who own a house leave as soon as the summer ends, so it grabbed my notice knowing this man lived two blocks from the Jersey shore, year round.

"I stroll to the end of this pier every day. I can't move as quickly as I used to though, so it takes me a lot longer to reach the end. I leave my house at 6:30 every morning to be outside. The summer is my favorite time of the year. I love watching families being families."

I grinned, thinking it was interesting he loved the summer so much. Most people who live in tourist communities tend not to enjoy the busy season, full of heavy traffic, more noise and crowded sidewalks and shops; it drastically disrupts their everyday lives. So I asked him: "Why do you love the summer so much?"

"Oh," he said. "I live all by myself. Most of my family has either died or moved far away. I don't have anyone to experience life with."

Our conversation quickly changed from surface level to intimate in a matter of moments. Now he certainly piqued my interest even more. Too often older folks aren't "listened to" as they should be; too often they get all but forgotten, their wisdom and perspectives are not respected. But interestingly enough, I believe they are the ones who have the most to offer, because they are the ones who have experienced life the most.

I turned to Sarah and my parents and said I was going to go up on the pier for a few minutes. They had already noticed I was engaged in conversation with the man and knew it was important to me to continue the discussion. Sarah knows in moments such as these I am saying, "I need to be present with this other person for a little while, fully dedicated."

So up on the pier I went. I sat down on the bench next to him, stuck out my hand, and exchanged more satisfactory greetings. For the next hour we sat and I listened. He related stories about his parents and how big of a risk they took moving from Italy to the United States during the Great Depression. He told me about his time in the service and how much it both shaped him and scarred him for the rest of his life. For an hour, time stood still. I can't remember all the details of what we talked about, but I do remember talking with him about faith. At one point in the conversation, I remember asking him about his spiritual beliefs. I said, "You must have a deep faith to have overcome what you have in this life."

He went on to comment about how he does have a strong faith in God:

"God has brought me through so much. I can't not believe in God. My wife and I lost a child when we were first married. He was only two years old. We were never the same afterwards. We couldn't work through our grief together. Everyone grieves differently, you know? So we got a divorce. I became an alcoholic because I couldn't handle the unhappiness. I thought we would have our entire lives together. One day, I remember feeling as if God had totally abandoned me. It was around Easter so I picked up my Bible and started reading the Easter story. It's one thing my parents always instilled in me, a deep desire to know and be loved by God. We were strong Catholics, so I went to mass every week, CCD, I read my Bible regularly, and we prayed at mealtimes and before bed. Anyway, I remember reading about Jesus' death and all he experienced in his last days. All of the damage I had been carrying was reconciled in that moment because for the very first time I realized God understood what it was like. God had felt it too, losing a child. I cleaned my life up. I met my second wife, an absolute godsend. There's a whole other story about how we met. Talk about miracles. She and I had two children together who now live far away. They are great kids and I love them very much. I just wish I could see them more frequently. One of them lives overseas and the other out west."

"So how about your wife," I inquired. "Is she still living?"

"She is still living, but not physically. She's alive and well in my heart and in my memories. She died 20 years ago. At least 20 years too soon."

"I'm sorry," I said.

"But, this is why I walk down to the pier every day. Sitting here is one of the ways I remember her, my son who died, and all of the other family memories we created here. I look up and down the beach and I watch as all of these families, just like yours, laugh and smile, cherishing their time together. Seeing all of you awards me joy. I guess you could say I get out of bed every morning to live vicariously, indirectly, through everyone else. Their memories are my memories."

"So what about church? Do you have a community of people you get to spend time with here in Ocean Grove?"

"I wish I could say that I do, but I don't. Most of my friends have all passed away. Again, this is why I love the summer so much. I actually hate it when the end of August arrives. It means most everyone will be leaving town until next year, while I'm all-alone here. The winter months are long."

There was a quiet, lingering pause. Almost awkwardly so. I sensed there was something else he wanted to tell, but wasn't sure if he was comfortable enough yet with me, or with anyone for that matter. For several moments we gazed out over the ocean vista, watching as motorboats thrust against the current, as if we were alternates in a daydream.

He broke the silence, "I stopped going to mass when I was 14 and I've never been able to step foot in a church building ever since. When I was 11 years old I attended Catholic school. The priest taught our class. After school finished, he would invite students into his living quarters. He started abusing us emotionally and verbally. I would even say spiritually."

He fought back tears. I put my arm on his shoulder. He whimpered a few times, and then whistled. "I never thought I would be disclosing this stuff today." We both chuckled, breaking the intensity of his revelation. "Talk about miracles, right?" I intoned, softly. Another few silent moments passed, but this time it wasn't so awkward.

"Yeah, I have never been able to reconcile the priest's actions. I've forgiven him. At least I think I have. But I just can't seem to bring myself to the place where I've been able to walk into a church building again. I've come close a couple of time, especially at holidays. Thankfully, I've had other friends who knew the story and have given me space. I always encouraged my wife to go, along with our two children, which she did. But I've never been able to. Maybe I haven't completely and fully forgiven God, I don't know?"

We sat there for a long time. We explored other things too, some of the less stark details of our lives.

Toward the end of our conversation, he asked: **"So what do you do for a living? What gets you out of bed in the morning?"**

I told him I was trained as a pastor and had co-founded a non-profit. I explained in greater detail about our mission and how we create a safe place for people. He then realized we had created a safe place for one another that special summer afternoon.

He wanted to know more and so he asked more personal questions.

"So how did you know you had this, if I can use the word, "calling," in your life?"

It was then when the conversation shifted. I told him I had served churches before starting our ministry. Now I had his sharp focus! I quickly made the connection that one of his burdens for most of his life had been with religious leaders. It was obvious they were the ones who had caused him his life's greatest torment.

He became silent, very silent; it felt as if I had said something I wish I hadn't in a crowded room heard by everyone.

Realizing the connection, I spoke up, "I am so, so sorry about what happened to you as a boy. I can't imagine the amount of confusion and grief it must have caused you. I can't imagine the feelings of betrayal you must have felt. I'm so sorry your priest stole so much of your adolescence and your innocence. It's obviously affected so much of your life. I'm glad you've been able to reconcile your relationship with God and you didn't project the priest's actions onto a perfectly loving and gracious God.

Sadly, I speak with a lot of people who can't help but project. They are abused, physically, emotionally, sexually, and spiritually, and cannot see God as being perfect, affectionate. I just want to remind you and reaffirm that I believe God loves you so much. God was with you through every solemn moment you have had—the abuse, the loss of your son, your divorce, your time in the service, your time away from the church. God was there for all of it. God knows; God comprehends."

We ended our time together shortly thereafter. He thanked me for the time we connected. I thanked him for the level of vulnerability and openness he provided. We hugged. Before I walked away he asked quietly, reticently: "Do you want to stop over before you go home this week? I'd love to show you my home. It's small, but it's a great location. Just a few blocks from the beach!"

I quickly and exuberantly responded, "Absolutely! I would love to stop by."

"I'm home every afternoon. I stay in the shade when it gets too hot outside," he said. "I'm looking forward to it."

"Me too."

"Enjoy the rest of the day with your beautiful family."

Our vacation was going to end in two days; I was intentional about visiting him. It was an opportunity, in my own small way, to break the epidemic of loneliness plaguing our society.

The next day our family went to the same spot underneath the pier at Ocean Grove. I looked for the man several times but didn't see him. After lunch, we put our children down for naps at my parents' home. I told everyone I was going for a walk. Sarah knew where I was headed; I had briefly expressed about my newfound friendship with the man. I arrived at his home and knocked on the door.

"Come in," he yelled from the kitchen. "So happy you decided to drop in."

"I wouldn't miss it," I said.

"Can I show you around my house? There isn't much, as you can see, but it's only me here and I don't get too many visitors. It's more than I need."

It only took a moment or two to see his one bedroom home, but I knew it was important to him. He enjoyed being noticed by someone, by anyone.

"I made some sweet tea; would you like a glass? I thought we could sit outside on the porch. I have that huge oak tree out front which provides some great shade in the afternoon."

The shade of the oak tree was suggestive of the shelter he felt with me.

It didn't take long for our conversation to go to a very intimate, private place. The fact that he invited me over said to me he trusted me, despite my religious title.

For the next two hours, I listened as he revealed other significant stories from his life, happier moments—how proud he was of his two children and six grandchildren, the successful career path he had chosen, his love for "our" beloved Yankees and all of the historic players he was fortunate to watch in person. He expanded upon the places he had traveled, the sights he had seen, and some of the more memorable moments of his life. I cherished every second of it.

Knowing our time would be coming to an end, I could see he had something else he wanted to divulge. For whatever reason, I could sense it had to do with our conversation at the beach, so I asked him: "You had some time to think about our conversation from yesterday. Is there anything else you wanted to say?"

There was a long silence, a silence of reflection and contemplation.

"Thank you for asking. And thank you for our conversation yesterday. At one point, you had mentioned that one of your philosophical views, if you want to call it that, is 'people don't heal if they don't first reveal.' Can you explain more for me what you mean?"

I told how I believe people need to convey the deeper stuff from their lives. If they don't convey the deeper stuff, often times the painful stuff, then the healing process cannot begin.

People don't heal, if they don't first reveal because you can't just forget about the past or things that have happened to you. It's almost impossible to forgive ourselves and forgive others without first talking it out with people we trust.

It was almost dinner time and he knew I needed to go. Before I left, he looked me in the eyes and announced,

"I know you speak with a lot of people in situations like mine. If I had words for them, tell them to forgive. Real, honest-to-goodness forgiveness. Tell them to move forward, to open up, and then to leave the past in the past. But definitely open up! Don't hold it in because you are only hurting yourself and those around you. You have helped me to realize how much sorrow I have been carrying around for most of my life just because I was afraid to talk about it, sorrow that could have been relieved long, long ago. I've realized in the last two days I thought I had forgiven the priest, but I haven't. I haven't been able to step foot in a church because I was angry. If I did, it was almost as if he had won, and I never wanted him to win. But in the end, he was still winning because I was missing out on the very things God stands for. By letting go today, I'm finally saying the past is in the past. The past doesn't define me. I guess . . . I guess I was angry at God without even knowing it. I'm now able to see the priest is God's child too and he was obviously in deep pain himself. He wouldn't have done something so horrific without having been hurt himself. It's crazy but it has taken me over 70 years to come to this place."

We said our last goodbyes. I told him I would write him and try to maintain a connection. I stepped off the porch. He yelled, **"One last thing. Tom, I know you are a writer and you often write other people's stories. Please write my story. Use my life as an example. This is one final way I feel like I can leave a legacy."**

And so I write his story today.

I wish I could say I maintained a strong relationship with the man, but days turned into weeks and weeks turned into months. I wrote him a few times, but never heard back. Writing was impossible for him because his eyesight had deteriorated rapidly.

When we returned to Ocean Grove the next summer, I walked down Broadway hoping I would see him out on his front porch. A neighbor was watering her plants. I asked if she had seen the man that day. She responded with a doleful look on her face, "He passed away several months ago. He was such a kind man. "

People in pain, unheeded and unheard have forgotten their intended reason for living, to fly, to soar on wings like seagulls. Compassion is about entering those places of pain, those places most troublesome, helping others to keep flying.

I'm thankful for our divine appointment on a picturesque summer day by the sea. The old man did leave a legacy; he left a legacy for me.

I write this for him, so his legacy can be larger, still.

Prison

"I was naked and you gave me clothing. I was sick, and you cared for me.
I was in prison, and you visited me."
-Matthew 25:36 New Living Version

"One of the best parts of being human is other humans. It's true, because
life is hard; but people get to show up for one another; as God told us to,
and remember we are loved and seen and God is here and we are not
alone. We can't deliver folks from their pits, but we can sure get in there
with them until God does."
-Jen Hatmaker

I T WAS RAINING HARD that morning. The cold was penetrating. A gloom pervaded the city. As we hurried through the rain and up the ramp to her door, there were two things we wondered about aloud—if she'd have any cats and if she was a smoker. We had never met her before. Both of us are allergic to cats and smoking tends to easily give us headaches.

We had the first part of an answer the moment she opened her back door—a cloud of smoke poured out and over us and into our lungs. Her apartment reeked of heavy smoke. Oh well. We could suck it up—literally—and endure it for the time we'd be there. We weren't there long when her cats ambled out of her bedroom and proceeded to rub themselves up against both of our legs. Repeatedly. All we could do was smile at each other discreetly, amused at the circumstances and go on.

A local social service agency had suggested to us she could use a visit. She was all alone, living in a city in which she had no relatives and no real friends. Confined with just her cats in the tiny apartment, overcrowded with her meager belongings, confined to a wheelchair, she described to us her life story.

Divorced, estranged from her son, her parents and siblings dead, starting over in a community she had moved to in an effort to escape her broken past, afflicted with multiple diseases, she felt utterly alone in this world. As we listened to her litany of indignities, disability and distress, we couldn't miss recognizing the endless sorrow she was feeling because life had turned out to be so cruel to her.

Before all this happened, she'd had a successful career in finance, she indicated. She'd made a lot of money. She traveled frequently. She had respect and prestige. She had friends and a life of activity and satisfaction. But now all of it was only a distant memory. It had all been destroyed. Gone. Never to return in her older age. She didn't explain how it was lost or why, just that it was. The question of "why" could come at another time. None of the memories could make up for the ache and emptiness she was feeling now. Her tiny apartment was, in essence, a prison, a place from which she could rarely escape.

Even worse, though, was the solitary confinement of her spirit and mind.

Her hurt was profound. Her longing for relief was palpable. Her broken life was seemingly without hope. We wondered how she could go on. We asked what sustained her in her affliction and loneliness.

"My faith," she answered.

It was mind-blowing for us to believe she still had any faith. After so much was gone, after so much seemed lost, it was hard for us to imagine how she wouldn't be bitter, indignant. But she wasn't. She still believed in the faith of her youth, hoping there was a God who was still with her and was with her even—or maybe especially—in the prison in which her circumstances confined her.

"Your visit today was a reminder that God does hear my prayers."

"I define connection as the energy that exists between people when they feel seen, heard, and valued; when they can give and receive without judgment; and when they derive sustenance and strength from the relationship." Brene' Brown

A postscript:

After leaving her, we were scheduled to attend a luncheon, one for which we needed to dress in shirts and ties. We reeked of smoke and had more cat hair on us than was good for us. The smoke penetrated everything we were wearing. So, we rushed to Tom's home, which was closest to us that morning, to quickly shower and change into something fresh and clean. There was no way we could go into such a public forum with the clothes we had on. Such is the life of meeting people where they are; we often don't know what we're getting into. It's a usual occurrence to need changes of clothes for the circumstances of different appointments each day. Entering into others' worlds isn't always neat nor is it always stress-free. But we wouldn't have it any other way. To create the context for other's comfort in opening up to us, they need to know we'll do our best to come to them in the places and ways most safe for them.

We met him in his home, too. He was in his early twenties. A family member of his had asked if we could visit; he didn't receive many visitors. We asked why? He couldn't leave his home because he was under house arrest. Several poor decisions were part of his past, which propelled him into the criminal justice system, several months before.

Answering the door wearing shorts, the monitoring device with a tiny red LED light was attached to one of his ankles. We tried not to pay undue attention to it; he quickly eased the tension by not shying away from the topic: "I made some bad choices. So now here I am under house arrest. The only time I can leave is to occasionally walk to the grocery store two blocks away or when I have to see my parole officer. I have to wear this thing for two more months. It's depressing because I'm stuck in this dark and stuffy apartment all day. Sometimes I feel like a caged animal. I don't have any visitors. Even animals have visitors in the zoo."

Two more months. No more visitors.

The apartment was dank. It was dirty. It made us a bit uncomfortable. But he was very pleasant and easy to talk to. Our time together took up most of the rest of the afternoon, which he needed. It was important, we thought, to make the time to visit with him. There were no bars on the windows or the doors. He wasn't locked up. Yet, his mistakes and the resulting ankle bracelet imprisoned him in other ways. It isolated him too, bringing loneliness and great limitations to his life. So we went to him, to sit with him, to help him be a little less alone in his prison, as Jesus asks us to do.

We had planned to devote a Friday afternoon to work on this book. The week had been full; we needed time to stay on track for the deadlines created for publishing it. It was a beautiful late spring day. We sat outside, took off our shoes, turned on some quiet music and started writing.

The most essential part of writing a book on compassion is actually being compassionate, living up to the principles about which we are writing. The compassionate way isn't always easy. In fact, most days, it can be downright uncomfortable and inconvenient.

We vowed to each other not to check email and to let phone calls go to voicemail through the afternoon so we could focus on the task at hand—writing the book. Not even 300 words into the first story we were working on, both of our phones buzzed—simultaneously—on the joint work line we share. We didn't pay much attention to the first call; we didn't recognize the number; it was from an unrecognizable area code. No message was left, so initially we figured the call wasn't urgent. But five successive calls later, all from the same number, mere minutes apart, we thought we should answer. Maybe it was urgent.

"Hello." we answered on speakerphone. "Hi. I was given your name by (another organization). Are you Someone To Talk To?"

"Yes. We are from Someone To Tell It To. This is Michael and Tom. How are you? How might we be able to help you?"

"I'm not very well. I'm not well at all," replied a woman with a downcast voice. "I've been homeless for the past seven weeks. I've been living out of my car. I'm not from around here and I don't have any family near by."

"We are so sorry to hear that. Would it help you if we got together?" "I would like that." We whispered to one another, "Let's look at the calendar."

The temptation in the moment was to suggest a date two or three weeks from then, but we sensed such a response wasn't what she needed. Michael was leaving for vacation the next Monday. Waiting a few weeks to meet her didn't seem reasonable or helpful—and certainly not compassionate.

Reluctantly, we looked at each other, knowing what we needed to do. Even though it would deeply cut into our writing afternoon, adding even more delays than we were already experiencing for the book to be published, we knew we needed to try to see her then, if she was able.

She was willing and able. "We could meet this afternoon. How about that? Where are you right now?

"I've had some issues with mental illness. I'm in the parking lot of the shopping center on the edge of town. Could you meet me somewhere close to here? I don't have much gas in my car or any money."

We weren't far at all from where she was. We chose a diner next to the shopping center, reasoning she was probably hungry and could use a decent meal. We were willing to pay.

At the diner she timidly shook our hands. Meeting two strangers, especially men, was understandably initially intimidating for her. But it didn't take long for her to warm up to us.

Quickly, she started in with her story: She had two sisters who aren't supportive. Her mental illness often debilitated her. She was deeply religious. She wanted to know a lot about what we do and who we are. She wanted to know our thoughts about God and how that affects the way we interact with people. She was extremely isolated. We talked a lot about God's grace. There was not much we could do practically for her. We gave her names and numbers of ministries dedicated to helping people experiencing homelessness. We said to use our names when she contacted them; the agencies would know who we were. We had an hour with her and at least for the hour she was safe, she wasn't alone, she was out of her car, and we hoped she knew she had two people who did care about what she was going through. For that hour, we hope she felt a connection with other people who would treat her with dignity and respect and would listen without judging her—even if not everything about her life made sense to us. We prayed with her; she wanted us to. It was important to her. We offered her the only thing we could offer her, God's love. We couldn't change her situation in a few brief moments. She also didn't want to accept the help we were giving when we offered names of homeless shelters and agencies. We couldn't force her to accept their help. The only thing we could do was to exhibit love and show her how her life counted for something. We offered to continue meeting with her, to continue reminding her of her merit, to continue reminding her that she isn't alone, because God is with her. She continued to reach out to us through text messages. We continued to respond to her outreach. Perhaps it helps her to step out of her prison of loneliness and homelessness at least for a little while when we do.

Each of these dear friends, children of God, is living in a prison of one kind or another. Prisons of loneliness and loss, isolation and heartache, separation and pain. Each of their circumstances is uncomfortable. Entering into their circumstances is uncomfortable, too. But none of us should go through the un-comfortableness alone. We haven't been created for that. We need each other. We need community. We need support. We need to know when others stand beside us to accompany us through the discomfort.

As Brené Brown has expressed, "I thought faith would say, I'll take away the pain and discomfort, but what it ended up saying is, I'll sit with you in it."

We all need someone to sit with us in it. That's exactly what Jesus did for us by walking this earth and moving into the neighborhood of our lives. That's what we who are Jesus' followers are called to do when we profess a faith in his love.

There is a challenging passage in the book of Acts that comes to our attention. The passage—in chapter three—concerns Peter and John, two of Jesus' closest friends and followers.

Headed to the Temple for one of their regular times of prayer, they encountered a man who had been born with a disability at the entrance to the Temple. He engaged the two men in conversation. He hoped to receive, as he so often had, a monetary handout. Here is what the text goes on to say:

*Peter and John **looked at him intently**, and Peter said, "Look at us!"*
The lame man looked at them eagerly, expecting some money. But Peter said,
"I don't have any silver or gold for you. But I'll give you what I have. In the
name of Jesus Christ the Nazarene, get up and walk!"
Then Peter took the lame man by the right hand and helped him up. And
as he did, the man's feet and ankles were instantly healed and strengthened.
He jumped up, stood on his feet, and began to walk! Then, walking, leaping,
and praising God, he went into the Temple with them. (Acts 3:4 NLT)

The message is countercultural. It coveys something worth noting: **Peter and John looked at him intently.**

In the original Greek, it literally means that Peter and John **looked hard** at him. No one had ever "looked hard" at him before. In that moment, these men were able to look beyond the man's situation and see him for who he was, a beloved child of God. It changed his life.

Peter and John didn't give the man what he had always been receiving—a quick handout. But they gave him something so much more meaningful—their time, their sense of empathy, their ears, their hearts and their prayers.

We are called to notice each other, to take a good, hard look at one another, to enter into emotional and spiritual prisons and to sit with each other behind the bars keeping our spirits from being free. We are called to "look hard at one another," to sit with one another as we seek to find the keys that may unlock the disease in our souls and accompany one another wherever we may need to go.

Author Shane Claiborne has written:

"And I think that's what our world is desperately in need of—lovers,
people who are building deep, genuine relationships with fellow strugglers
along the way, and who actually know the faces of the people behind the issues
they are concerned about."

This is the way, perhaps the only way, for the bars imprisoning any of us to truly open up.

What Did i Do to Deserve This?

"I had a dream my life would be so different from this hell I'm living,
so different now from what it seemed.
Now life has killed the dream, I dreamed."
-HERBERT KRETZMER, LYRICIST,
"I DREAMED A DREAM," FROM *LES MISERABLE*

*O*K HERE'S MY THING . . . i was in a bad car accident where it put me in a coma . . . broke my arm, hip and nose. Plus took an eye . . . Also took a baby i was 4 months pregnant with . . . so here's the thing i want to believe in God. I'm just so mad at him right now. i know i believe in him cuz i'm so mad at him, but don't know what to think.

Her plea for a way to understand grabbed us immediately. We had never gotten such a searing message through Facebook before. We answered immediately:

Thanks so much for reaching out and expressing as you have. We are terribly sorry to learn of your situation today. We can't imagine how much of a risk this is for you. If you would like to tell us more, please feel free. You can email us. Also, if you would like to meet face to face, we can certainly do that too, whatever you are most comfortable with at this point. Our hearts are heavy for you.

It didn't take long for her reply. We knew her questions were haunting her.

i'm just basically asking why in the world it happened to me. i mean, what did i do to deserve this? Is God mad at me for something i did before? i just don't understand what i did to deserve this.

We responded again:

We are very grateful that you are willing to offer your feelings as you have. We believe God has "broad shoulders" and can handle it. We wish we had easy answers for you, but unfortunately there is much in life that doesn't make sense. We don't believe you deserved this and that God is mad at you in any way. We don't believe in that kind of a God. The God we believe in is perfectly loving; God loves you deeply. God is here to be present with us and to help us through these very painful times in our lives. God doesn't cause them to happen, but walks with us through each challenge on the journey.

The heart of her concern came out,

i just feel God is mad at me cuz years ago i did something that i really regret. That's why he keeps taking pregnancies. i know i shouldn't have and regret it big time but that's what i feel . . .

We continue to applaud you for being so vulnerable and willing to share all of this with us. Part of our calling, with you, and with everyone else we speak with every day, is to remind you of your beloved status in God's eyes. God is incredibly proud of you and loves you so, so much. God thinks you are very special and God doesn't hold past actions against you. That isn't the way God operates. It's sad to hear that you have that way of thinking ingrained inside of you, but we understand why you do. So much of society and even our religious communities have taught a message that "God is ready to pounce on us when we make the choices we make." But that isn't the kind of God we see in the Bible. We see a God who is loaded with so much grace, empathy, and compassion for us and our situations. Maybe we could set up a time to meet face to face to discuss this further? We can meet wherever? Maybe a coffee shop? Keep writing and keep exploring your feelings . . .

She was searching, desperately, for answers to why her life had turned the way it did. Her story, and her guilt, haunted us. Her perception of God—and of God's vengeance—troubled us. Her life and the terrible traumas she endured simply broke our hearts.

On the day she agreed to meet us, we recognized her immediately as she walked into the coffee shop. She walked slowly and methodically, limping, grasping a cane for balance. The moment she sat down with us at the small table in the corner, away from other customers, she let loose:

She watched her father die from lymphoma when she was 12. A recreational vehicle accident damaged her teeth and face. She had to sue the friend driving the vehicle to pay her medical expenses. She lost the friendship. Two more pregnancies followed, both ending in miscarriage. Then, there was the car accident where she hit a pole driving home for lunch one day. Flown by helicopter to the nearest trauma center, she was in a coma for three days. When she came to consciousness again, she had no recollection of what had happened, or of the previous year. But she learned a third pregnancy ended, because of the accident. Months and months of rehabilitation and therapy followed. Her speech was garbled. She couldn't drive or work. She lost her fiancé, who couldn't accept her new disabilities and who called her a "baby killer."

Most significantly, she lost her dreams. Her new reality, tempered by physical and cognitive disability, was now characterized by boredom, loneliness and anger toward a God she previously wasn't certain existed.

"I'm so mad at God." Then she chuckled, "Yet, how could I be mad at God when I'm not even sure God exists?"

We asked her what she thought about God. Who did she believe God is? Did she believe that God caused all her traumas? We explained that we didn't believe God caused her disabilities. We told her it's also okay to be mad at God; God is absolutely big enough to handle and understand our questions and our anguish.

Why did this happen? Did God do this to me? Was i being punished for what i did years ago? i'm just so angry. i want to have a husband. i want to have children. i want to work.

People think i'm stupid. They don't talk to me directly, often. In front of me, they'll ask my mother how i'm doing, if i'm ok. Just because i don't talk clearly and i have trouble walking doesn't mean i can't think or hear them or answer for myself. They treat me like i don't know anything. i don't like that. It makes me angry.

We couldn't help but love her. At age 32, she had suffered much more than seemed fair. Her dreams were destroyed and she was living an endlessness of regret and confusion. Her once vibrant life was diminished.

Her messages to us were telling, too. All her "i's" were typed in lower case. It was as if she wasn't of worth, as if she wasn't substantial. Not capitalizing the "i" was an apt symbol of how she felt others perceived her—and maybe how she perceived herself.

She told us she had never talked about these things with anyone before, except with her mother, with whom she lived and depended upon for transportation and care.

What emerged when she talked about it was an endearing sense of humor. She was able to laugh at her circumstances and put them in perspective. She was alive. She was grateful for life.

She was grateful we were willing to listen. She appreciated how we did not tell her what she had to do, but simply allowed her to tell us what it's been like living with all she's been through.

"It was good," she said, "to ask these questions about God." She was searching to make sense of her life and her circumstances. She was trying to understand the idea of God and who God is in her life.

She believed. But her belief was based on things she had heard about God's nature and being: God is a punisher. God keeps an account of our sins and faults. God repays us for the decisions we make that many perceive as wrong.

She seemed to know nothing about God's compassion, unfailing love and kindness. We tried to reassure her. We reminded her that she is infinitely beloved by God. Just because she is here. We reminded her nothing she has done or could do would take this fact away. We reminded her God wipes away our mistakes and shortcomings:

They are forgotten.

We are continually given chance after chance after chance to live a loving life.

God knows the depth of our attentions, anguishes and questions.

Nothing we can do will ever take God's love away.

God doesn't take away our babies because we may have done something we regret.

God just doesn't work that way.

God is about the work of helping us to live with joy, in peace, offering hope and experiencing love.

We conveyed to her that God has been walking with her every step of the way. We conveyed to her:

God was with her as she lay broken and bleeding beside the road. God was there on the emergency helicopter ride to the hospital. God was with her in the coma. God was there during her eight-hour surgery.

God was present in the miscarriages. God was with her still as she questioned and wondered and expressed her anger. God never leaves us or forsakes us. We also told her God is about the business of miracles:

In the love and devotion of her mother who cared for her.

In the friend who connected us with her, to allow her to share as she'd never shared before.

In the surgeons and nurses and technicians and therapists and counselors who helped her over the years to get to this place in her life.

In the complete and utter love that God has for her.

We also had the privilege of talking with her mother who has been such a source of support and strength for her through each of these ordeals. We asked her if she ever lost hope for her daughter, especially in the darkest days after her daughter's last and most devastating accident.

"No, I never really did," she recalled. "I was scared at times. I'll never forget where I was when I received the call that she was in the accident. I was outside doing some work in the yard. When I got to the hospital I had no idea I'd find her so broken and helpless. The doctor said every single bone in her face was broken. She was in a coma. She was hurt so badly. But for some reason, I never thought she would die."

"Tell them about that day with my tongue," her daughter urged her.

"That day with your tongue?" her mother questioned. "Oh yeah. Now I remember." For days, she lay perfectly still, not moving, not opening her eyes, not responding to any noise or stimulation. Because of that, most of the medical staff came into her room, did what they had to do without saying much of anything to her and left. It was as if there wasn't a person beyond all the tubes and wires and beeping machines.

"But there was one nurse, who was different. She would always talk with her, ask her questions, tell her what she was doing. Even though she wasn't responding, the nurse still talked with her as if she could hear and understand. She'd wash and comb her hair, put ribbons in it, try to fix her up. This particular day, she asked my daughter if she could hear her to stick her tongue out.

"She did!

"That's the day I realized she was in there. It was the sign I needed to believe that she had the strength to fight. I knew deep inside she wasn't lost to us, that she was still here, she would make it."

She certainly has.

"Just before her first nose surgery her surgeon did an x-ray of her face and every single bone had healed. She only needed nose surgery. I knew deep in my heart it was because we had so many people praying for her. The surgeon was absolutely amazed! Most, if not all of the doctors didn't think she would make it through the first night because of her severe head trauma. Her life has opened their eyes to what God can do."

The young woman sent us this quote by an unknown author that summed up her feelings about who she is and where she is on her journey toward healing:

I've seen better days, but I've also seen worse. I don't have everything I want, but I do have all I need. I woke up with some aches and pains, but I woke up. My life may not be perfect, but I am blessed. God is with you through the good times and bad times.

On her birthday, we invited her to lunch. She seemed to enjoy a nice time; we know we did. We learned more about her that day and more about the journey she has been on. As we were leaving the restaurant, she suddenly stopped and pointed to a photo, among many other photos of local events, by the door: "There I am. That's me!" she exclaimed, more animated than we'd ever seen her. "That was the year we won the state field hockey championship. There I am, right there. In the third row. See? It was so cool!"

"You were a state field hockey champion when you were in high school? Wow! That's awesome. That *must* have been so cool!" we echoed.

"It really was."

"We never knew about it. What a great memory for you."

"I was also the homecoming queen my senior year." She paused momentarily. "I used to be pretty."

She used to be pretty. Used to be an athlete. Used to be popular. Used to have a future. Now she didn't believe she had any of those gifts anymore. It was all in the past—the glory, the fun, the hope for a happy and good life.

We saw a young woman who desperately wanted to regain her life and her dreams again. She was not stupid. Her intelligence and dignity broke through the difficulties she had talking and walking and as she tried to sort it all out.

We saw a young woman who just needed to know that whatever she had done before, whatever regrets she had, all that mattered was how she was loved. It was the essence of compassion: this compassionate love is the foundation for a new dream, a new life from God.

We believe in this unbelievable love. We pray she can learn to believe it too.

SECTION 4

"When Have You Not Seen
the Presence of *Compassion*?"

Backslapping

"Authenticity is a collection of choices that we have to make every day.
It's about the choice to show up and be real. The choice to be honest. The
choice to let our true selves be seen."
-Brené Brown

"What happens when people open their hearts? They get better."
-Haruki Murakami

In talking about our ministry and mission at various community groups, civic clubs and churches, we have been troubled by the superficiality we often see. Kidding and time-worn jokes and "backslapping" so often takes the place of actual real, honest-to-goodness conversations.

It's especially evident in the groups we have visited more than one time. The jokes are predictable; the ribbing seems routine and almost scripted. The same people are often "called out" in the same way each time. We can see it coming: the punch lines and the all-knowing laughter. We anticipate the dialogue threads woven through the all-too-familiar fabric of the group:

"What kind of trouble have you gotten into again this week, Harry?"

"Same old, same old. You know how it goes, Steve."

"Getting enough to eat, Karen? It's your own fault if you go away from here hungry."

"What did you think about the game last Sunday, Kev? Your boys didn't look too good."

"Yeah, they disappointed me again, Jen. I don't know why I watch. They give me heartburn, especially this season."

And so it goes . . .

The connections lack depth and intimacy. In fact, they are barely connections at all. What passes for camaraderie and friendship barely penetrates the spirit or the heart.

In one particular luncheon meeting, a gentleman gave a short presentation. Afterward, after most others had left, he quietly lamented to us, "I've been in this group for more than 20 years. This is the first time I've actually been asked to address them."

His statement, tinged with sadness, spoke poignantly about how little connection there was among even its longest-serving members.

Another woman, whom we know well, confided in us about her recent job loss and the depressed state it is leaving her in. Yet, week after week, she continues to return to her civic organization's luncheon in her finest dress, hiding behind her attire. No one in the group has any true idea about how terribly isolating her unemployment is for her.

A woman lingered off to the side in her church's sanctuary one Sunday morning as we shook hands at the door, following the end of the service and our presentation. We had just spoken to the congregation about forgiveness and reconciliation. She waited until we were the only three persons left in the room. She wanted no one else to hear what she had to divulge; she asked us to write it to prove a point:

"My husband died three months ago. I still leave a place for him in the pew beside me. I feel his presence there, and I like that. But there's something I can't forgive him for. Something he did years ago. Something that got him in big trouble. No one else here knows but one other woman and the pastor. I didn't even tell the pastor until after my husband died. He couldn't believe what I told him. I still can barely believe it. My own children don't even know. I couldn't bear to tell them such news about their father . . . "

She went on to tell us the story.

"The reason I haven't told anyone else here is that they talk too much. They gossip. I know them too well. I can't talk about it with them."

Her greatest burden. Her deepest shame. Her private struggle. Her broken heart.

It couldn't be expressed, for it didn't feel safe. In her own community of faith, her own need to unburden herself was left unfulfilled.

What her marriage appeared to be on the surface wasn't the reality within it or in her heart. She wrestled with a brokenness that couldn't be told to those with whom she interacted most closely. How sad we felt for her.

At another church, the pastor lamented with us that the members of her congregation couldn't truly reveal deeper questions of faith to one another. One woman, a 40-year member, had recently confided in her that she has always had questions about the literal nature of the Bible. She just wasn't certain that it was inerrant, word for word, absolutely true. She was afraid to reveal her doubts to anyone else, afraid she would be judged to be unfaithful, heretical, misguided. She was a 40-year member! And still she didn't feel safe enough to ask a theological question, to explore a basic matter of belief. If not there, after all that time, then when and where could she ask it?

How sad it is for her, too, that she feared the criticism of her fellow church members for a profound question about the faith she was trying authentically to live out. What she was always taught had haunted and troubled her; she wanted to explore those feelings in an atmosphere of acceptance and in an attitude of growth. But it was too frightening, too intimidating. To us, it's the last thing a church—or any true community of people—should be—frightening and intimidating.

As we ate lunch with another group before having a dialogue about our mission with them, a "get-well" card was passed around the table for the members to sign. Amidst the backslapping and joking around, one member, admirably, wanted to remember another member of the group who was in the hospital for surgery. She wanted to wish the other woman well and to let her know the group was thinking of her. When the card was passed to one of the men, he suddenly became agitated and barked to the woman who initiated the signing,

"I don't appreciate us doing this. My wife has had multiple surgeries over the last few years. Not once did she get a card. Not once did this group send anything to her. If you want to know why she doesn't come to these meetings anymore, well, there's the reason why!"

An awkward silence fell around the table. The host who had invited us, looked at us self-consciously, embarrassed we had to witness this outburst. Perhaps too, he was embarrassed that the group had failed to reach out to one of its members when she was in need of encouragement and support. They met together every week for lunch. Yet apparently they never let her know they were thinking of her during the moments of her greatest need. Her husband's resentment was palpable, a long-simmering hostility evident throughout the rest of the meeting, as he made sarcastic, caustic comments to the others and about the business at hand. The unmistakable superficiality of the group, after so much time together, had obviously angered him. Lying just below the surface, a "get-well" card circulated among the group caused the resentment to bubble over. What was this group, after all? Was it not a community in which the members were connected? Were their interactions merely surface level? In his mind, apparently so.

Why do we belong to groups—civic, community, church? What are our reasons for entering in and expressing a commitment as one of the members?

Are the jokes and the laughs reason enough? The food we may eat, the drinks we may drink together? Is the mission of the group, its work and outreach, enough? Are the connections merely for business and to fill out our résumés?

Is the backslapping enough? Does it fill our souls? Does it touch our hearts? Does it bring us fulfillment? Is there a larger devotion?

What is a community for? For us, a community—of faith, of those who hold similar values, of common purpose—is a place for us to know that we are not alone, that we are in this life together, that we are bound to one another in commitment and, we hope, in respect, trust and love.

No, every member of every community of whatever kind can't and doesn't need to be our best friend. But don't we all desire—and need—deeper bonds, greater connections, more fulfilling relationships? Compassion always means we move into the neighborhoods of others' lives.

Backslapping only gets us so far. It doesn't deeply connect us with those around us and simply fosters superficial relationships. But by not being afraid to connect more closely with another person around us—by asking questions of depth, by being willing to actually be present enough to listen to the answers and by showing another person how we want to know them and how we connect with their lives, we begin to develop relationships of real depth, which enriches and values us all.

Aren't we called to delight in one another as God delights in us, and to reach out to one another in real and intentional ways?

Look Up

"One of the most beautiful qualities of true friendship
is to understand and to be understood."
-Lucius Annaeus Seneca

REGRETTABLY, far too few of us have relationships in which we truly understand and are understood.

During a question and answer time after a noontime talk we gave to a civic group, a man in his 80s, quietly confessed,

"I absolutely understand what your organization is about. But I'll be honest with you, the only "one" in my life who actually listens to me right now is my dog. My dog never responds with criticism or judgment when I tell him things. He simply sits there and let's me voice my troubles and my worries. He's the one who does it best. He gives me what I need."

Utter silence followed.

After a few moments, people began to chuckle, nervously breaking the awkwardness of the silence. A few others nodded in agreement. They were beginning to absorb his point. We all need a sounding board, non-critical ears to take in our insecurities, questions and failures.

Since his admission, we've done a lot of reflecting on his profound wisdom and vulnerability in offering it. It was a brave thing for him to do.

Dogs are wonderful, absolutely. But don't we need those qualities in people too, so much more? Don't we all need someone who will simply love us for who we are, who will see through our fallible, imperfect exteriors and into our hearts and souls and minds? Someone who can simply see and celebrate the wonder of creation who each of us are?

There is a book of quotes by the late Fred Rogers called, *The World According to Mister Rogers: Important Things to Remember.* In it there is a story about Mr. Rogers' connection with his dog when he was a boy:

> *My own friend and companion, when I was little and didn't yet have*
> *a sister, was Mitzi, a brown, wire-haired mongrel. We played and had lone*

conversations during which she heard many of my secrets and shared my joys and sadnesses. We ran in the fields and huddled together through thunderstorms. I gave a great deal of myself to Mitzi, and she faithfully reflected that self back to me, helping me learn more about who I was and, in those early days, what I was feeling. When she died, she went on teaching me—about loss and grief . . . and about the renewal of hope and joy.

The gifts we treasure most over the years are often small and simple. In easy times and in tough times, what seems to matter most is the way we show those around us and nearest to us that we've been listening to their needs, to their joys and to their challenges.

What we see be in today's society is a generation of people who want to learn what it means to vulnerable, to be more authentic. Years ago, many individuals weren't vulnerable with one another, not because they didn't want to be, but because they didn't know how to be.

The rallying cry then was "buck up or shut up," "boys don't cry," and "have a stiff upper lip." With that standard in mind, many people didn't have readily confidential or reliably authentic emotional relationships. Yet, in our culture today—in an effort to be more open, more vulnerable, people sometimes go to the other extreme, voicing (or "vomiting") their political, religious, or other views and feelings for the entire world to hear and read—especially on social media—regardless of the consequences. It may be because too many of us don't know how to open up healthily or judiciously. This isn't necessarily helpful or healing either. It actually masks vulnerability and authenticity because there's no real personal connection. It's a form of hiding and keeping a distance to avoid intimate relationships.

There is a word we want to highlight here. It's *obedience*, which often evokes negative feelings and ideas and conjures images of someone ordering us to do something without us having any say or input. A parent yelling at a child to clean up his room. A husband or a wife demanding the other work harder to bring in more money. A boss telling an employee to do something she believes is unethical. A master commanding a dog to sit or to heal.

But in reality, the word obedience derives from the Latin word *audire*, which means "to listen." It means to "give attention to" without hesitation or limitation, to be "all ear." It means to be fully engaged in the situation of the other. It doesn't mean "searching for a response" while another person in talking, but allowing the other person to fully express what he or she is thinking, feeling and experiencing. It means to be patient and accepting of a person's history. It means not to judge or be critical, but willing to be equally open to the joy and the sorrow, the laughter and the tears. Obedience reminds us about the need to "show up" and to be "real" with one another.

Sometimes it is frightening and awkward and risky to be real. A friend told a story in which she and a group of friends were talking about their week. One friend opened with the painful news that his wife who has cancer is losing her job. This was a devastating development for his family financially and emotionally. Our friend said there was a stunned silence as if no one knew what to say. Their stunned silence wasn't an empathetic silence—as if they were listening and being "all ear" for their friend and his family. Instead, it was an unpleasant, deadened, silence.

Our friend told us after a moment, someone spoke up and extolled the news of something pleasant that had happened, which redirected the conversation off the trying news their other friend had disclosed. It was as if by ignoring the depth of what was disclosed it would somehow "go away."

Our friend expressed regret that she didn't speak up and acknowledge the great anxiety the man expressed. She rightly realizes the weight of the silence and the damage it can do. She understands that the group's silence in essence said to the man, "your troubles, your circumstances, your heartache, aren't valid and important." More than likely, she feels he will be very reluctant to uncover something so personal and weighty again.

Our friend is a considerate and thoughtful person. His friends are as well. None of them purposefully wished to hurt or ignore him as he disclosed his devastating news. They just didn't know what to say, so they said nothing.

Technology can add to our social discomfort. It can get in the way of human connections. One afternoon we were speaking at a chapel service to a group of teenagers. We showed a YouTube video clip, called "Look Up," that had gone viral with 50 million views. Using rhyme, the narrator encourages viewers to "look up" from their electronic devices to engage more personally with the world. After completing our talk, we took time to answer some questions. Some of the students made comments such as:

That video is incredibly sad, but true.

Technology is creating a culture of inauthenticity, of shallowness.

Most of us lack depth in our relationships and don't feel like we have safe outlets to express our feelings. So we really appreciate your mission and we "get" why you started it.

In a follow-up message to us, the adult leader of the group corresponded how meaningful the morning was for her and her students. She offered a quote by author Kurt Vonnegut: "What should young people do with their lives today? Many things, obviously. But the most daring thing is to create stable communities in which the terrible disease of loneliness can be cured."

We couldn't agree more.

Healing? (Michael)

"If we knew each other's secrets,
what comforts we should find."
-JOHN CHURTON COLLINS

THE GRAY AND BITTER CHILL of the late winter afternoon penetrated both of us to the core. Neither of us had the fortitude to stand outside the movie theater to linger for long. But we knew we needed to explore our reactions to the film we had just seen—*Spotlight*—based on the fact-based story of the *Boston Globe's* investigation into the Boston diocese of the Roman Catholic Church's decades-long child sex abuse cover-up. The movie's searing subject underscored the hidden realities of the church's and the culture's proclivity to deny and evade the damning truth. The movie's message was haunting. Neither of us knew just what to say about it at first.

Tom broke the reflective silence as we stood momentarily on the sidewalk, "What did you think? How are you feeling about the movie? Was it uncomfortable for you to watch?"

Insightfully, he knew it must have had a strong effect on me. Because of my own story, he was concerned about what was going through my mind, what might be piercing my heart.

"It's too complex to begin to convey it all right here, right now. I need to let it sink in," I responded. "But I *do* want to talk about this. I also know we both need to get home. It's freezing out here. Let's pick up the conversation tomorrow morning after we've had the chance to properly digest what we just saw."

"Sounds good to me. I hope you'll have a good night. What an intense story. I'm anxious to know your reaction."

In our first book, I related a story about the sexual intimidation and unwanted advances I endured when I was 16 and 17. The story was called "Healing."

In short, I wrote about the part-time job I had on a few weeknights and on Saturdays in my great uncle's clothing store, when I was a senior in high school. A man twice my age also worked there. We were often the only two working in the store on Wednesday nights. Throughout the year, he became increasingly more aggressive at ambushing me in storerooms and hiding around corners, "lying in wait" for me. Routinely and with greater boldness, he would rub up against me, lingering as he did, touching me in inappropriate places. Twice as big as I, he'd grab my hands, forcing me to touch him inappropriately. He pulled down his zipper, as if he was going to expose himself and told me very personal details of his sexual relationship with his wife. It was uncomfortable and dehumanizing, and I dreaded the hours we were scheduled to work alone together. I tried my best to avoid him and to resist, keeping as wide a berth around him as I could and still do my job.

For 18 years I was quiet. I never told anyone about what he did to me or how I felt about it. Then in 1991, when the nation was tuning into the hearings for Clarence Thomas' U.S. Supreme Court nomination, I told my wife, Kathy. Across the country people were focused on Anita Hill's accusations of how Thomas had sexually harassed and intimidated her when she worked for him years before. The attention those hearings received shook loose in me the experience that I had buried for more than half my life.

I was ashamed, embarrassed and afraid that I would be blamed for what had gone on. It just wasn't something anyone talked about when I was growing up. Ever. So I kept it to myself, deep inside. I thought I was alone; this just didn't happen to others, especially to boys. I felt weak and powerless to change the situation.

Things are different four decades later, in so many ways. More and more people are admitting their experiences of the sexual harassment and abuse they endured. It is astonishing how many people tell Tom and me they were abused when they were growing up. So many of their stories are far more intense and intrusive, even violent, than my story. Our hearts break for them, for the scars that linger, for the wounds that are still open and raw, decades after the actual abuse ended. But the emotion that remains often grows heavier with the years—especially when it is not given a voice.

When we submitted the story to our publisher, a Christian publisher, the company requested we tone down the details of the situation. References to being touched "between my legs," to the man "pulling down his zipper" and to the "socks he'd stick in the front of his pants to create noticeable bulges" had to be deleted from the story.

The reason was fear, fear that those details might offend the publisher's readers. In all truth, those details were hardly explicit. They were discreetly toned down from the actual reality of what happened. I never described the more graphic and highly inappropriate things he said to me, a minor half his age. I didn't detail every sordid nuance of his attempts to intimidate and take advantage of me. But I thought at least some of the details needed to be described for readers to have a reasonable picture of what I had experienced. Still, I was asked to soften the description, to decrease the chances for people to be offended.

The request offended *me.*

The offense doesn't come because I couldn't tell my story in the exact way it happened and the way I wanted. The offense comes from the fact that the publisher deemed it inappropriate for Christians, or people of any faith, to read about, know about, or talk about the difficult truths of sexual harassment and abuse going on around them.

The man who harassed me was a church organist. He was a professing Christian. He was involved intimately in church life. Yet the church doesn't always want to recognize the realities of what its own people have done to hurt and scar one another.

It offends me that there are millions of stories such as mine, most far worse, and far more damaging. If we as a community of concern for one another cannot talk openly about what has gone on and what still goes on around us, how can the abuse be stopped? How can healing begin?

The fact is, there are millions of boys and girls and men and women of every age, who harbor secrets about what was done to them or what is currently happening to them. If light cannot be shed into the darkest corners of those secrets, then the secrets hold a perverse and damning power over those who hide behind them— both for the victims and their perpetrators. If the church, or any faith community, cannot be a safe place in which to talk about our experiences and shame, then what place is? If people of faith are not allowed space to express their most intimate and personal stories of hurt and sadness, then how can we be reminded that the "Lord is near to the brokenhearted, and saves the crushed in spirit," as Psalm 34:18 and countless other passages like it promise?

What offends me is when religion, and by extension, religious people, ignore the very real truths of life—and cannot or will not talk about them. Tom and I both believe all of us are created in the image of an unconditionally loving, gracious, compassionate God. This belief is at the core of our faith. We believe this God is intimately connected to us and is within us. We believe this God desires for all of us to have life lived in wholeness and in peace, and have it abundantly.

As Christians, we believe in a God who lived our life—in all its beauty and in all its ugliness—in the person of Jesus Christ, a God who infinitely and perfectly understands what we experience and what we suffer. This God, we believe, wants deeply and passionately, for us to heal from our emotional, physical, and spiritual wounds and gives us the power to help each other do so. But we cannot do it when we are not allowed to open up and give voice to the intimate realities of our lives.

A secret kept is a secret denied. A secret denied is a secret buried. A secret buried keeps us from abundant life and holds us hostage to its monstrous power and indignities. And that, we believe, is not God's intention for us.

That, we believe, is not why Jesus came to us. He came, we believe, to set us free.

Why are we so so reluctant to hear or talk about these kinds of issues? Why can't we be more open and sensitive to the very real, very unyielding realities of others' lives?

While it is uncomfortable to come face to face with those unyielding realities, it is the only way we can help each other begin to heal.

It is also how compassion moves us to be. Compassion is the living embodiment of what the church is called to be—an open heart to those who feel rootless and need a home, an outstretched hand to those who are lonely and lost, a source of acceptance to those who are seized by overwhelming demons and fears, a common place of safety and comfort for those who are deep in torment and affliction.

We long for the church to *always* be a place of safety and comfort.

Tom's sensitivity that cold winter's afternoon warmed my soul. In understanding that *Spotlight* would evoke strong feelings for me meant he had empathy for my experience, even one from decades before. Such concern takes away all manner of pain and isolation. It is a healing solace.

If only we all had friends who can be sensitive and empathetic for us every day.

"Are We Measuring Up?"
(An Essay in Two Parts)

"The only people I know who pray well are those who continue to pray. Perseverance is the only mark of "success" in prayer."
-RICHARD ROHR

"Relying on God has to begin all over again every day as if nothing had yet been done."
-C.S. LEWIS

"The moment you wake up each morning, all your wishes and hopes for the day rush at you like wild animals. And the first job each morning consists in shoving it all back; in listening to that other voice, taking that other point of view, letting that other, larger, stronger, quieter life come flowing in."
-C.S. LEWIS

HEART TO HEART CONVERSATIONS (TOM)

SARAH TOOK A DAY for herself and I was happy she did. Being the mom of four small children may be among the most demanding jobs the world has to offer—and she does it beautifully! However, we both realize in order to continue to do it beautifully, it's vitally important that she invests some of her energy into being attentive to her own needs for self-preservation. It reminds me of the adage—if you were sitting on an airplane and it was to go down, make sure you put the oxygen mask on yourself first, otherwise you won't be helpful to anyone else on the plane—you will be dead! It's such a great principle, but most of us are resistant to living it out in practice.

Since I was with the kids by myself for the day, my expectations were minimal for the dreary January Saturday. I went to bed Friday night, reminding myself to set the bar very low for the next day.

Our new cat, and first pet, Elsa, was in heat and peeing all over the place. First thing in the morning I rolled over on my pillow to a face full of cat urine.

159

I went downstairs to make coffee and stepped in a giant pool of water. The roof above our kitchen was leaking extensively. Apparently the ice storm two days before had clogged our gutters and the water wasn't draining properly. All four of our kids didn't sleep well the night before and sounded like a bunch of whimpering puppy dogs when they awoke—far too early. It's on those days when I need an extra special amount of grace for myself and for the kids. But more often than not, it's often on those days when I wrestle to give and receive the grace I need.

By mid-morning I already felt as if the day had been a long one. My mind was a million miles away. I was scheduled to preach the next day, which was creating some anxiety, as it always does. And not only that, I had received a phone call from my dad; he wasn't feeling well. He had recently undergone major heart surgery, causing added stress to our family. Each of those issues was causing my mind to wander. But there was a deeper, more pressing issue going on below the surface. Michael and I often talk about how there is always a "thing behind a thing" for most of us. For example, most of us get angry over the normal stressors of life—an unexpected bill in the mail, a sudden knocking noise from the car engine, a broken dishwasher or similar irritants. But more often than not, those externals only cause us minor distress; it's the deeper issues, the internal ones, which cause us to go to some very dark, lonesome and gloomy places.

The deeper issue for me that morning was I wasn't feeling as if I was "cutting it" as a dad or as a man. I'd be lying if I said this was the only day I ever felt such instability. At times Lillian, who was then eight, and I had a tendency to butt heads—which is the sarcasm of the year. Studies show our children who can cause the most grief are often times the ones who are most like us. I guess it means Lillian is most like me.

I texted Sarah in the middle of the day with the declaration (in all caps):
"I LITERALLY DON'T KNOW WHAT I AM DOING!"

Occasionally, I wish there was a "how to" manual for parents—although, if there was, then I'd have to actually follow it—and I'm not always the best at following directions. Comedian Jim Gaffigan and fellow father of "many" (at the time I wrote this he and his wife were expecting their fifth) put it this way:

"Having four small children is like drowning and having someone hand you a baby."

But in our case, it's like drowning and having someone hand us two babies with our hands tied behind our backs while blindfolded. The joy of twins!

The day was an especially grinding one and not just because of the relational disconnect between Lillian and me, but because of the many other paper cuts I was feeling in my life. Paper cuts don't hurt too badly if you get just one of them at a time. But if you get enough paper cuts at once, you will eventually be bleeding all over the place.

Earlier in the day, I was becoming increasingly short-tempered. We needed to get out of the house so I took all four kids to the local library. The peaceful library went from a place of absolute silence to one filled with pandemonium in a heartbeat after we burst in. One of the twins started pulling books off the shelves; one by one, an entire row fell on the floor. The other twin was undergoing potty training and needed a bathroom ASAP! I had a dilemma: Do I take the one twin to the restroom before she wets herself OR do I grab the other twin before she knocks over an entire bookshelf?

Shortly thereafter, an older woman stated very sharply, "Wow, you could definitely use a mom's touch here."

We left the library with only minimal physical damages done. But, the damage to my self-esteem was *not* minimal. After the woman's comment, I thought about causing a little destruction myself. Her statement was a reflection on how I was already feeling on the inside—inadequate, overwhelmed and out of place. It made me feel worse. Censured. Emasculated.

All of which leads to the deeper issue raging inside me that day—the raging feeling I wasn't measuring up, cutting it. My mind was elsewhere; I wasn't mentally or emotionally present with my kids. I was short-tempered. And I knew I wasn't providing enough financially for my family; all of it contributed to the dark and negative tenor of the day.

In his book *Abba's Child*, Brennan Manning shares a story giving us pause to reflect on the ways in which we instantly, often unfairly, judge others around us:

> *Author Stephen Covey recalled an incident while riding the New York City subway one Sunday morning. The few passengers aboard were reading the newspaper or dozing. It was a quiet, almost somnolent ride through the bowels of the Big Apple. Covey was engrossed in reading when a man accompanied by several small children boarded at the next stop. In less than a minute, bedlam erupted. The kids ran up and down the aisle shouting, screaming, and wrestling with one another on the floor. Their father made no attempt to intervene.*
>
> *The elderly passengers shifted nervously. Stress became distress. Covey waited patiently. Surely the father would do something to restore some expression of paternal authority—anything. Nothing was forthcoming. Frustration mounted. After an unduly generous pause, Covey turned to the father and said kindly, "Sir, perhaps you could restore order here by telling your children*

to come back and sit down." "I know I should do something," the man re-
plied. "We just came from the hospital. Their mother died an hour ago. I just
don't know what to do."

Brennan Manning also wrote:

> *The heartfelt compassion that hastens forgiveness matures when we dis-*
> *cover where our enemy cries.*

For whatever reason, I felt as if no one understood my situation. I was crying
on the inside, all alone.

By no means am I comparing my situation to the man who had just lost his
wife in this story. But I resonated with it because it was a day during which I felt
totally overmatched.

Sarah arrived home later in the evening. Lillian had posted a note on the front
door for her to read:

Dear mommy, daddy has been
mean tonight. He gave me a padil
(paddle) when we all wanted brown
sugar on our sweet patato (potato).
I did not like it at all, he gave me
3 or 4 spankings for no reson (rea-
son). Mean daddy. From Lilly,
Thank you.

Our refrigerator and pantry were nearly empty. We needed groceries, so when
Sarah came home I volunteered to make the trip.

"You don't need to go now; we can always go after church tomorrow," Sarah
suggested.

"No, I need to go now (which was code for 'I needed a little time to do something, anything, alone')." Sarah and I know how to speak in code these days. We
often tell young married couples who are thinking about having kids, the two greatest transitions with small children are a decrease in adequate sleep and an increase in
a home's noise level. It was an especially "noisy" day and Sarah understood it.

I arrived at the grocery store and nearly every spot in the parking lot was filled. It
didn't make sense to me because it was a Saturday night in the middle of winter. Who
wants to shop on a Saturday night? Apparently, everyone who has children does!

I got an additional answer when just before getting out the car the radio announcer pronounced:

Expect six to eight inches of snow tomorrow if you live in Cumberland, Dauphin, Perry, York, and Adams Counties.

I put in my headphones and turned on Pandora on my phone to listen to some Christmas carols. Even though the season had ended, on such a fraught night, I needed the inspiration, which Christmas music gives to me. Besides, I also needed silence—but not the kind of silence a packed out supermarket brings the night before an apocalypse of a snowstorm (I use the word "apocalypse" sarcastically; so many people in our area react to any amount of snow as if it's a major catastrophe). Up and down the aisles I went, grabbing items of necessity. I remembered Sarah saying we didn't have much money left in our account before we received her paycheck the next week. Only the essentials went in the cart, milk, eggs, juice, yogurt, cereal, etc. I was in a trance and wasn't sure how long I was in the store. But I hoped the lines would have died down by time I reached the checkout. Sadly, they hadn't. I looked for the shortest line. But it didn't matter; it was going to be a long wait regardless. Now that I was actually thinking about the time, I started checking the clock on my phone every five minutes. Thirty-five minutes later I reached the register. One by one I pulled out each item and placed it on the conveyer belt. One by one the bagger placed the items back in the cart.

"$82.31" the young girl behind the register informed me.

I swiped my card.

"Your card isn't reading," the clerk reported, a little too loudly for my dignity.

I'm sure you could see the redness increasing on my face as a line full of people behind me were impatiently waiting their turns.

"Your card isn't reading," she related for the second time. Another hit to my dignity. "But let me try another trick."

She proceeded to grab a plastic bag and wrap the card and then try to swipe it.

"Sometimes this works. I don't understand why." It didn't work and I knew it wouldn't. The embarrassment was increasing.

"Uh, oh. Ok," I replied. "Can we keep the cart off to the side; I need to run home and grab another card."

Truth be told, there wasn't another card. I wanted to grab one of the brown bags and put it over my head. I grabbed my phone to call Sarah to see if she could check our bank account. My phone was dead. The embarrassment quickly turned to anger.

"What a day! @#%*"

I walked back to my car in a fit of rage.

"Ugh. This sucks!!!"

On the drive home I had a heart to heart conversation with God. I remember reading a small book in college by a guy named Brother Lawrence. Brother Lawrence wrote:

> *There is not in the world a kind of life more sweet and delightful than that of a continual conversation with God.*

So I had my own "conversation" with God:

> *God, I don't understand why this has to be so freakin' complicated. First off, why is everyone freaking out over 6-8 inches of snow!!! Even a simple trip to the grocery store has been a real pain. It's been one issue after another today and I don't have a clue about what to do about it. I'm in way over my head. Why can't this be easier for me . . . for us! It's inconvenient to follow your leading. I feel like I've given up so much to do it. The lack of connection I've felt with Lillian has made me feel less than adequate as a dad; I wonder constantly if I am cutting it as a dad. Then the lack of money in our account tonight is the icing on the cake. To be totally honest, I'm feeling worthless as a man, that I'm not providing for my family.*
>
> *It seems like you aren't listening and that my words are falling on deaf ears. The Christmas music I was just listening to talks about you coming near, that you are with us. You don't feel very near to me right now.*
>
> *You've taught me, especially over the last few months, that life isn't always what it is cracked up to be. I've learned and experienced the wilderness firsthand. I've learned what it's like to wander, to ask and feel as if we're not receiving what we asked for.*
>
> *I've complained and grumbled like the Israelites during their 40-year journey in the wilderness, and I'm sorry about that. But I just don't know what else to do sometimes.*
>
> *I'm simply overwhelmed by all of this.*
>
> *The Bible says "give thanks to the Lord and rejoice in all situations." But honestly, I'm having a back-breaking time giving thanks and rejoicing. I am sick and tired of it all. Rejoice! I don't want to rejoice in all situations . . . that seems so forced.*
>
> *God, if you hear me and are near, answer me. I need to know that there's a reason to have hope.*

I just want things to work out, (with a big gulp) even if that means things don't go my way at all. I can't imagine wandering my whole life in the wilderness, waiting and watching for the moment when we reach this so called "Promised Land."

I don't understand all of this, but I choose to trust you. You have always showed up before, and I trust you will show up again. Please, please, help me to remember all the times you have showed up before—and given me even more than I need.

Amen.

It felt so healthy to get all of that off my chest. Arriving home 20 minutes later I felt so "free." It felt like God had heard my prayer, and the especially good news —God let me pour it out, all of it. No judgment, no condemnation, no anger. Simply understanding in response.

Walking through the door "empty handed," I honestly felt at peace and emptied of all the raging emotions and feelings I'd had inside."

I explained the situation to Sarah and she was very apologetic and also very understanding. We even laughed about it.

She looked at the bank account and realized we had about $60 left. She also remembered she had a $20 bill left in her wallet. We opened the jar of coins sitting on our kitchen counter and counted out the remaining $2.31.

We had exactly what we needed . . . as we have had so many times before.

Sarah left to go back to the grocery store and I continued my conversation with God.

God, You know I have a tough time giving thanks for what you provide. I'm asking for your help to live in gratitude for what you provide. Thank you for reminding me tonight of your constant provision and abiding presence. Thank you for loving me when I don't feel loveable or good or worthy or gracious. I love you.

People often ask us: "What does prayer mean to you?"

Prayer is about continually showing up and letting ourselves be seen, it's about inviting God into whatever space we find ourselves in. Lots of us hide our pains and function as if life is relaxed and unruffled. But what I've been realizing about prayer the past few years is that God cares about the deeper stuff. God knows the deeper stuff already, so we might as well express it. God knows what makes us insecure, what keeps us up at night, what makes us angry or stressed. God knows it all.

And here is the especially good news: God's shoulders are broad enough to carry it and God's heart is big enough to lament all of it with us. The real work of prayer is to keep praying, waiting, watching and listening for God to say good things about us and to us. Prayer is being with God and simply spending time nurturing the relationship, being unguarded, genuine, and candid.

God hears. God listens. God responds. With kindheartedness. With goodwill. With gentleness.

To all the raging emotions inside each one of us.

Our hope is to remember and live with that assurance, a little more with every new day.

WHAT'S WRONG WITH HIM? (MICHAEL)

He didn't want to leave.

As Kathy and I each took one of Matthew's arms to help steady him as we walked off the beach, it was obvious he didn't want to go. He kept plopping down, every few steps along the way. The boardwalk, where his transport chair awaited, seemed an increasing long distance away, every time he fell to the sand, obstinate.

"Do you need my help?" A man bounded over to us, obviously witnessing our dilemma. We did need the help, so I answered, "Yes. We would love it. Your help would be great."

Picking him up together, he and I carried Matthew off the sand, to the boardwalk and placed him in his chair. I thanked him profusely when we were finished and he responded that he was glad to help.

Kathy and I were grateful for his graciousness and concern.

But nearly three weeks after the encounter, I was still haunted by the question he asked me as we carried Matthew off the beach,

"What's wrong with him?"

"Well, he has severe intellectual disabilities and autism. He lost his ability to walk on his own over three years ago when he had spinal cord compression. He also loves the beach and just doesn't want to leave."

My answer was factually accurate. But I wish that I could have responded differently. After all, the man went out of his way to help us. He was doing something very compassionate; few others ever stop to help us when we are wrestling with Matthew. In the moment, I was immediately concerned with the scuffle at hand, getting Matthew off the beach. In the moment I realized it wasn't the time to lecture him on the premise of his question or the unartful wording he used to ask it.

Instead, I wish I had responded,

"Oh, there's nothing wrong with him. He just loves the beach so much he doesn't want to leave it. But if you're asking why he needs our help, he can't walk due to spinal compression and related nerve damage."

Period.

There's nothing wrong with him. This is who he was created to be. For better or for worse, this is who he is. We don't despair about him. We don't wish for him to be different. Yes, our lives would be much easier—and different—if he didn't live with disabilities. But, we embrace him and love him, adore him, actually. For who he is—a beloved, beautiful, often beaming child of God.

There is nothing wrong with him . . .

The year before. The same beach. Matthew sits at the surf's edge. Kathy and I are a few yards behind him; we don't like the water splashing up over us like he does. He's supremely happy and content. We watch him with awe; there's no more joyful sight than seeing him laughing passionately as the tide swirls around his legs and occasionally up over his lap.

I leave the beach for a few minutes to go back to our the place we were staying, about a block and a half away, to get some snacks for us to eat. In my absence, a man sitting with his family nearby comes over to Kathy to ask if Matthew is okay sitting where he is at the water's edge. Could he help move him back so the water wouldn't wash up over him? Kathy explains, no; Matthew loves sitting where he is. It's his favorite place to be and thing to be doing. She thanks him for his concern and reiterates Matthew is quite comfortable and peaceful where he is. His placement by the water is intentional, purposeful. He is safe. We have our eyes on him. When he is content, so are we.

She tells me about the encounter when I return.

Not more than a half hour later, as the tide begins noticeably to come in, a sudden larger wave breaks fairly closely to Matthew, splashing up over him. He roars with delight, looking back at us with his mouth wide open, all teeth and tonsils, eyes squinting, sparkling. Communicating, "Look at me, Mom and Dad. Look what the water did! Isn't it great?! I love being here!"

We laugh, knowing this is what he lives for every summer.

A few minutes later, another wave. This time bigger, closer. The tide is rapidly encroaching. We say to one another, it might be time to pull Matthew back a few yards. Before we can do it, another wave, another break, this time right at Matthew. The rising tide lifts Matthew and his chair up into the air, pivots him around and dumps him face down in the sand as it recedes again. Engulfed in the surf, covered from head to toe with sand, Matthew looks up shrieking with abandon; nirvana, heaven, has been seen. He is beside himself with rapture.

We quickly jump up to right his chair and pull him back, at the same time celebrating with him his wild ride in the wave.

Our neighbor, the man who questioned Matthew's position at the water's edge, as the water hit and lifted Matthew with its forceful energy, shrieks. Not with delight, as Matthew has, but with horror. He jumps up and rushes over to save him. He seems horrified at seeing Matthew planted face down in the sand.

We get it. To the uninitiated and unfamiliar, it definitely can look as if Matthew is suffering, in danger. Not knowing what we know about Matthew's profound love of the beach and all its splendors, it can appear as if he is being harmed or is uncomfortable.

But the man's shrieks, his gasps, his jumping up to "save" Matthew, can also make us feel as if we are neglectful, irresponsible, bad parents. As if we need to keep Matthew right by our sides, far from the encroaching sea, cocooned and protected. Sometimes I feel as if we are expected to be helicopter parents with him, always hovering over, whirling around him to keep him safe and secure. The fact is, we do watch him like hawks. We have to; he needs protecting, often from himself. He doesn't understand danger.

He also needs to live—with exuberance and joy, doing the things he loves and lives for. There is so very little in his life he is able to do as others do. There are so few activities he obviously lives for and delights in. Going to the beach, as I've written about so many times before, is one of them.

Yes, he's a sight on the beach. His flapping arms and kicking legs. His gleeful bellowing and cackling laugh. His wild rides on a few waves as the tide rushes in. His face planted into the sand. He revels in it all like nothing else in his life. We know something the casual observers don't. We know how much it means to him, how much he anticipates and waits for those few brief shining moments every year, all year.

So, while some people's well-meaning queries, reactions and offers to help, may make us feel a bit judged and viewed as inadequate, we have to remind ourselves why we do what we believe we have to do with and for Matthew. And be okay with whatever negative judgments come.

We know there's nothing wrong with Matthew—and that a good wave, a wild ride, is what he loves most in life.

I Loved You Best (Michael)

*"Love is so unconditional; love liberates; love is the reason why I do
what I do, and so I think it is the greatest gift we have."*
-BeBe Winans

IT WAS MOTHER'S DAY. I was scheduled to preach. This day is often a complicated one for pastors. Culturally, even though Mother's Day is not a religious holiday, there is still considerable expectation in churches for at least some references to be made to the holiday and it's importance. Tom and I have had great mothers, grandmothers and wives who have been wonderful role models for our children and us. But we are also very aware that many people have not had such healthy, warm relationships and experiences. Many people carry considerable emotional baggage with regard to their mothers. In addition, fractured and painful relationships, loss and grief, the inability to have children, and many other circumstances can make Mother's Day a tenuous one. For those reasons, preaching on Mother's Day is always fraught with the balancing act of how to reach the most people with an inclusive message recognizing the joys of celebrating mothers as well as the brokenness of human relationships.

I chose to recount a portion of a short story written by the late humorist Erma Bombeck. The story tells of the legacy a 48-year-old mother leaves her three sons on the day of her funeral. I believe it illustrates both the deep and abiding love a mother can have for all of her children and the even greater love God has for all of us.

The mom had written a letter to each of her sons before she died, and each of them carried the letter, secretly, in his pocket as they sat together at her service. None of the boys had been perfect, of course, as none of us ever are. Each posed his own frustrations to his mother. The eldest son possessed an arrogance and an air of superiority. The middle son had a rebellious and reckless spirit. The youngest carried resentment for coming along so much later than his brothers and, as a result, felt he didn't get the best of his brothers or his parents. Each son, as he sat in the pew, felt a sense of guilt for not having been a "better" son.

But, the letters they carried in their pockets didn't mention the idiosyncrasies that tested their mother's patience.

Instead, each one detailed the qualities for which his mother was grateful. Each letter was a testament to forbearance, mercy, and unqualified affection. And in each letter, their mother declared: **"I loved you best."**

The message of that story resonates strongly with me. It's certainly how I feel about my three sons. I love each of them best. It's also, according to my understanding of God, exactly how God feels about each one of us. God loves each one of us best. Only infinitely more than we ever can.

Forbearance. Mercy. Unqualified affection.

These are the essence and the indispensible aspects of living and leading a compassionate life. That was the message I was trying to convey on Mother's Day—a message about an infinitely compassionate God. I was also presenting every one with a call to action to respond to this divine gift with compassion for others and ourselves.

After the service, when I stood shaking hands as people left the church, I received many warm and appreciative comments about the message. But I don't remember the specifics of any of them. I only remember one comment I received. The critical one. The negative one. The one cutting sharply into my confidence and self-esteem.

It was from a member of the congregation who was a prominent leader in the community. I didn't know him well. I was still fairly new at the church.

He handed me his business card as he shook my hand, and announced, "I'd like you to call me. I want to discuss your sermon."

He wasn't smiling.

"In regard to it, you were dead wrong. Those boys were ungrateful. They didn't deserve their mother's grace. Your message of forgiveness is all wrong."

My stomach immediately churned. My heart felt as if it leapt into my throat and sunk at the same time. My pulse quickened, substantially. I don't remember anything else he said after that. His words cut into my soul, wounding me. I felt diminished and dismissed.

The businessman's wife looked at me sheepishly, saying nothing. I was embarrassed as the line of people behind him lengthened. Most of them heard his rant. It was an incredibly awkward and dreadful moment for me.

Mustering politeness, not wanting to create a scene, I remember thanking him for letting me know his thoughts, even though I wasn't the least bit thankful. I just wanted the moment to end. Immediately. I was grateful when it did.

I still had another service to preach. Now I questioned whether my sermon was any good and whether I was "dead wrong." I asked my pastoral colleague what he thought. He reassured me there was nothing I said that was wrong or bad. He told me this parishioner always "has issues" when it comes to the topic of forgiveness. He had a troubled relationship with his own mother and given that it was Mother's Day, his conflicted feelings were probably only intensified and brought to the surface. My colleague's words were calming and helped me get through the next service. But, the criticism stayed with me. The rest of the day was a blur.

I remember that my extended family got together to celebrate Mother's Day with our mother. While I was present physically, I wasn't especially present mentally or emotionally. For the rest of the day, I replayed over and over and over again, the words "you were dead wrong" in my mind.

I felt weak, like I wasn't strong enough to withstand a critique or a disagreement someone had with me. I questioned my abilities and myself. I questioned my theology. I questioned my understanding of grace, forgiveness and unconditional love. I felt discouraged and disheartened. I despaired that the man and others might not like me.

I felt angry with myself for allowing his comments to ruin my day. More than 20 years later, I still haven't forgotten his words and how they made me feel.

But since then, I have gotten better about receiving criticism. While it's always been a weaker spot for me, I manage it better and try to learn from it. Experience, maturity, forgiveness and deciding that I just can't carry everyone's hurtful actions help it to be better. Harsh comments, or even perceived harsh comments, such as those I received on Mother's Day years ago, still sting and I can still obsess over them for long periods of time. But, I try not to let the words seep in.

Being sensitive is both a great gift and a considerable curse.

To be highly attuned to others' feelings and empathize well with them is a tremendous plus for a pastor and a compassionate listener. Empathy is the key to leading a compassionate life. But the flip side is the same sensitivity allowing me to empathize deeply with others also makes me sensitive to criticism and easily wounded. Sometimes I take things much too personally. The compassionate personal empathy and attention I can give to someone in distress has a dark underbelly. The same sensitivity to another's feelings works against my own feelings. There are times when I struggle to remind myself most people's actions and reactions, especially the critical ones, are not so much about me, but more about them and the burdens they carry. But most people would never know the internal turmoil it produces in me.

It's burdensome facing those who hurt, criticize, confront, or diminish us. My natural, gut reaction isn't to lash back or even defend myself when someone says, "You are dead wrong." I don't get angry with them. I don't hold grudges, or have any desire to get even, seek revenge or give someone "a piece of my mind." I've never felt the need to do any of those things.

Instead I examine and reexamine my actions, my words and my motives, and try to understand what caused someone to say what they've said or do what they've done. I continue to be outwardly kind, polite, gracious, diplomatic, discreet and compassionate toward those who injure me, as much as I humanly can. But the internal struggle is a fierce one most of the time.

A few days later, I called the man at home. My heart raced as I dialed. My blood pressure rose. I could feel the anxiety in my stomach as I braced for a lecture on why I was wrong. I expected to be hurt again.

His wife answered the phone. She told me he wasn't home. (I said a silent prayer of thanks.) I asked when I could call back to reach him. She said he probably expressed what he wanted to say and there was no need to call him again about the matter.

Then she said, "He's very direct. It's been an interesting marriage."

There it was. I wasn't the only one he was critical of; it wasn't necessarily personal. It was the way he was. When I coupled that observation with what my pastoral colleague had told me about the man's troubled relationship with his mother and his wrestling with the concept of forgiveness, I began to see a more complete picture of the man. I saw his humanness, his vulnerability and his conflict to be compassionate.

And, I felt more compassion for him. Everyone else has a struggle (or two or three or fifty) we rarely know about. It's all the more reason to express compassion for everyone we meet. Everyone needs compassion to help face the trials.

I have since come to realize what distressed me the most about his comments were that the subjects about which I had spoken—mercy, goodwill and kindheartedness —are integral to my belief system, my faith and my way of life, and he criticized all of it. Tom and I both believe that mercy, goodwill and kindheartedness are essential to living compassionately. Compassion requires them; compassion is impossible without them.

His words struck at the core of who I was (and am). They struck at the core of what I believe faith compels of me—of all of us. Our faith calls us all to live compassionately. To live compassionately requires that we practice goodwill, that we offer mercy, and that we are kindhearted. It's not easy.

Often, it's exasperating to practice goodwill with someone who doesn't show goodwill to us. It seems nearly impossible to offer mercy to someone who might not be willing to be merciful in return. It is exceedingly arduous to try to be kindhearted, when someone is not kindhearted with us. We can't deny it.

But there's also no denying we are called to try. And as tough as it is, ultimately, extending goodwill, being merciful and kindhearted is far easier than carrying the weight and burden of resentment, bitterness, self-doubt, or grudges on our hearts every day. Physical exercise, which can be painful and exhausting, especially at first, gets easier with practice. The more we exercise, the better we feel, the more energy we have, and the healthier we become. It is the same with goodwill, mercy and kindheartedness. The more we practice exhibiting them, the better we will feel about ourselves and others, the more energy we will have to live with greater freedom, joy and peace, and the healthier we will become, emotionally, mentally and spiritually, and possibly, physically.

As we practice doing our best to model this way of living, in our ministry and in our lives, we know we do not do any of it perfectly. We can judge others, hold onto slights, be impatient, lack understanding and not show empathy. But that's where we can also help each other to be more intentional and to persevere when we don't quite get it right. In fact, we fall short in many ways every single day. But the important thing is we try.

We believe without reservation, God shows endless goodwill, extends limitless mercy and exhibits kindhearted love for us. We believe God loves us every one of us, no matter who we are or what we have done (or not done). God loves all of us best.

It's the greatest gift we can receive and a message we believe we all constantly need to hear. Maybe when we do, we will eventually believe in its truth.

The Party Wouldn't Be a Party Without You

"To be yourself in a world that is constantly trying to make you something else is the greatest accomplishment."
-Ralph Waldo Emerson

"Today you are You, that is truer than true. There is no one alive who is Youer than You."
-Dr. Seuss

"SO, YOU . . . **just** listen?" We certainly didn't expect the response we received to the question about what we do professionally.

We were attending a World Leaders Conference with some of the deepest thinkers, activists, and social change agents from around the world. We had been gifted with two complimentary tickets to the conference and felt advantaged to be "invited to the party," to listen, for three days, as others extolled their BIG ideas and how those ideas were making a noteworthy difference in the lives of others.

The first morning started off well. Several key communicators spoke with conviction and vulnerability. The conference was doing exactly what we hoped it would—it was beginning to reenergize us to go back into our mission field with passion and enthusiasm. But things quickly shifted as the lunch hour approached. The host of the conference invited us to get our lunches and assemble around a table with six or eight other attendees. One by one, we went around the table introducing ourselves and describing our areas of expertise.

The first leader spoke about his gifts in engineering and how those gifts were helping to create irrigation systems in third world countries for water preservation. The second leader discussed her gifts relating to public relations and described how those skills were helping children learn English as a second language on the Internet. The third leader expressed her qualities in leadership development and explained the curriculum she had created to prepare teenagers to enter the business world in foreign marketplaces.

More and more BIG ideas flowed. Economics. Healthcare. Politics. Communications. Each idea was unique; each idea was noteworthy. It seemed to us as if everyone around our table was impressed by the contributions and ideas of the others.

Then it was our turn. We introduced ourselves. We explained our mission of creating a caring culture that accompanies others on the path toward meaningful connections. We explained that we offer a compassionate presence and a listening ear to those who need a safe place to share their stories. Silence. We could hear each inhale and exhale. It wasn't because they were overwhelmed by what we said. Or that they were intently listening! They simply didn't know how to respond. The awkward silence went on for a few seconds until one of the women, like a lifeguard throwing a verbal life preserver, saved everyone else at the table by inviting them to eat their lunches. Our time to voice our idea has passed.

Another woman sitting next to us reticently made eye contact. She re-introduced herself knowing we would be sitting next to one another for the rest of the afternoon. We couldn't be "avoided" even if it's what she wanted.

After a few pleasantries, she asked us a question:

"*So, you. . .just listen?*" She emphasized the word, "JUST" as if our mission was trivial; it felt fairly dismissive.

It seemed as if she was asking the question everyone else around the table wanted to ask, but didn't or wouldn't.

We both looked at each other, bashfully, wondering which one of us would react. Truly, it wasn't the first time we had been asked this question, so we weren't completely caught off-guard. Tom spoke up first:

"We think often times we are too quick to try to fix others. We offer platitudes and wise sounding advice as if we have a "magic bullet" to solve someone's problems. Most of us like to see cure and change in someone else's life. But what we don't want to see is other people's problems not able to be fixed as quickly as possible."

Michael added, "What most of us need most of the time, instead of problem solving, is someone to care for us by walking with us through our pain and brokenness. To accompany us as we work through the things that trouble us. We believe we can all do this by listening well and entering those dark, difficult places with others."

Tom continued, "In fact, the word "care" finds its roots in the word "lament." We can all lament with those who have experienced loss, those who are feeling lonely, those who are uncertain or doubtful, those who are searching for meaning. We can mourn with them. We give them a shoulder to cry on. We can cry out in anguish with them."

She didn't seem too interested in our response; her head started scanning the room as if she was planning her exit strategy in an "escape room."

Knowing there wasn't an easy exit, we decided instead to engage her in conversation. We asked her a question about her area of expertise: communications. She had voiced, just a few moments before, about the books, seminars and trainings she does for organizations to empower better communication with investors and employees. Later in the week we would be speaking to a large group of our financial supporters at our annual fundraiser and we thought she might be able to help focus our message. We told her about it and requested,

"So how might we best approach things?" The question was barely finished when she chimed in, "Ok, so, you need to do this. . ." "Do this. . .." "Do this, this and this. . ." "Make sure. . .you don't do this. . ." "And definitely, definitely, don't do that. . ." "Oh yeah, and one more thing, make sure you do this!!!"

By the time she had finished her debriefing, our heads hurt. Lunchtime was over and so was her instruction. Tom whispered, "What just happened?" Even though she offered some valuable inspiration and wisdom and gave us a few things to ponder, we were stunned. She had gone into "fixer" mode without blinking an eye. She never took the time to listen to our interests and needs for the event.

With our minds (and hearts) still spinning, the afternoon session commenced. The next speaker spoke about valuing those around us by celebrating their individuality. He asked a question of the audience, "Who on earth needs encouragement?"

He waited a few moments, letting his question sink in, knowing everyone in the room needed to hear his answer.

"EVERYONE—ON—EARTH—DOES!"

We weren't sure if the speaker's words spoke to everyone else in the room but they were a therapeutic remedy to us.

During an afternoon break, we joined a huddle outside the restroom with several others. Again, the same inevitable question comes up: "So, what do you do?"

"I am an architect. I design eco-friendly skyscrapers in Asia," a woman responds. Another man chimes in, "I am the CEO of a food chain. I work with government officials to get food distributed to countries where people are malnourished."

"That's wonderful! That sounds like very satisfying and imperative work. We have no doubt you are making change happen," Tom says.

They ask us what we do. "We listen and help bear other peoples' burdens." "So, you. . .**just** listen to people? Do you offer advice or solutions?" the CEO retorts.

What alarms us about the question is not the words themselves, but rather the tone with which it is often asked. What we have found, quite often, is that those who ask the question are typically not the best listeners.

We aren't offended by the question; in fact, we appreciate being asked about what we do because it helps us better communicate the importance of our ministry and how we use our spiritual gifts. But like everyone else, there are days when we don't feel as if who we are and what we provide is relevant.

In those moments, we have been offended and discouraged by the skeptical, condescending nature of some peoples' responses. Maybe it's because everyone else seems to be "producing" something tangible, something material. What we offer is intangible and many times intangibles seem to be devalued by the world. Consistently, we remind one another our gifts come from God, not from anyone else, and so God obviously thinks they are important enough to give them to us! We also realize deep down that others do not convey worth on any of us. Only God can. Each one of us has gifts and abilities the world needs. We celebrate and believe every one of us has something of great value to offer and we are called to encourage one another to use our gifts to the best ability we can.

Theologian Dietrich Bonheoffer, before dying in a Nazi prison, wrote an amazing book about Christian community called, *Life Together*. In the book, Bonheoffer addresses the art of listening to one another (as opposed to "**just**" listening). He states,

Christians, especially ministers, so often think they must always contribute something when they are in the company of others, that this is the one service they have to render. They forget that listening can be a greater service than speaking.

Many people are looking for an ear that will listen. . . One who cannot listen long and patiently will presently be talking beside the point and be never really speaking to others, albeit he be not conscious of it. Anyone who thinks that his time is too valuable to spend keeping quiet will eventually have no time for God and his brother, but only for himself and for his own follies.

Surely, we aren't taking anything away from what others bring to the world. In fact, we celebrate, very much so, the uniqueness of all of our skillsets. The apostle Paul, in 1 Corinthians 12 (New Living Translation) used the illustration of a body to talk about the significance of what each of us presents and how the body wouldn't be a body without all of us:

The human body has many parts, but the many parts make up one whole body. . .

Yes, the body has many different parts, not just one part. If the foot says, "I am not a part of the body because I am not a hand," that does not make it any less a part of the body. And if the ear says, "I am not part of the body because I am not an eye," would that make it any less a part of the body? If the whole body were an eye, how would you hear? Or if your whole body were an ear, how would you smell anything?

But our bodies have many parts, and God has put each part just where he wants it . . .

This makes for harmony among the members, so that all the members care for each other. If one part suffers, all the parts suffer with it, and if one part is honored, all the parts are glad.

All of you together are Christ's body, and each of you is a part of it.

Some of us may not be wired in such a way as to be able to build bridges, cook magnificent meals, write plans and procedures to design things, but others of us can. (We especially thank those of you who are mathematicians because Lord knows we don't have that gift! You can ask our wives!!)

Some of us have been given the gift of being present and offering a listening ear. Here is a thought:

What if you looked at every person you interact with, no matter where they find themselves on life's journey, as if they have something important to teach you? Wouldn't such a perspective level the playing field?

We all have unique gifts, important gifts. And one of the primary ways we show compassion to one another is by celebrating each other's exceptionality. Everyone has something to offer and deserves to be invited to the party.

Author Frederick Buechner, another champion of ours, has said:

The grace of God means something like: Here is your life. You might never have been, but you are because the party wouldn't have been complete without you. Here is the world. Beautiful and terrible things will happen. Don't be afraid. I am with you. Nothing can ever separate us. It's for you I created the universe. I love you. There's only one catch. Like any other gift, the gift of grace can be yours only if you'll reach out and take it. Maybe being able to reach out and take it is a gift too.

If you find yourself doubting your graces or questioning whether or not what you bring to the party is of importance, we invite you to surround yourself with people (as we do for one another), who can remind you the party wouldn't be a party without you. Using the body illustration, each of us plays an imperative role in making the body a body; without eyes, we couldn't see where God wants to take us; without feet, we couldn't go to those places God has asked us to go; without minds, we would lack creativity in how to get to those special places. All of us are of sacred worth. All of us bring value to the world. All of us make a party, a party worth attending.

Here's something we believe is fundamental to our identity: successful and satisfied people love what they do, their work is not work. It's a privilege, a gift, a statement of who they are. It gives them energy. It gives them life.

Every one of us is incomparably, matchlessly and generously made. We have all been endowed with very special graces to offer to the world. When we are able to recognize our gifts and are given the encouragement and chance to offer them to others, we will delight in what we are empowered to do. We will love each day, even the hard-hitting days. When we are able to do what we have been created to do, it is remarkable what can be accomplished and how much we can welcome the journey.

The two of us are fortunate to have such an experience every day. Some days are tedious, wearisome and long. They're not always fun. But because we are able to do what we know we've been created to do and can certainly delight in it, even those grueling days are gifts which make us more resilient, stronger and better listeners, caregivers and men.

It brings fulfillment to be at this "party," doing what God has called and invited us to do. We wouldn't have it any other way. We are supremely grateful we know who we are, why we're here and who God calls us—always—to be.

Every one of us brings something far-reaching and needed "to the party." When we can recognize this fact about one another, and ourselves, "the party" is infinitely richer and more joyous because of it.

Play the Hand You've Been Dealt (Tom)

"There is no greater agony than bearing an untold story inside of you."
-MAYA ANGELOU

DRIVING TO MY FIRST writer's retreat, my sweaty palms grip the steering wheel. I take a few deep breaths, hoping to calm the increasing nervousness I am feeling. The hesitations creep in:

"Why am I attending a writer's retreat? I don't belong in such a special company of people."

I turn on the radio. There is an interview with an author who had "hit the jackpot" with her first book. The interviewer asked her how she handles the pressure of having written an international bestselling novel. (She sold millions of copies worldwide in eight different languages.) She talks about how she, as a writer, doesn't put that kind of pressure on herself. Clarifying, she said, she "simply does what she has always done. She writes from her heart. She writes her story."

It just so happened her story resonated with an audience of more than 10 million people! Her words are inspirational to me. I'm reminded of a lesson God has been trying to teach me in a variety of ways—outcomes aren't in my control; God just asks me to be faithful. The same principle applies to my writing. I don't write to gain a following; I write because writing keeps me grounded in who I am.

I drive up to the farmhouse where I will be spending most of the day with about six other authors, bloggers, and poets. We will be "writing our stories." Michael will be there too.

The leader of the retreat introduces herself and for the bulk of the morning we talk about the practicalities of writing our stories, along with the techniques, disciplines and habits of what makes a strong writer. The leader is obviously well schooled, and I'm glad to be one of the students in her class, for the day. One of the other "students" asks her about what we should be revealing publically in our writing.

Her response is tough to grasp. She says, "As writers we may not want to put things out there for others to read if we are still wounded."

We are invited to take a short recess. I need all 15 minutes of the break to process the conversation so far. I walk outside to get some fresh air. It's cold. But I hardly notice as I consider the essence of her statement about a writer's wounds.

Break time is over. I sit down on the sofa in the corner of the room with my second cup of coffee in hand, spilling a portion of it all over my shirt. I am still nervous being there; I still don't feel as if I belong in a writer's retreat. The leader of the retreat asks us, for the first time, to pick up our journals and start writing for 15 minutes about "the thing we are most scared to write about."

For the second time already this morning, my palms get sweaty. I take a long sip of coffee, wishing I were in the confines of my own living room, alone. My eyes scan the room to see how the other writers are reacting to the assignment. I feel much like the Tom Cruise character in the *Mission Impossible* movie series, who has been summoned into an important assignment— "should I choose to accept it." I'd almost rather not.

I've written about some of my personal experiences, emotions, fears, hardships and disappointments, and I have expressed some of them publically. In this book, I've written about me livng with depression and anxiety and how those conditions shape me each day. Writing about each of those frailties was daring in its own way, especially knowing that other eyes would be reading them. But this topic, which I have now been asked to write about, is quite possibly the most ambitious so far.

I open my journal, pick up a pen, and reluctantly start writing.

The words suddenly start devouring the page:

> *For the past three years, I have been a part-time, stay-at-home dad, and most days I am quite embarrassed admitting it.*
>
> *As a young boy, I always pictured myself scaling mountains like Everest, landing on the moon like Armstrong, being a professional photographer for National Geographic magazine; something adventurous, something risky, something I could "hang my hat on" in this life and say, "Tom Kaden did this. . .accomplished this. . .built this. . ."*
>
> *That's not exactly how things turned out. The only mountains I seem to climb are mountains of dirty laundry scattered across our living room floor. The only moon I land on is the full moon of a child's dirty bottom. The only pictures I take are the photo bombs of the twins with hand lotion running through their hair.*

The words kept coming and I kept writing. I wrote about a memorably exasperating day two weeks before. I was having an especially tenuous time resting in the place God had for me that day—which just so happened to be home with all four children for another 12-hour shift while Sarah was working at the hospital.

The day began noisily. The clattering of the snowplow across the street awakened me. Sarah had already left for work. My phone buzzed with a text message from her: *Lilly has a snow day.*

"Are you serious? Another snow day! There is only like three inches of snow on the ground. When I was a child growing up in New York State we would have been cancelling snow every day, literally every day, if we cancelled at three inches!"

Luckily, I only said those words in my head; I sounded too much like a grandfather, who is fond of saying, "I used to walk four miles in two feet of snow when I was your age."

Lilly, in blissful exhilaration over the possibility of another snow day, walked in and interrupted my thoughts. I'm glad she was feeling excited because I sure wasn't. A snow day meant I would be cramped inside the house for the entire day. Even a 1,600 square foot home can make me feel like I'm trapped in an avalanche.

I walk downstairs. Madeline, one of our two-year-old twins, is reclining on the couch. She is watching a movie Sarah and I had recently watched on Netflix, one not suited for such a young child, and is eating an uncooked frozen waffle. She had managed to turn on the TV and Netflix, and also "make" herself breakfast. She makes me laugh!

A few hours later, following the assembly breakfast line, I start drinking my first sips of ice-cold coffee. I put the coffee back in the microwave for the third time. In walks one of the twins asking for more juice. I shout, "Can't I just finish my coffee? Leave me the *bleep* alone."

Only I didn't say *bleep*. Suddenly, I hear an adult voice in the living room. An adult voice!? Immediately, I could feel the sweat beading on my forehead.

"Oh no, what did I say! What did he hear?!"

I felt like the kid in the movie *A Christmas Story*, after having yelled out the mother of all curse words, which I just did. I remember the shame he felt knowing his dad had heard him. I felt the same shame too.

My father-in-law, walks into the kitchen and greets me with a smile, "Good morning. How are you doing today? Another snow day? Isn't this crazy?!"

My mind was reeling. "Did he hear me a few minutes ago or is he hiding the fact that he just heard me a few minutes ago?" I thought to myself.

After a few awkward moments of small talk, he leaves. I don't know if he heard me or not.

I need to get out of here because I am seriously feeling like a caged lion at the National Zoo. I put on a long sleeve T-shirt from a friend of ours who co-founded a non-profit helping people with mental illness. The shirt reads:

Be Brave. Storytelling Saves Lives.

I tell the kids we're going out. Before leaving, I quickly check to see if there are any new emails. A woman sent us a message.

I just finished reading your book! Thank you for writing it. It reminded me that I'm not such an oddball after all."

Although I'm not in a laughing mood, her words make me chuckle.

I pile all four kids into the van and decide to drive to Bass Pro Shop, a sporting/outdoors store. "At least at Bass Pro I'll be in good company," I think to myself.

On the way to the mall I pass a church sign, which reads:

Mom's Morning Out: drop your kids off from 9—noon on Fridays and enjoy the morning by yourself.

It just so happened to be a Friday morning. But I'm not a mom. Could I drop the kids off, too?

As a part-time stay-at-home dad there doesn't seem to be any MOPS (Mothers of Preschoolers) groups or men's Bible studies to participate in. Or maybe there are and men are too embarrassed to publicize them. Or maybe, just maybe, I'm too embarrassed to attend one.

A line of 4 x 4 trucks passes me on the highway.

"The hits just keep on coming!" I mutter. I'm feeling completely emasculated, alone, out of place.

"What did you say, Daddy?" asks Lilly.

"Nothing. I didn't say anything."

At this point, my self-esteem, my self-worth, my manhood are all at an all-time low.

We arrive in the parking lot of Bass Pro Shop. I yank on the door handle of the van and it breaks.

"Are you kidding me!!!? What a piece a crap!"

Mercifully, my kids don't hear my fuming. I've tried to work on not letting them see my discontent. Not just the malfunctioning of our van, but the general dissatisfaction in my soul.

We get to the entrance of the store and are greeted by a huge sign: WELCOME FISHERMAN, HUNTERS, AND OTHER LIARS.

"I'm at home," I think to myself! "A guy's store. A place of refuge and grounding for me. For the next few hours I can take a deep breath and be at peace. I don't have to be embarrassed. I don't have to live in shame. I can simply BE."

This isn't the life I would have chosen for myself. I didn't go to college for four years and grad school for four more to be a part-time, stay-at-home-dad. I always expected my paycheck to be a little more representative of how many hours I work and how much value I bring to the world.

But this isn't the hand I have been dealt.

In a poker match, every player sitting at the table is dealt the same number of cards and has the same number of options as every other player. With each hand, each player only has three options when it's time to bet:

1. Fold (You can give up and hope for a better hand next time, which may or may not happen); 2. Bluff (You can act as if you actually have a good hand. The hope is that the other players around the table don't suspect the truth. This may work once or twice throughout the match, but the other players learn who bluffs and who doesn't. It's not a lasting move); or 3. Play the hand you have been dealt (since you can't change the cards you have been dealt you choose to give it your best shot with what you've got).

Most of us can probably resonate with each one of these options at various times in our lives. Possibly it's a tough diagnosis and folding—or giving up—seems like the most viable option. Life isn't a flush, hardly ever in fact, and hoping for a better "hand"—which may or may not happen—seems like the way to go. But what I am discovering is that a better hand may never come. We can go on living in discouragement, fear or longing and wait. Or we can simply rest and BE in what IS rather than what could be.

Bluffing also seems like a reasonable option, at least for a little while. Just act as if the hand you have been dealt isn't your hand, and don't tell anyone. But this approach only lasts for a while, because eventually other people figure you out. And more times than not, this approach only leads to hiding, shame, self-loathing, and self-pity because you are not living authentically.

Living the hand you've been dealt is the best option. It's the only option that can bring us the greatest amount of fulfillment and joy in life. All of us have been dealt a specific hand. (And here is a secret: THERE IS NOTHING YOU CAN DO ABOUT IT.)

I'm not saying there aren't times when we can make a change in our lives or we can't or shouldn't make wise choices. God has given us minds to think and bodies to act. However, the life we have been given is OUR LIFE. That's the deal. Certainly, playing the hand we have been dealt can bring about fear, failure and disappointment and even disgrace: disgrace which we allow other people to place on us OR, even more harsh, the disgrace we place on ourselves.

But again, this is your hand. If others are placing discredit on us because of their own wounds and issues, we can accept their discredit or refuse it. Beyond that, the only thing we can do is to accept what God has presented to us. We can either choose to find delight, fulfillment and gratitude, and God in it, or we can continue living with regret, sadness and resentment.

I have also learned how important it is to find someone or just a few people we can trust and with whom we can be real about the hand we have been dealt. We need to tell them when we are scared, lonely, disappointed, sad and even frustrated by the hand we have been dealt. We need to ask them to help us see the good in the hand.

My children are one of the greatest blessings I have in my life, without a doubt. Yes, it is also isolating on the days when I have to stay at home with them alone. It isn't exactly the hand I would have like to have been dealt by the dealer. But I'm learning. I'm choosing, on a good day, to find the love and grace of God in it. I know this can almost sound like a cliché—and I hate clichés— but the "dealer" knows what the dealer is doing. This is exactly what God has gifted me to do. Even though it's exasperating to be a stay at home dad most days, not making enough money to allow my wife to be at home more where she'd like to be, I know that is what I need to be doing until we get all the financial support we need. Being a founder of a non-profit is very formidable and demanding. It takes time for most non-profits to be sustainable and viable in the long term. But we continue to do this because it's not all about the money for us. It's about the hand we've been dealt—the calling from God to connect with those who are brokenhearted, lonely and searching for connections. I could choose a different path. But even though this path is often a roller coaster and every aspect of it isn't exactly what I thought it would be, I still sense this is the path I am meant to be on. And in spite of all the precariousness, I am grateful to be chosen to follow this path. Sometimes choosing the right path is the most daunting path. But it's still the right one—and always the most fulfilling.

I get all four kids out of the van like a cowboy herding cattle. Sometimes I wish I was a cowboy, actually herding cattle, it seems so much more "manly." I wonder if King David felt that way. The Bible doesn't talk much about the fact that he was a shepherd before he became a king. I wonder if he contemplated his own future:

"What am I doing here caring for sheep?! Surely there has to be something more impactful I should be doing or could be doing with my time and talents, right??"

But it's not what the Bible says. Here is the story it tells about David:

> When they arrived, Samuel took one look at Eliab and thought, "Surely this is the Lord's anointed!" But the Lord said to Samuel, "Don't judge by his appearance or height, for I have rejected him. The Lord doesn't see things the way you see them. People judge by outward appearance, but the Lord looks at the heart." Then Jesse told his son Abinadab to step forward and walk in front of Samuel. But Samuel said, "This is not the one the Lord has chosen." Next Jesse summoned Shimea, but Samuel said, "Neither is this the one the Lord has chosen." In the same way all seven of Jesse's sons were presented to Samuel. But Samuel said to Jesse, "The Lord has not chosen any of these." Then Samuel asked, "Are these all the sons you have?" "There is still the youngest," Jesse replied. "But he's out in the fields watching the sheep and goats." "Send for him at once," Samuel said. "We will not sit down to eat until he arrives." So Jesse sent for him. He was dark and handsome, with beautiful eyes. And the Lord said, "This is the one; anoint him." So as David stood there among his brothers, Samuel took the flask of olive oil he had brought and anointed David with the oil. And the Spirit of the Lord came powerfully upon David from that day on. Then Samuel returned to Ramah.
> 1 Samuel 16: 4 - 13, New Living Translation

Its been two years since that day. That season of being a part-time stay-at-home dad taught me to think about God, to talk with God, to hear from God, and to learn of God's will for my life. At various times in all of our lives, we are put in situations in which we didn't expect to find ourselves. I'm sure David felt it often throughout his life. As did David, I'm watching the "sheep" God has entrusted to me—my beloved, beautiful children—to the best of my ability.

I'm learning, day-by-day, to live in the grace of the day, embracing all God has for me. There are days when I don't get it right. There are days, (like that day when I piled the kids in the van to go to the Bass Pro Shop) when I long to be somewhere, anywhere, other than the day-to-day routine God has given me. But I'm getting better. Thank God it has gotten so much easier for me to accept and delight in those days.

I know God loves me and is proud of me on those good days and on those when it's not as good as I would like them to be.

Sabbath

"If you keep the Sabbath, you start to see creation not as somewhere to get away from your ordinary life, but a place to frame an attentiveness to your life."
-Eugene H. Peterson

"Injustice anywhere is a threat to justice everywhere."
-Martin Luther King Jr.

W E NEEDED A DAY OFF. We had just been through several intense weeks and we longed for a break. The severity of the stories we had had been hearing was profound. Suicide, divorce, the loss of a child, yet another stage 4 cancer diagnosis, and a growing list of deep and intractable problems weighed us down. The emotional strain had left us severely depleted and worn. So we decided to step away for a day. Do something fun. Get out of town and focus our minds on other matters. There's a reason why so much of scripture implores us all to take a rest, to step away from our everyday pressures, to observe a Sabbath.

We had recently preached on the topic of the importance of seeking solitude and rest in order for our spirits to be re-ignited. We knew we needed to put our own words into practice. In the gospel of Mark, chapter six, from which we preached, the passage tells the story of Jesus' disciples gathering together with Jesus to tell him all they had accomplished. Jesus says to them:

"You must come away to some lonely place all by yourselves and rest for a while," for there were so many coming and going that the apostles had no time even to eat. So they went off in a boat to a lonely place where they could be by themselves.

"Yes," we said to each other. "We definitely need to do the same thing too."

So, we scheduled a day-long retreat in Washington, D.C., a city we both love for its history and prominence. The weather promised to be beautiful. We were excited to go.

But before we had traveled even 20 miles, the reality of life's fragile nature hit us in the face, nearly literally.

In a blur before our eyes, a pick-up truck turned to the right to exit the limited access roadway. The car following it, immediately in front of us, didn't see it begin to turn and hit its left bumper, causing the truck to swerve precariously. Pieces of both the car and truck, flew into the air, like shrapnel, around us. Several slammed into our car and bounced off. We watched, stunned, as the car in front of us appeared to be headed into the opposing lanes of traffic, before it righted itself, was able to slow and limp off the road. We pulled off too, as witnesses to the scene and to assess any damage to our car, with hearts pounding from the adrenaline rush pulsing through us.

The drivers and their passengers were all physically unscathed, just badly shaken up. The police were called and came fairly quickly. Incredibly, there was no discernible damage to our car. After the police checked with us and got our account of the accident, they indicated we could leave. We were grateful the situation was no worse than it was.

But the suddenness and close call unnerved us greatly. A fairly silent ride followed for miles. It was an inauspicious start to a day designed to help us pull back from the stress and burdens we bear with others. Yet, as the miles went by and we crossed the Mason-Dixon Line into Maryland, we slowly began to calm and anticipate again the sites we hoped to see in the city.

The incident on the road highlighted to us, again, what we already knew—throughout all of life, there always run currents of both good and bad, joy and sorrow, excitement and fear. Often all at the same time. Hit almost immediately with stress in the midst of a day of "escape," as we like to call days such as those, we were reminded of life's very rare absence of stress, curve balls or problems.

Washington's flowers were in full bloom, offering hues of purples, pinks and whites and sweet fragrances around every corner. Birds were chirping in the trees. People were smiling and the world seemed at peace, and so were we, on a spectacular May morning. The surge of anxiety from the accident was, thankfully, gone.

Our first stop in the city was at the Korean War Veterans Memorial, near the Lincoln Memorial. Even though both of us are admirers of history and are well versed in much of our nation's story, neither of us knew a great deal about the horrific specifics of the Korean conflict. We made certain we took time to read the inscriptions on each of the memorial's statues and were moved by the story they told. The main part of the memorial, a giant triangle, features 20 larger than life sized soldiers in full combat gear walking amidst juniper bushes. Another section features a long granite wall depicting images of more soldiers and symbols affiliated with the conflict. There is the "Pool of Remembrance" inscribed with the number of soldiers killed in action, along with those wounded, missing in action. So many had been long forgotten. A very powerful and stark reminder of how freedom has come with a devastating cost. Sadly.

At the Martin Luther King Jr. Memorial on the far southwest corner of the National Mall, our next stop, we viewed the Stone of Hope, a huge piece of granite standing approximately 30 feet in the air with Dr. King's visage carved into it. We were reflective and inspired to remember a life well lived, a life filled with eloquence, influence and inspiration. Dr. King stood for what is right and good and important in this life: dignity, compassion, honor, integrity, grace, understanding, empathy, equality, justice, righteousness, and love for every human being.

Inscribed into the stone are two of King's most famous quotes:

> *If you want to say that I was a drum major, say that I was a drum major for justice. Say that I was a drum major for peace. I was a drum major for righteousness. And all of the other shallow things will not matter.*
> *Out of the Mountain of Despair, a Stone of Hope.*

Across from the central stone, is a long granite wall listing many quotes from Dr. King's most famous sermons and speeches. As we took time to read his words and to consider their rich, timeless meaning, we were filled with gratitude and awe for what his life's work set in motion—and sadness, for so much still left undone.

We needed a pause after absorbing the gravity of both memorials, and were hungry too. It was the perfect time for lunch, as we paused to recall, together, what we had read and seen throughout the morning.

We came across a Mexican restaurant and decided to stop for burritos. The restaurant had outdoor seating, which beckoned to us on such a splendid day. Our conversation began quite seriously, as we talked about Dr. King's life and legacy. We engaged in a sober conversation over what it means to stand for justice, as we allowed the losses we read about during the Korean conflict to wash over us. We also discussed a book we had been reading together concerning spiritual friendships, which detailed the need we all have for those types of friendships in our lives. It is those very friendships, which can help motivate and inspire us to keep on the path of justice and righteousness, the book's author wrote.

As we were enjoying our burritos and the time of introspection, a large African-American man, who seemed to be in his 30's, wearing a well-worn Lakers basketball jersey and sweatpants, sat down at our table. His eyes were bloodshot, as if he hadn't slept in days. His teeth were permanently stained yellow, as if he hadn't brushed them in months. He carried a bowl of cornflakes and a small half-empty bottle of milk. We greeted him and smiled politely, although we weren't smiling on the inside. Honestly, we were uncomfortable, not knowing what to expect from him. One of us asked, "How are you doing?"

He didn't respond to our question. Instead he asked if we could buy him another bottle of milk to cover all of the flakes in his bowl. Not knowing how the other wanted to respond, we awkwardly intoned simultaneously,

"We don't have any cash in our wallets."

It wasn't the total truth. Although neither of us carry much cash these days, we could have come up with enough to cover the milk he needed.

This certainly wasn't the first time either one of us had engaged with what appeared to be someone who was living in homelessness. But echoing in our ears was the admonition we'd both heard so many times before,

Don't ever give them money. They will simply spend it on booze or crack or something else that will make them worse off than they already are.

There we were, two guys who have devoted our lives to bearing other peoples' burdens by creating a safe place for them to express who they are. We commit our time to listen, to support and to encourage. It is a foundational part of our call, especially, to reach out to those who live in poverty of spirit, of resources and of love. We say that we offer everyone grace, compassion and unconditional love. But on that day, we didn't get it right. We didn't offer this child of God much grace, any discernible compassion or evidence of unconditional love—the very things God has first offered to us.

We had just come from remembering Martin Luther King, who had devoted his life to calling attention to the needs of those living in poverty, those who felt beaten down and those who are brokenhearted. Yet, just an hour later, when we had been given a perfect opportunity to live out those very same values, we didn't respond with equanimity. Because it was our "sabbath," our day of "rest," we were not able to muster the ability to engage with someone who needed something as simple and basic as some milk for his cereal. We regret it still today.

People have asked, "So, what should we do for those experiencing homelessness? Should we give them money? Buy them food? If not, then how can we help?" Should we help or should we just let the job to the 'professionals'?"

We understand many of us don't know what to do. It can be intimidating to come across someone who appears to be very different from us. Compassion might nudge us into feeling as if we should do something. But practicalities and self-preservation speak more loudly and forcefully and often cause us to walk on by, letting the risky work of engaging someone who is frightening to others. Being compassionate can be threatening. It can be uncomfortable. There is no doubt about it.

Yet, we also know and believe every person, regardless of his or her appearance, manner, economic status, sexual orientation, race, religion and nationality, is a child of God. Wholly precious. Completely treasured. Infinitely, innately, possesed of the sacred and divine within.

Believing this does compel us to do something when such a person as that comes into our midst. Different circumstances and abilities will certainly require different reactions. But, in the end, the least we can do – and could have done that day—was engage the man in our midst more enthusiastically. We could have scraped the little bit of money he requested to buy enough milk to cover his corn flakes. Maybe even have a little left over for another meal, another drink to quench his thirst. It's the least we could have done for one of "the least of God's children," one of God's holy and beloved sons.

We were in a very public place. We were together; we weren't alone. The risks were very minimal.

The opportunity for compassion was great.

Yet, we didn't respond to the opportunity. If only for one meal, we could have shown this man he was respected, deserving of concern and warranting of love. But we didn't.

As we look back, we are reminded of Jesus' words in Mark 2:27 (NET Bible),

The Sabbath was made for (people), not (people for) the Sabbath.

Sabbath rest is important. We believe this very strongly. It is vital. But we also need to be reminded how even on Jesus' days of rest, he still had compassion for people who needed to be loved.

We don't write this to shame ourselves, blame ourselves or beat ourselves up over a missed opportunity. Ultimately, it doesn't help any of us. Rather, we write this to acknowledge when we don't always get it right; sometimes we miss an opportunity. Thank God, we are given grace when we falter. Sometimes we're just tired or not thinking or not sure of what to do. Compassion can also extend to our own selves when we miss the mark or fall short of an ideal.

But it's also another opportunity to be reminded of the One who quoted the prophet Isaiah, in Luke 4:18 (NET Bible):

The Spirit of the Lord is upon me, because he has anointed me to pro-

claim good news to the poor. (The Spirit) has sent me to proclaim release to the captives and the regaining of sight to the blind, to set free those who are oppressed.

Being authentic, we want compassion, but we want compassion on our terms, without uncomfortability or sacrifice; we want the nice, easy, clean, sanitized version. There are times, many times actually, when we (all) have missed opportunities to be examples of God's mercy and benevolence through our lives. It is in those times when we can invite God to fill us up more and more with a compassionate spirit - to make us strong when we feel weak, to give us hope when we feel hopeless, to give us encouragement when we feel guilty and insecure about missing the mark.

Shame's Antidote (Tom)
(An Essay in Five Parts)

"Shame is a soul eating emotion."
-C.G. JUNG

*"If we can share our story with someone who responds
with empathy and understanding, shame can't survive."*
-BRENÉ BROWN

GUILT AND SHAME

WHAT SARAH and I posted on our Facebook timelines one evening didn't come close to telling the story behind the story. According to the pictures we put out there, the fall colors were radiant, the scenery was stunning and our four children were ecstatic. But behind all those photos was the "real" story—where tears were shed, pain was sensed and shame was felt.

It was a beautiful fall afternoon. We decided to venture to the top of one of our favorite mountain peaks in Central Pennsylvania, with all four children—ages eight, six and three-year-old twins, at the time. A climb normally taking a grown adult approximately 45 minutes, took our family a grueling two hours to make it to the top. But our kids made it; we were proud of them. We knew it wasn't easy for them.

After taking a few panoramic photos and selfies with each of the kids, we found a cool spot in the shade to recharge our batteries. We pulled out juice boxes, fruit snacks, granola bars and peanuts. Despite the length of the climb, the day was moving along seamlessly.

The summit had lots of visitors that day, expectedly so, with the breathtaking beauty of the fall foliage nearing its prime. On the far side of one of the cliffs, Sarah and I noticed several ropes hanging over the edge. It was obvious to us (and the other adults around) there were rock climbers below scaling the side of the mountain. It wasn't so obvious to our eight-year-old daughter.

Prior to starting our descent down the mountain, we thought we would take one more family photo to remind us of our time on the summit, knowing such a moment is priceless. Lillian and I started scouting out the perfect spot; she suggested one close to the ropes lying on the ground. But I told her we should probably find another spot because we didn't want to interrupt the climbers down below. Before moving away, Lillian noticed a glass bottle glistening in the sunshine. Suddenly, she did something very much out of her character: she picked up the bottle and threw it over the edge of the cliff. It shattered on a rock, showering glass over the climbers, causing a huge uproar on the mountain. My hands grasped my head. I couldn't believe what she had just done.

Like rubberneckers on a highway, the other families around us watched the whole scene take place. I could feel the heat of shame and embarrassment burn through our daughter and me. She started sobbing, her cries echoing throughout the countryside. Both of us would have loved nothing more in the moment than to crawl underneath one of the rocks we were stepping on—to escape and hide from the humiliation we were feeling.

Moments such as these happen throughout our lives, often times without any anticipation or warning signals.

How did we respond?

In the moment, we can honestly say we handled it "well." But we would be lying if we said we always handled those situations "well."

One of the things I keep learning is about the difference between guilt and shame. Guilt is when we feel bad for something we have done, knowing we may not have made the best decision. Shame, on the other hand, is feeling horrible about ourselves, not just about a decision, but about our very existence.

A few moments later, one of the climbers made it to the top of the mountain, asking who had caused such a huge disruption for him and his friends below.

Standing off in the distance, Sarah and I bent down and talked gently to Lillian,

"Lilly, I know you don't want to do this right now . . . and we don't want to do it either . . . but we are in this together. We know this is going to be scary for you, for all of us, but we need to go and apologize to the climber and ask if anyone was injured."

Louder and louder she sobbed. She didn't want to do it. I didn't want to do it either. We continued our conversation,

"Sometimes we do things without thinking and we can hurt people. When that happens, we need to ask for forgiveness for our mistakes. It's upsetting, but this is the right thing to do. You don't have to be frightened. We forgive you and so does God! We love you very much."

So, off we went to ask for forgiveness. The climber received Lilly's apology with grace and no further harm was done. It was an important learning experience for all of us.

The entire way down the mountain we reminded Lilly about how proud we were of her for her response. We reminded her what she did was one of the most courageous, gutsy, brave things she had ever done in her life.

HYSTERICAL, HORRIFYING, MORTIFYING MOMENTS

For whatever reason, the topic of shame came up day after day for several weeks. I couldn't seem to avoid it. I could smell it in the air. I could sense it in my spirit. I could feel it in my bones.

It all started on a trip we had taken to my parents' beach house in New Jersey, just a few weeks after the cliff experience. It was a Thursday, heading into a long holiday weekend.

We had spent a spectacular morning on the beach. The day couldn't have been more enjoyable. It was almost naptime for the twins and they were tired. So we headed back to my parents' house.

After unhooking each of the girls from their car seats, we started grabbing bags and chairs to unload the van. Just before shutting one of the van doors, one of the twins reached her arm back in the van and the door slammed on her wrist. In one of my "not so finer" moments, I snapped at Sarah, "You know the twins do that, you need to pay attention!"

It was a shameful statement; I knew it was an accident. I quickly apologized. The swelling in Madelyn's arm subsided after a few minutes, so we decided to forego a trip to the ER.

A few hours later, we had just finished eating dinner. My dad and I announced we would be heading outside to play a lawn game we had been looking forward to playing together. Somehow there was a lack of communication between Sarah and me. She thought I would be watching the children while she cleaned up after dinner. I thought she had heard me say I would clean the kitchen after I played the game with my dad, if she watched the kids while we played. Because of a simple miscommunication, chaos and hysteria ensued.

Lillian was riding her bicycle around the house and up and down the block. I could keep my eye on her as we played. One of the twins, on the other hand, started following Lillian on her bicycle and I didn't grasp it. My dad, realizing he had seen Mya at one point, asked if I knew where she was. I didn't, because I didn't know she had come outside the house. Frantically, we started searching for her. My heart sank.

Lilly spoke up and said that Mya had been following her on her bicycle. So together, retracing her bike trail, I found her off in the distance, three blocks away. Sprinting as fast as I could and yelling her name as loudly as I could, I got her to turn around. She stopped in her tracks. It was a horrifying moment. Thank God we found her so quickly; she didn't get hit by a car or wasn't snatched away by someone sinister. I felt ashamed about what happened.

Once we were back home from the beach trip Sarah had two days of working at the hospital; I was home with all four kids by myself. I was doing my best to have an "uneventful" rest of the weekend. Things didn't go as planned.

After lunch on Saturday afternoon, it was time for the twins to take their naps and I was looking forward to some down time (if there is such a thing). Both of the girls, in order to go to sleep smoothly, needed their blanket and pacifiers. One of the twins' blankets was nowhere to be found and I started feverishly searching the house. I looked everywhere, but couldn't find it. Trying to retrace her tiny steps, I eventually ended up outside the house in the driveway, knowing we had made a trip to the Farmer's Market earlier in the day. Next to the trash can in the driveway was her pink blanket.

When I went back in the kitchen door, I caught Madelyn, the other twin, with an open bottle of allergy medicine, chomping on and swallowing what appeared to be several pills. Rushing to her, I firmly told her to spit out the pills. Not knowing how to proceed, I read the label on the back of the bottle. It stated if a small child eats any of the pills you (I) should call Poison Control. So I did. While on the phone with a woman from Poison Control, Mya grabbed a bottle of sunscreen, covering her face and eyes. She started screaming. I didn't know what to do. The woman from Poison Control reminded me to stay calm, but to immediately take Madelyn to the ER. I'm thankful my father-in-law arrived to attend to Mya's needs.

We spent several hours in the ER together. Praise God she was okay and no harm was done to her. But harm was done to my emotions. I started to feel very guilty about my parenting abilities, as if each of these situations somehow confirmed what I already thought about myself—ridiculously incompetent and unfit.

After Sarah arrived home later than evening, I left home to go to her Nana's house to help cut her grass. Nana surprised us with a $100 for my efforts. Before heading home, I had to make one last stop at a close friend's house. He asked how I was doing and I briefly voiced how my day had gone. He did the same. He said he was sensitive place because he and his wife were tight financially and their oven had just broken. I sighed, because I knew the feeling, and I said so. Leaving his house, I remembered we had been given an extra $100. So I called Sarah and asked if we could bless our friend's family. She said yes.

The next day on our way home from church, I stopped at the grocery store.

People often ask, "How do you take all four kids to the grocery store with you?" as if we actually have any choice in the matter.

Knowing we didn't have much money to help us through the rest of the week I started grabbing the essentials—milk, juice, eggs and yogurt. The grocery store was packed. There were several people in the lines next to ours, who started saying hello, "So, you are here all by yourself. That's pretty impressive."

Acting as if I hadn't heard that statement a hundred times before, I smiled and said, "I enjoy a good adventure."

Waiting in line with four kids is the most trying part of the adventure. One of them always picks up a piece of candy and places it in the cart. I pick up the same piece of candy and place it back on the shelf. This process goes on until it's finally our turn to check out. Since the line was so long this happened about 25 times. The kids started helping me to place the items on the conveyer belt. In the meantime, I pulled out my wallet to swipe my debit card. The card didn't work.

"Oh, please, not again! Please God, not again." I thought to myself.

Embarrassment started washing over me. I had been in this very same situation, in the same store, with the same clerk just a few months before. It seemed as if everyone in line was staring at me, waiting to see how I would respond. There were people in the checkout lanes on either side of us whom I knew, which only added to the embarrassment. I wanted to grab one of the paper bags and put it over my head—again. The kids started complaining, "Daddy, what's going on?"

"Ugh, nothing kids. I need to go back out in the car and grab another card," I told the clerk.

Truth be told again, there still wasn't another card. Piling all four kids back in the van, they started questioning, "Daddy, what about the groceries?!"

"We will have to come back later," I snarled, knowing there wouldn't be a later.

The next day was a Monday. Michael and I were together again.

"How did the weekend go?" he asked, knowing I had the kids alone throughout.

"It was hellish." I responded.

"Really, how so?"

I told him about our beach trip and all that had transpired there. I told him about my unexpected ER trip the previous day. I told him about the grocery store adventure. I told him about the insensitive comments, the shocking looks and the shame I had placed on myself. He listened, quietly.

We took a walk to the post office. It was a nice day outside. But just before we left the office, I happened to look at my Facebook page. Someone had hacked into another friend's account and in turn a very vulgar picture appeared on the wall of my page and many of his friends'. I was mortified. I felt sick to my stomach.

"What would people think of me? I wonder how many people saw that and thought I posted it? I'm so embarrassed" I admitted to Michael.

Michael asked, "What would help you right now? I'm sorry this has happened. It sucks."

As best as he could, he responded with compassion.

"Honestly, I don't know. I guess just sit with me until the uncertainty goes away. Maybe remind me this is all a part of life and I'm normal. I am 'normal', right?!"

"Of course you are." He knew it was no time for joking.

"What if I actually did post the picture? It's sad to think people wouldn't respond to me with compassion, because it's all any of us need, isn't it?"

Nothing ever seemed to result from the Facebook post; at least no one ever said anything to my face, thankfully. It took a few days for me to "get over it." But until it did, until the mortification subsided, I wanted to crawl away and leave for some South Pacific island where no one knew about Facebook or knew anything about me.

"I'M HERE FOR THE CAKE"

A week later I attended a bi-weekly men's group with some guys from our church. It's a great group of guys who are trying to model healthy, vulnerable relationships. We love one another. The topic of shame came up in conversation. One by one we went around the circle and everyone offered the story of a time when he felt shamed by someone else or shame he had put on themselves. I felt compelled to expound upon about my adventure at the grocery store. One of my good friends in the group, who is also a pastor, related this:

> *After months of premarital counseling, the big day for a groom and his bride came. They were married by a lake at a gazebo, followed by a huge blow-out of a reception in a fancy converted barn. It was a sunny day, and it felt good to be included in this life-changing event for this young couple whom I have become close friends with.*
>
> *As we had rehearsed, the bride's dad walked her along the path of the lake, and he stopped just short of the gazebo. I stepped away from the small podium I had set up in the gazebo, down three steps to join the father and his beloved daughter. I'm up.*

All I need to say is "Who gives this woman to be married?" So simple, but in this moment, with the father looking at me increasingly nervous, and the bride wondering what's up, I'm stalled. My mind is blank, and my notes are up three stairs and twenty feet behind me. I breathe, hoping it'll come to me, but nothing comes. It's been longer than a pregnant pause, it's now full-on embarrassing, and the bride and her dad are frozen. I finally shrug, turn around, and get my notes. Sheepishly I re-take my place, check my notes, and say "Who gives this woman to be married?" Now the entire audience knows that the insurmountable phrase was seven words. I make some excuse about making the first gaffe, and now we have THAT out of the way we can get down to business. The audience, the bride, and her father laughed, and comedy has rescued me again.

The rest of the wedding went fine, and I only felt the occasional pinch of shame, which would come as a question in my mind,

"Who are you fooling? You suck at this." I looked at the happy couple, or talked to one of the guests and the feeling would fade quickly.

The reception was in the haymow of a fancy converted barn, and the seating other than the head table was arbitrary. I sat with a couple in their sixties with their young adult daughter, and our conversation was friendly and light. The gentleman was seated directly across a folding table from me, and my seat was between the table and a smaller table behind me, which sat a few inches taller than ours. Before dinner was served, I was mid-sentence asking a benign question when the gentleman across from me leapt across the table, directly at me, as if we were in a bar fight. I was shocked and froze. His body passed by me a little to my left. It all seemed to be in slow motion. But as I leaned away, my head turned and I saw a horrific moment frozen in time. On the rickety table behind me, balanced on a single 18" spindle, was the wedding cake. I had bumped the table with my elbow, and the man across from me was leaping to save this cake from toppling to the floor. Despite his valiant effort, the cake wobbled, and then slowly passed the point of no return, and with a clatter, landed on the barn floor. The place is dead silent, 200 or so guests alerted by a middle aged man diving across the table, and then by the cake crashing to the floor. I stood, with the cake at my feet, two hundred pairs of eyes on me, everyone shocked, and I felt the familiar rush of shame over my entire body. Hot shame. In the past, I would have waited a half beat and headed for the door, never to return. These days, I have a secret weapon. I name shame. In my mind, as the shame washed over me, I said to myself, "I'm awash with shame." By admitting it, I can more easily choose a response. For a split second I thought of invoking the "five second rule." But the level of baked destruction, and the remnants of barn straw in the cake canceled that option. The faces around me were frozen in the moment, and truth is most of the horror in their eyes was empathetic horror, as in, "There but for the grace of God go I."

But in the moment their horror registered in my mind as revulsion, or rage. I felt like people must have been thinking what a fat idiot I am. In the past, I wouldn't have waited to sort it out. I took a deep breath, and I bent down and started to put the cake in the garbage can. It took a while. People were talking by the time I finished.

I stayed until the end of the night, and was one of the last folks to leave. The shame lasted a half hour, at least the burning shame, and by the end of the night I had mostly let it go.

The bride and groom had spent extravagantly on the wedding, and one of the options they bought was an old style photo booth, in which one poses for four pictures, and the machine drops a four picture strip out the side after a few minutes. This machine was programmed to drop the four picture strip, as well as a second exact copy that the guests were invited to tape into a photo album for the bride and groom, There were all kinds of costumes and signs one could hold for the pictures. I picked a simple sign to hold for the pictures I left for them. . . the sign said, "I'm here for the cake."

His story was a powerful one. I couldn't imagine a more socially dreadful scene. Knocking over a wedding cake has to be up there with one of the seven deadly sins! You never want to be the one to "ruin" someone's perfect wedding day.

"I WILL NEVER FORGET"

Michael and I met a good friend of ours for lunch. Again, for whatever reason, the topic of shame came up in conversation. She revealed a time in her own life where she felt the deepest amount of shame she had ever felt, and sadly, it came from her own family. Brought up in a conservative Christian home, our friend was taught divorce was a sin. When she entered into a marriage at a very young age she had the same value.

"I was young and so was he. Neither one of us knew our selves or each other. We sort of fell in love, but didn't have any idea what love truly meant. We didn't know what we were actually looking for in a relationship. Anyway, it didn't take very long before we realized we weren't compatible at all. The worst part is we didn't know how to work through our different values and temperaments. So our marriage ended abruptly.

"My grandfather said to me, 'I'm just glad your great-grandmother isn't alive to see this.'"

"My parents said, 'We want you to know you are certainly welcome to come back home and live with us, because we know you can't make it living on your own.'"

Shame.

"So how did you make it through?" we asked her.

"I had an aunt who simply loved me unconditionally. She spent a lot of time with me, reminding me of my merit and dignity, reminding me God loves me, reminding me I'm forgiven. She loved me well. I desperately needed the reminders at a time when I didn't feel lovable at all.

"During that terrible period I had stopped going to church. I turned my back on everything I ever believed. Including God. I felt as if I had already done the worst thing that I could do, by getting divorced, so why bother trying to be good anymore? I drank a lot more, partied heavily. Since I was a "horrible person" I decided to live like one. I dated a lot of men who weren't good for me. I was already so bad; I didn't need to be good.

"The church did nothing to support or help me after my divorce. No one ever reached out to me. No one ever asked me if I was okay. If the people of the church aren't there in my deepest pain, then what is the church? I grew up in that place and the church still didn't help me.

"I was running away. Meeting my new husband calmed my life down a lot.

"The whole experience changed me. I believe now God saved me from myself. I believe God never let go of me, never turned away from me even though I turned away from God."

"Have you ever gotten over what happened?" we asked.

"The topic still comes up from time to time in conversation. Every time I'm in a Bible study class and the mention of divorce arises there is inevitably someone in the group who goes on a long rant about how wrong divorce is. Those comments hurt. I know I have to be prepared for those situations. But I also know I need other people in my life who will do what my aunt did for me years ago.

"I'm happily married now. But I can honestly say I will never forget how my parents, despite their best intentions, spoke to me in the moment and the very hurtful comment my grandfather made. I will also never forget the aunt who loved me through that difficult time, showing me empathy, understanding and infinite patience."

SHAME IS STRONG. BUT LOVE IS STRONGER

One of our favorite authors and speakers, Dr. Brené Brown was interviewed on the *Morning Joe* program on MSNBC. She talked about the difference between shame and guilt. Here is some of what she expressed about living in our unforgiving, hypercritical culture:

"Shame makes us believe that we are not enough . . . The difference between shame and guilt is this:"

"Guilt is—'I did something bad.' Shame is—'Something is wrong with me.' Our fear of failure is so great."

Shame plays a shocking role in our lives. Shame is one of the most toxic moralities we can experience in this life, because shame can figuratively suck the life out of us. Shame makes us feel as if our life doesn't matter, as if we are evil. Nothing less than evil.

As we read the Bible we are amazed (or maybe not so amazed . . . because this is who God is) at the unique cast of characters chosen to bear God's message of grace and of love:

Abraham and Sarah—the spiritual father and mother of the nation of Israel – doubted God's creative power and laughed in God's face when God declared they would have a son in their old age.

Moses—who led God's chosen people from slavery to freedom in the Promised Land—was an imposter, a murderer and a slave driver.

David—a "man after God's own heart"—slept with another man's wife and then had the man killed to hide his duplicity and shame.

Peter—one of Jesus' closest friends and confidants—turned his back on Jesus in a time of his deepest need, denying he knew him. At a time when he could have written Peter off, Jesus says he is the person with whom he will start to build his church.

Mary Magdelene—a woman from a society in which women were regarded as mere property—when Jesus' male friends abandoned him at the hour of mortal danger, she stayed with him, even to the crucifixion and was the first person to whom Jesus appeared after his resurrection.

The Apostle Paul—a man who made a living persecuting and killing Christians—became arguably one of the most prolific and influential writers of all time, having written well more than half of the New Testament we read today.

The list goes on and on. The Bible is loaded with a cast of characters who occasionally made some spectacularly bad choices; they were human like the rest of us.

Yet in the places of their deepest shame, God invited them to continue to be a part of a transformative mission of love and compassion for the world.

So, a few good questions to ask are these:

Why are we so good at shaming each other? Why are we so good at shaming our selves? Why are we so quick to criticize and condemn and so slow to show compassion and grace for one another's humanness?

Why are we so often our own worst enemies, so slow to forgive our selves for our imperfections and mistakes? Why do we have such a dilemma accepting we are constant recipients of the grace and compassion of God? Why are we in such a quandary about imparting God's gifts with others and accepting them for ourselves? Shame sticks with us when it enters our lives. We rarely ever forget the person who shames us.

But grace and compassion can stick with us too. We also rarely forget the person who loves us in the middle of our deepest shame, who doesn't add shame upon shame, who offers grace in recognition of our common humanity.

Shame destroys our spirits. Shame darkens our souls. Shame depresses our ability to accept God's gifts of grace and compassion.

But these generous, infinite gifts of God continue to be given by a God who wants us to know forgiveness is stronger than shame, grace is stronger than judgment and compassion is stronger than condemnation. They are given by a God who announces unequivocally—love is stronger than blame and hate. Always.

We Need Each Other (Tom)

"To be human is to be a person in relation."
-Elisabeth T. Vasko

WHEN I WAS A STUDENT in seminary, I worked at a hotel on campus 30 hours a week to help pay my way through school. It was a regimented time in our life. Sarah was a full-time RN. She would leave for work at 6:00 a.m.; shortly thereafter, I would leave for class and later, my job.

In the middle of one of the semesters, we were blessed, surprisingly, with the news we were expecting our first child, Lillian. I often tell people, our first two children, Lillian and Luke, were both a total surprise, truly miracle babies—that's a whole other story. (On a side note, we actually planned our third child and we ended up having twins. It's such a good reminder how in this life so much is totally out of our control!)

Lillian and I spent a lot of time together. She would come to class with me some days, crying and cooing in the middle of my professor's lectures about free will versus predestination. She didn't seem too interested; quite frankly, I wasn't much interested in some of it either.

Following my last class of the day, I would walk across campus to the hotel, pushing Lillian in her stroller, to start my evening job. On occasion, in the middle of my shift, my manager would present opportunities for me to earn some extra money driving guests to and from the local airport. One evening, he asked if I wanted to pick up a guest the next day. Slowly and precisely, he said the name of the guest, a pastor and author. When I wasn't enthusiastic about this very special opportunity, he asked, "Don't you know the pastor?"

"Actually, no, I don't," I said. "Should I?"

"He is the pastor of the fastest growing church in the country. He is speaking on campus tomorrow," he replied. "I can't believe you have never heard of him."

I turned on the computer to do a little research. Sure enough, as soon as I typed the pastor's name on the Google search bar, his picture was everywhere.

"Thanks for the opportunity," I said. "I'll pick him up."

When I got home I told Sarah what I was asked to do.

"Are you excited?" she asked amusingly.

"I guess? I just hope it doesn't take too long; I have a huge paper to write by Friday. Maybe he will give me a big tip!"

We both laughed.

The next day I arrived at the hotel extra early. It was a 25-minute drive to the airport and I didn't want to be late. People were counting on me to make sure the pastor made it to campus on time.

The pastor's flight was scheduled to arrive at 3:15pm. Just before leaving the hotel at 2:30, my manager stressed: "Remember, you aren't picking him up at the 'normal' airport. You have to go to the private airport just up the road."

He gave me the address along with a map. "Make sure you are there by 3:15! Got it?"

I assured him and hopped in the shuttle (a.k.a. the Dodge minivan) and drove to the airport. I glanced at the map a second time.

Then, 3 pm came and went. 3:15 came and went. I started to panic. "Crap! I must be going in the wrong location." A few minutes later I arrived. Gratefully.

When I did, I started frantically circling, hoping and praying I would recognize the pastor's face from the Internet photos. He wasn't anywhere to be found. I called my manager and asked him if he had heard anything.

"We haven't heard anything, but will let you know if we do," he said.

3:30 came and went and now I was starting to freak out. I drove around some more, praying he would magically appear.

At 3:45 I received a call from my manager,

"TOM, WHERE ARE YOU! THE GUESTS ARRIVED 15 MINUTES AGO!!!!"

"I'm sorry. I don't know where he is," I responded dejectedly. "He's where I told you to be. Go there!" barked my manager.

Feverishly driving back to the first location I had been, I looked in all directions but there still wasn't a soul in sight, only a jet parked on the runway. I did notice a building next to the runway. I parked the car and walked through the revolving door into the building. Looking to my left I spotted the pastor, with his (what I like to call them) "cronies." They were seated with their feet propped up in front of a fireplace. Timidly, I walked up to them, stuck out my hand, and introduced myself to the pastor.

"Good afternoon, my name is Tom." "Here are our bags," he replied. "Aren't you a few minutes late?" I apologized, quickly grabbed his bag and started walking toward the van. Approaching the van I heard laughing. "No Lincoln town car or Limo?" they snickered. "No, sorry. This is what the hotel provides," I replied.

A few moments later we started our 25-minute drive toward campus. I called my manager and told him we were finally on our way. He said to hurry up because we were already late and there was a huge line of people waiting in eager expectation of the pastor's arrival.

"What's your name again?" said the pastor. "You've heard of our church, right?"

Nervously, I replied, "Actually, I'm sorry. I hadn't heard of your church until my supervisor mentioned it to me yesterday."

"Do you have a TV?!" he pronounced, half kiddingly. "Have you heard of *me*?"

Now I was thoroughly embarrassed. It crossed my mind to tell a little white lie, but I thought better of it.

"I'm sorry, but I hadn't heard of you until yesterday afternoon. I guess I need to get my head out of the books more often."

He changed the subject.

"TIM? Can we stop for some coffee? This is going to be a long night and we need some caffeine."

I responded quickly, "Tom. My name is Tom. There is a McDonald's on the way; we can go through the drive-thru. We are running a little late and from what I have heard you have a book signing on campus scheduled to start 10 minutes ago."

Looking at each other with comical looks on their faces, they burst out laughing.

"We don't drink McDonalds coffee," the pastor declared. "We only drink Starbucks. Can you take us to Starbucks?"

"I guess I can take you to Starbucks, but it's all the way on the other side of the city. You are going to be extremely late," I explained, anxiously.

"It would be nice to go there," he declared.

A few awkward moments passed. He then queried, "Is this what you do for a living?"

The feeling of anxiety running through my veins quickly changed to anger. I wanted to say, outlandishly, "I'm a student, moron," but thought better of it. "I'm a student at Asbury. I'm in the Master of Divinity Program."

"You are!" he exclaimed. "And what are you hoping to do with your degree?"

I sensed condescension in his voice, but I answered directly, "I'm not sure exactly. I guess I'll be a pastor."

I can't remember all we talked about the rest of the trip to campus. I know we talked at length about his perspectives on church. He was quick to add, several times, about his church being the fastest growing church in America.

Forty-five minutes later, we had arrived back on campus.

Before getting out of the van, he asked me what I was going to do next. I thought he might be curious if I was going to attend his book signing.

"I'm going home. I'm already late for dinner," I said.

"What are you eating for dinner?" he asked, amusingly.

"Beef barley soup," I responded. "It's one of our family favorites."

"Beef barley soup!" Chuckling, he said, "Did you guys hear that?! He is eating beef barley soup tonight."

They all laughed as if our dinner selection was a poor one.

Now I was extremely frustrated and embarrassed. Beef barley soup is a family recipe passed down for generations. I tried my best to maintain my composure.

Parting ways, I intoned, irritated, "I'll be at this exact spot to pick you up at 7:15. Your plane leaves at 7:45."

When I got home, I sat down to enjoy beef barley soup with Sarah and Lillian. "He isn't going to bother me," I voiced to myself. "So how did it go?" Sarah asked. "Let's put it this way, it didn't go anything like I hoped it would."

After dinner I drove back to campus. Fully expecting the pastor to arrive late, I sat down and picked up the most recent issue of our seminary's newsletter. On the cover of the magazine was a picture of the pastor.

"I guess I missed this issue?" I thought to myself and smirked. 7:15. 7:25. 7:30.

I was pacing back and forth. I'm only staying 10 more minutes, I told myself.

7:39. He and his cronies, in their gator skin boots and suede jackets, walked into the lobby. I offer them a half smile and walk straight toward the van.

"So, Tim, how was your soup dinner? Did it fill you up?"

"This guy is unbelievable," I thought to myself. "He just doesn't quit."

"My name is Tom. It was great. Thanks for asking."

"How was your book signing?" I asked.

"It was a waste of time, I only sold like 80 books," he replied. "How many students are on campus?"

Trying to ignore his question, I focused on the traffic in front of me. "Hey buddy, can we stop and get something to eat? We're hungry."

"Isn't your plane leaving in 10 minutes? We are already going to be a few minutes late," I declared.

"Oh, don't worry about it; it's my plane. The pilot can wait."

Almost crashing my car into the car in front of me, I shouted, "That's *your* plane?!!!"

"Yeah, that's my private jet. Do you like it?" he asked proudly.

Now I was the one who found myself laughing out loud.

"This is amazing," I whispered.

He heard me.

"Yeah, it is amazing, isn't it! Tim, is there anywhere we can grab something to eat?" he barked.

"There aren't any other restaurants within 20 minutes unless you want a sit-down meal."

Why did I say that out loud, I thought. I don't want to have a sit-down meal with this guy. It would be too painful!

"It's ok, Tim. We will just eat on the plane." I let out a huge sigh of relief.

When we arrived back at the airport, I hopped out of the vehicle and started unloading their bags. I smiled, shook their hands, and said, half-heartedly, it was good to meet them. To be honest, I hoped to get a big tip from the pastor to ease my pain and suffering.

The pastor stuck out his hand and said, "Jim, it was good to meet you. Maybe our paths will cross again sometime."

"That would be wonderful, wouldn't it?" I replied, sarcastically.

The pastor walked away, then turned around.

Here is my big moment, I thought! A tip.

"Hey, Jim, I forgot to give you something. Here is a copy of my recent book. Do you want me to sign it for you?"

On the front cover of the book was a huge picture of his smiling face. Smiling, I responded, dejectedly, "Thanks so much! God bless your ministry." The following day I was back at the hotel and my manager asked how the trip went.

I chuckled and started telling him about the preceding day's festivities. He laughed too. He spoke of others who also had a negative experience with the pastor. He recalled, "Yeah, he showed up 45 minutes late to his book signing. Signed 80 books and refused to sign copies for the other 80 people standing in line. He was then supposed to speak for 30 minutes, plus Q and A. He spoke for 15 and answered two questions—literally two questions! Do you believe that?!"

Later in the evening, just before my shift was coming to a close, a bearded man with glasses walked up to the counter to check in. He was wearing sandals on his feet, blue jeans with holes in the knees, and a "Life is Good" T-shirt with a picture of a hammock on the front.

"Hi," he said emphatically, with a huge smile on face. "What's your name?" "Tom," I replied, as I continued with his check-in.

"It's so nice to meet you Tom. This is my first time to Asbury. I'm happy to be here. I'm guessing you are a student on campus. Where are you from?" he asked, curiously.

"I'm from New Jersey," I responded.

"Wow! I think it's incredible you are giving up so much to follow this call upon your life. It's a big sacrifice for your family, isn't it?" he continued.

"Yeah, I guess it has been a pretty big sacrifice. I've never thought about it that way. But I guess so."

"How are your studies going?" he asked. "I know how challenging the M. Div. program can be."

"It's going pretty well. There's a lot of work and a ton of reading—way more than I have ever had to read before." Sitting on the counter next to me was a stack of books.

Talking for several minutes, he ended the conversation by asking if he could pray for me and my studies.

Sighing, I responded, "After the day I've had, I could use some prayer." Placing his hand in my hand, he started praying, and I mean REALLY praying.

I didn't look at my watch, but if I had to guess, he prayed for more than five minutes. It was one of the most genuine, heartfelt and gracious prayers I have ever received.

I thanked him and wished him a nice stay at Asbury.

The next day my manager approached me and noticed the book I was reading for class. Beneath the title of the book, were the words:

Over 20 million copies sold.

"Did you know the author of your book is staying at the hotel?"

Laughing out loud, I exclaimed, "You have to be kidding me! I spoke with him for like 15 minutes last night and I never made the connection. He was the most kind, gentle, humble person I have ever met."

Moments later, the author walked up to the front desk. "Tom, how are you doing? What classes did you have today?" He seemed very interested, and I replied honestly and thoughtfully.

"Tom, I wanted to apologize. I completely forgot to ask about your wife. What's her name? I'd like to pray for her too. I'm sure this is a huge commitment on her part."

He seemed to genuinely care and was eager to listen. On and on our conversation went.

At the end of our time together, I told him about how much I loved his book and how often I had referred to it throughout my spiritual journey.

His response was one I will never forget:

"You know Tom, that means so much coming from you, probably far more than you will ever know. Most of my life I have had severe self-doubt. In fact, I still wrestle with whether or not I should even be a writer and if my writing even matters to anyone. I'm always amazed at what God has done with that book because I still don't even think it is very good. So thank you so much, you really made my day and made my trip here at Asbury an important one. I've added you and your wife's name to my prayer journal and I will pray for you every day."

I believed him.

It's been quite a few years since this story unfolded. It's been a challenge not to tell this story in such a way as to make it appear like I am "throwing (the pastor) under the bus" and showing a lack of grace toward him. Years ago, I didn't see what I see now. For the longest time I held a grudge against the pastor with the private jet. He seemed so arrogant, over-confident and self- assured. He didn't seem as if he had much interest in others. He didn't seem as if he had much interest in me. And in some ways, it may have been true in the moment.

But as time has passed and I have grown, I realize he has a story too. It's probably a story marked by regret and heartache just like the rest of us. Did he grow up without anyone who was present enough, affirming enough or thoughtful enough? Did he learn that success in the world's eyes is more important than anything else? Did he have problems with his dad? Was his idea of self- worth based on a model of putting other people down? Was his mom overbearing and critical? Was he still trying to overcome the circumstances of his life? Who knows?

Whatever the case may be, the pastor with the private jet was still searching, just like the rest of us, to find his way in this life. Like the successful author, he was probably incredibly insecure. Unlike the author, he masked his insecurity with over-confidence. Both men were on a journey to find themselves—to find their way—just like the rest of us.

Behind every character trait there is always another side to the trait. The other side is what makes us well-rounded individuals. Truth be told, we need one another. We need pastors such as the confident pastor with the fastest growing church in America. We need authors like the author who sometimes lacks self-confidence. The pastor's confidence is what helped him to run such an impressive operation—and probably touch a lot of lives through it. The author's humility, expressed through his writings, is what made people want to hear what he had to say; his sensitive side is what gave him a voice.

I know for myself, those individuals who come across as overconfident have been some of the toughest people for me to love and offer grace. At times during my life, I have wrestled with an extreme lack of self-confidence. So it's been unnerving connecting with people who seem so self-assured. But as I have gotten older and experienced more, I have begun to appreciate both types of people.

We all need to treat each other well. Confident people have the chance to treat people who lack self-confidence with respect by offering words building up rather than tearing down; confident people have the chance to instill confidence in others. Insecure people also need to treat confident people with respect by offering words pointing out when they are making a difference. They need to hear it, as we all need to hear it. Insecure people have the chance to make confident people feel even more confident and use their confidence in a way that brings about the most good in the world and affects the most lives positively.

Those individuals with self-confidence give me confidence. Those individuals with a lack of self- confidence can give confident people a sense of humility and help keep them from running over people as they put their plans, visions, and dreams into action. Both parties need God's grace and to be reminded that we are all God's beloved children.

Glennon Doyle Melton, in her book, *Carry On Warrior,* writes,

> *If I am humble but lack confidence, it is because I haven't accepted that there is a divine spark inside me. It means that I don't believe in the miracle that I was made by God for a purpose all my own, and so I am worthy of the space that I occupy on this earth. And that as a child of God, no one deserves more respect, joy, or peace than I. As a child of God, I have the right to speak, to feel, to think, and to believe what I believe. Those dreams in my heart, those ideas in my head, they are real and they have a divine origin, and so they are worth exploring. Just because I am a child of God. And thankfully, there is nothing I can to do lose that title. I am confident not because I am pretty or smart or athletic or talented or kind. Those things change and can be given and taken. I am confident simply because I am a child of God. . .If I am confident but not humble, it is because I have not fully accepted that everyone has won the lottery. Because everyone has the same amount of God in her. If I am in the habit of turning my back on others, it is because I haven't learned that God approaches us in the disguise of other people. If I am confident but not humble, my mind is closed. If my mind is closed, my heart is closed. A closed heart is so sad. It is the end. A heart cannot grow any larger if it decides not to let more God in. There is always room for more. A heart expands exactly as much as her owner allows.*

Yes, there is always room for more. All of us are insecure about a lot of things. But we have the potential to bring out the best in each other and to allow greater love, humility, tenderness, gratitude and acceptance into our lives. It's quite easy for humble people to connect on a deeper level with other humble people; just like it's quite easy for confident people to connect with other confident people. But the truly remarkable thing is for us to show love and grace toward people who are different—and to ourselves. It reminds me of Jesus' words in Luke 6:32:

If you love only those who love you, why should you get credit for that?

In the future, I hope I can treat the confident pastor with respect by pointing out his successes. I hope I can bring about even more good by offering words of affirmation and not take his comments personally based on my own insecurities. I know for myself, my lack of self-confidence has, at times, kept me from all God wants me to be. But it's people with confidence who have walked alongside me, reminding me of the confidence God gives us through Jesus. Because at the end of the day, our confidence, for all of us, doesn't come from external things anyway; our confidence always, always, always comes from God first.

All of us need to know we are God's beloved sons and daughters. All of us have exclusive gifts and talents. All of us have a story defining us and making us who we are. Each story is important—very important. It is each unique story showing us more about the love God has for us and the remarkably unique ways in which God has created every one of us.

"What Does It *Mean* to Be Compassionate?"

A Nonjudgmental Life

*"One of the hardest spiritual tasks is to live without prejudices.
Sometimes we aren't even aware how deeply rooted our prejudices
are . . . Strangers, people different than we are, stir up fear,
discomfort, suspicion, and hostility. They make us lose our sense
of security just by being 'other.'"*
-Henri Nouwen

*"We put labels on life all the time. 'Right,' 'wrong,' 'success,' 'failure,'
'lucky,' 'unlucky' may be as limiting a way of seeing things as 'diabetic,'
'epileptic,' 'manic-depressive,' or even 'invalid.' "*
-Rachel Naomi Remen, M.D.

"I was a stranger and you did not welcome me . . ."
-Matthew 25:43a ESV

PREJUDICES.
Everyone has them. No matter how much we say and try to embody the
golden rule of doing unto others, as we would have them do unto us, we love our
neighbors in limited ways because we are all limited in our own ways.

When someone says or does something other than what we would have said or
done in a similar situation, harsh judgments, cruel criticisms and unforgiving con-
victions can erupt seemingly out of nowhere. We think we are open-minded until
we are the ones who feel threatened. It is then when our real perceptions of those
who are not like us stand out. This has been our personal experience.

What we have also discovered from our own readings and understandings is
this: often the people who have felt the most marginalized in society are the ones
who are consoling, compassionate, sensitive, loving and welcoming. Perhaps they
readily model these things because they so often fail to receive it from others. They
know what is desperately needed.

The ballroom that night was beautifully decorated and everyone was dressed
well for the region's annual LGBT Chamber of Commerce banquet.

During the pre-dinner cocktail hour, we noticed a man walk past us scanning the room as if he was looking for someone. When he returned, he stopped next to us. We said hello and introduced ourselves. He did the same.

"So, how did you guys get connected with the LGBT Chamber?" he asked.

"One of our friends invited us and we are grateful he did. We are happy to be here to support him. It is a privilege to be asked."

"I'm happy to be here too!" he responded, smiling.

"How about yourself? How long have you been connected with the Chamber?" we questioned.

"I started coming to the chamber this past year and have been a part of the group ever since. They were very welcoming to me."

"How were they welcoming? We're always interested in how people help others feel included, connected."

He hesitated. Then, with a cautious and almost reluctant look on his face, he offered his story.

"Last year my son was killed. It was horrific. I desperately needed some sense of community to hold me up. Many of my religious friends and the religious community disappointed me deeply. People kept telling me that 'my child is in a better place,' 'God works all things together for good,' 'God doesn't give me more than I can handle,' and many other unhelpful clichés."

He continued, "I know most of them meant well, but statements like those made me feel more alone, hurt, depressed, and lonely. I didn't know where to go with my feelings. In looking for others to meet, I tried attending the regional Chamber of Commerce events. But the groups weren't welcoming. They didn't seem to make an effort to connect with me. I never felt as if I belonged. It felt like an old boys club."

"I'm not gay," he said. "But one of my friends invited me to one of the LGBT Chamber gatherings. Many of the people in the group already knew my story because they heard about it from my friend. But they didn't know me.

He paused and then went on. "Yet, they were warm. They simply consoled me in my pain. I didn't hear the clichés. And they have continued to welcome me ever since. No one tried to take my pain away as so many others tried to do; they simply reminded me I wasn't alone in it."

His story is an example of how people who know what it is like to be marginalized and excluded, who know what it feels like to be negatively labeled, to be hurt, often harshly. They, so often, can be the ones who will reach out to include and welcome others in their midst.

He shifted the conversation to us and we indicated we weren't gay, either. "So why are you here?" he asked.

"We wanted to be supportive because we know what it feels like to be left out and feeling lonely. We want our gay friends to know we regard them with respect and recognize it still isn't easy for them to be included, fully, in the community."

"What do you guys do for a living?" Now we were the ones with the cautious, reluctant look on our faces. "We are both pastors; we have a compassionate listening ministry."

Sometimes we aren't proud of the religious title we possess because we know some people who bear religious titles and affiliations have hurt others, badly. This was one such moment. Knowing he had been hurt by his religious community, we would have preferred to tell him we are builders, engineers, or store managers—anything other than pastor.

The look on his face confirmed our reluctance and reinforced our uneasiness. Instantly, his expression turned; he seemed more cautious, wary. He was visibly uncomfortable. We understood why and we were sorry. We felt deeply for him.

In the English dictionary, the word **consolation** means "to be" (con) "with the lonely one" (solus). Offering consolation is one of the deepest and most powerful expressions of attending to the needs of another individual. Consolation helps break down the barriers and the prejudices we all carry. Consolation means no longer looking at another individual as if his or her pain is something far removed from our own pain. We are no longer individuals on an individual journey; we are human beings on a human journey with one another. Consolation helps us respond to the woman who is lonely and has lost her son, the friend who is gay and has been treated as an outcast, the teenager who feel as if she has a will to live, and the old man who lies in a nursing home with no one to visit him. When we offer consolation, the stranger is no longer a stranger, but rather our friend.

Why do we label people?

What compels us to define others and ourselves by (often) narrow parameters, putting one another into categories based on our jobs, looks, sexual orientation, religion or race? Is it because it's easier to label, to define others with stereotypes? Is it because going beneath the surface may take us to uncomfortable places? Is it because going deeper into the core of our own or someone's being may threaten our cherished beliefs or challenge our expectations?

After touring a church with several outreaches, including an outreach to those who were gay and HIV positive or living with AIDS, we overheard one of our group members criticizing that particular aspect of the church's ministry:

"The church shouldn't be open to just anyone. It's not 'Y'all come.' I don't believe we should be welcoming those who are gay. Not unless they change their ways."

This comment came from a woman who was married and divorced three times. Was she feeling a need to put down others in order to make herself feel better about her own history and the circumstances which may have marginalized her? We wondered if others failed to show compassion to her during her seasons of broken relationships and turmoil. Why was it impossible for her to show compassion to others whose lives aren't considered the preferred norm?

Have you ever been labeled "slow," "fat," "bad," "selfish," "lazy," or "incompetent"? If so, how did it feel? Did it hold you back or keep you down? Have those labels—and countless others—made you feel unworthy, insignificant, ashamed, or disregarded? Have they made you feel restricted, inauthentic, or imprisoned?

Think about it.

When have labels hurt you and kept you from being who you really are? When have they sent the message that you are simply not respected? Considered worthy of goodness? Loved?

We wonder, how have the labels we place on one another kept us from truly being who we are meant and gifted to be? How much of life's wonder, beauty and richness have we actually missed because our labels have blinded us to the magnificence inherently within us and around us, as endowed by our creator?

One of the labels we've experienced as most daunting to bear personally is that of "pastor," as we've alluded to. When some people hear we are pastors and have served in churches, they make certain assumptions about who we are and what we believe. They assume we are against certain things and in support of other things. They believe we have certain political beliefs. They assume we won't be open to listening to them and their stories because they believe that we will automatically be judgmental or critical. They assume pastors have narrow interests and, often, rigid opinions. They, many times, don't see us as fully human—with emotions, fears, needs, insecurities and brokenness just like everyone else.

A few years ago I (Michael) officiated at a wedding. At the reception following, Kathy and I were seated next to a man who had strong opinions on many subjects; the table conversation was certainly entertaining. I enjoyed listening to him and offering my own observations on many of the issues he brought up. At one point during the conversation he paused and very seriously exclaimed to me, "You know, you're the first pastor I've ever talked to who didn't make me want to vomit!"

I had never received a "compliment" quite like that one before. Bombastic as it was, though, I actually appreciated it. He saw me as likable, easy to talk with and as an actual human being, and not a stereotype of a pastor. But, it was too bad he didn't see other pastors before me in the same way. It was odious for him to shake the negative label about pastors I fear was sadly and unfortunately well earned.

How have labels hurt or affected you? How might you reflect on the labels you place on others, especially as you remember how Christ welcomed, touched, broke the rules for and loved the very people who were marginalized, scorned and labeled as outcasts in his era and time?

We remember Jesus spending so much of his time with or speaking kindly about people whom the culture in his day devalued—tax collectors, women, children, lepers, Samaritans, prostitutes, those who lived with disabilities of many kinds, for example. He did not discriminate against them. In fact, the people he seemed most frustrated with were those with power, those who were self-righteous—those who shunned and harshly judged others and who attempted to exclude others from God's love. They were the ones who received rebukes from him. Those who were culturally and historically marginalized received his compassion and his grace. He spent time with them, against the cultural dictates of his day, and knew the reasons leading to their circumstances. He treated others with dignity and grace, especially those whom the culture didn't, thereby helping them to believe in their sacred distinctiveness, showing them ways to live and to be, enabling them to see a better way of living was possible. He wanted no one to be excluded from the goodness and presence of God and the abundant life of the spirit God wants us all to possess.

In the church we often spend so much time focusing on the cross that we can sometimes forget what led Jesus to the cross. He showed love to people who were shunned. He touched those who were considered untouchable. And, he proclaimed everyone belonged to God's kingdom. It was all the rigid rules he broke which ultimately got him in trouble and sent him to Calvary. Remembering how he loved, we are given a deeper and fuller understanding of the cross and its compassionate revelation for us.

In writing this story about our involvement in an event with people who have historically been marginalized and excluded in our culture and in the church, we had some fears. Knowing many people who have strong opinions about LGBT issues, especially as it relates to some religious understandings, we recognize there will be people who dispute our involvement with those in the LGBT community. But our reading of scripture, especially in the life of Jesus, and in our experience listening to people's stories, we see a very clear mandate to simply love one another and to offer grace in all circumstances. Jesus, in our understanding, was consistently about including people, offering compassion, accepting differences and loving others no matter their station in life, lifestyle or life circumstances. He respected and nurtured, giving himself to the people of his time and place, especially those whom his culture dismissed. It was his kind, inclusive actions that gave him the authority to speak words into their lives which could help them to grow in the grace and love of God.

We also see a clear message about grace. God is, above all things, gracious. God welcomes and loves all of us and desires for all of us to live an abundant life—abundant in love, abundant in satisfaction, abundant in peace, and abundant in relationship with God and with one another.

We believe in a God who has created each one of us and who loves each of us unconditionally, with all of our different experiences, gifts, and lives. God wants none of us to be left out, nor left behind. Ever. We believe God desires for every one of us to experience the eternal wonder and glory of God's blessings and infinite goodness. Just because we may not always agree with someone else's opinion or perspective on any given issue, doesn't mean we should diminish him or her.

We'll never forget the retired Southern Baptist pastor who sat before us and confessed that throughout his ministry he had always believed that people who were gay were outside the Kingdom of God. He believed it until his own son admitted he was gay, was diagnosed with AIDS and, sadly, died from the disease. With tears in his eyes, the pastor told us his opinion had changed when he was confronted with the realities of the child he dearly, unconditionally loved. Grace is born through this kind of love, the kind of a father for his son, for all the children he created.

In the words of Brother Robert L'Esperance, of the Society of Saint John the Evangelist:

This is what Christ calls us to do by his own word and example: to affirm the worth and dignity of every human being we come in contact with. Not to label others, not to dismiss them with a category and demean their humanity, but to call others by name as our God calls each of us by name. To value with compassion every other human being.

Nearly everyone we meet has expressed the same human feelings to one degree or another—separateness, uneasiness, and disquietedness. No matter the circumstances or station of one's life, all of us have likely felt undervalued and unworthy, unloved and unimportant at one time or another. Perhaps many times throughout our lives.

So, what do we do with those feelings? We believe because of our common humanity and vulnerability, we need to offer grace to one another. We need to have humility and an attitude of generosity and compassion for our very common experiences.

No matter what our culture indicates, the Bible tells us Jesus loves us all. No matter what. It is this divine love that breaks down barriers when we allow it to wash over us. It is this divine love that can guide our relationships with one another.

The civil rights icon Rosa Parks once proclaimed, "You must never be fearful about what you are doing when it is right."

She also said, "Each person must live their life as a model for others."

It's simply how we all need to be—looking at every person in this world as equally loved by God, modeling God's incalculable reservoir of affection for each of us, we who are divinely made.

The Church Is Not a Museum

"Whatever happens to me in life, I must believe that somewhere,
in the mess or madness of it all, there is a sacred potential—a possibility
for wondrous redemption in the embracing of all that is."
-EDWINA GATELEY

"Compassion is the wish for another being to be free from suffering."
-THE DALAI LAMA

ST. PAUL'S (EPISCOPAL) CHAPEL in New York City sits in the shadow of the World Trade Center complex. Dwarfed by the dozens of skyscrapers surrounding it in the heart of Manhattan's financial district, it was the most unlikely of buildings to remain intact and standing when the towers and other buildings nearby collapsed on September 11, 2001.

On the night of September 10, 2001, St. Paul's windows were open. Those open windows helped to save the structure when the other buildings fell.

St. Paul's, built in 1766, is the oldest standing church in the city and the place where George Washington came to pray after his inauguration as the first President of the United States. Several other U.S. presidents have also worshipped there. Not content to rest on its illustrious history, as a congregation, it made a decision to open its doors to people who were experiencing homelessness. Night after night, the church gave shelter to those who needed a safe, clean place to sleep. When we toured the beautiful sanctuary, a guide told us this story:

It was very warm on September 10, 2001. The chapel's windows were open to allow fresh, cooler night air to circulate through the building, making the stay more comfortable for the overnight guests. On the morning of September 11, those windows were still open when the planes hit the towers and the buildings crashed violently, horrifically to the ground.

Immediately, St. Paul's and the small centuries-old cemetery around it were covered in dense smoke, smoldering ashes and unimaginable debris. Yet the church remained standing.

Those open windows helped to save it.

The open windows allowed the intense and deafening sound waves from the collapsing towers to pass through the church sanctuary, sparing it from destruction. Had they been closed, the resulting pressure from the blast should have knocked the old building over, destroying the historic place of worship and killing everyone inside.

In this lies a cautionary message for all of us, particularly those of us in the church.

St. Paul's decided not to be just a museum, a historic place, with quaint colonial architecture, that played an important role in the birth of America. It decided not to rest on its laurels. It decided to be a living, breathing, vibrant church, a manifestation of the call to serve from Jesus Christ.

It was the decision, the compassion—to open its doors to people who had no safe place to lay their heads at night, to open its windows to provide them with fresh air, to open their hearts to those who were hurting, alone and afraid—which helped to save many people and the building from an awful, deadly fate.

Simply doing good things does not necessarily save us from destruction. As one of St. Paul's associates, The Reverend Lyndon Harris, wrote after the attacks: *It was not because we were holier than anyone who died across the street; it was because we now had a big job to do.*

In the days and months following the attacks on New York, thousands of first responders, police officers, firefighters, medical personnel and so many other compassionate people came to the site of the gaping wound in the city's soul to begin to bind it up. When they did, St. Paul's opened its doors, windows and hearts to them. Thousands upon thousands of volunteers were welcomed into its sanctuary for a safe place to sojourn. They found stillness and savored a few precious moments of relief from the unrelenting recovery and restoration efforts. Indeed, it was a big job to do.

When we visited the site together several years after the attacks, Michael had already been there a few times before, with his wife and parents, his brother and his family, with his church youth group and a few other friends. Tom hadn't been ready to visit the site in the years before our visit together. Growing up across the Hudson River in New Jersey, he knew many families in his community who had lost members on September 11. He had eaten lunch with a friend on the plaza outside the towers just one week before their fall. It had been too raw, too real, to return. But on this day together, he was ready.

The smoke, ashes and debris were gone. The buildings remaining in the area were in the process of being restored. The new skyscraper replacing the twin towers was under construction and already dozens of stories tall. This place of death and profound violence was once again vibrant and growing ever healthier. We toured the new museum opened to chronicle the events of September 11 and its aftermath. We stepped inside the sacred walls of St. Paul's to hear its story of those fateful days.

We were deeply moved . . .

We know of another church in which a colleague and mentor once served. It is in Vienna, Austria. The pastor and his family lived in a home next to the church. From their windows, they could see an apartment in which one of modern history's most famous persons had once lived. As a young man, a failed art student studying in Vienna—Adolf Hitler—lived in the apartment. Our colleague often pondered, *What if the church had reached out to Adolf Hitler when he was living in its shadow? What if someone from the church had shown him some attention? What if someone exhibited to him the love of Christ? How different might the world have been if Adolf Hitler had heard a different message than one of loneliness, rejection and shame? What if . . .?*

We will never know.

But we do know this—when people are moved by compassion to open the windows of their hearts to show love and grace to those who are lonely, defeated, heartbroken, rudderless and in distress, others' lives will change. When we take notice of and reach out to those who need hope we begin to affect the movement of a spirit of healing and of peace. When we are intentional about using our faith as an instrument of soothing, redemptive power, people's souls start to transform. Instead of dying in despair and defeat they are massaged into reviving with joy and hope.

It is in such a revival where sacred hope for all humankind is born . . .

We listened to his story. His was a harsh, embattled life. He was an alcoholic. His excessive drinking had caused countless broken relationships with women, estrangement from children he hadn't seen in years, leading him into homelessness and poverty. The decades of abuse to his body and spirit had put him into a downward spiral from which he could find no relief. Desperate for any salvation from his emptiness, he wandered into a church one Sunday morning.

With him, he brought his best friend—a bottle of Jack Daniels.

They took a seat in the back row of the sanctuary. He and Jack. Openly, throughout the service, he and Jack "communed." Without trying to hide the fact, he drank from the bottle until Jack was gone.

He thought to himself, "I know they're going to kick me the hell out of here. There's no way a church will let me stay, drinking a whole bottle of Jack."

But the church did.

So, he came back. Week after week, he returned, sitting in the same place in the back row, with a new bottle of Jack Daniels in hand. By the end of each service, Jack was gone.

They never kicked him out.

As each Sunday came around, worshippers in the church began to connect with him. They sat with him, learned his name, got to know him and asked if they could pray with him. He accepted. Week after week, he came back and they welcomed him and Jack in.

He felt wanted, accepted, not judged.

Now, years later, he is sober. His sobriety enables him to mentor others and help them find a way to sobriety too.

The church simply loved the man into recovery. The compassion, patience and acceptance its people showed him, helped him to realize he mattered. It helped him to realize there was a better way—he was worth receiving recovery. That church's love and grace enabled him to start all over again.

It's not always easy, living in recovery. Old demons are always present. But the church's love surrounds him and upholds him when the temptations and the setbacks rage in his soul . . .

Over the last few years we have developed a meaningful correspondence with a gracious man living in the mid-eastern Muslim world. Incredibly, he reached out separately through email to both of us, months apart. He had read stories that each of us had written for different *Chicken Soup for the Soul* books. He had no idea we knew each other or we were partners in a non-profit. But he wrote to tell both of us our stories were meaningful to him.

When we reached back to him, separately at first, until we realized we were corresponding with the same person, he wrote to us about some details of his life—he had a wife and was the father of a young daughter. One day, this message came in:

> *On January 4th my father was born to another world. He was taken to Heaven. Deep sadness and emotional distress penetrated my heart. I experienced an unbearable pain in my soul. I spent 45 days with them during the pilgrimage season when he was sick. One month after coming back from there, he passed away. Thankfully, I was given another 15 days vacation to go back to console my mother, brothers, and sisters. Even though the family home was full of people, it was empty and very small in my eyes with my fa-*

ther's absence. I wished I was only 2 years old when he died. At least, I would
not have known the beauty of life or the bitterness of death . . . Please pray
for his soul, peace and rest.

We felt deeply his sadness, as he so eloquently wrote to us. We expressed our
empathy. We promised to pray as he asked. We kept in touch. He mentioned his
father in many of the subsequent messages. His acute sorrow lingered.

Months later, this welcome message arrived:

We are all well. My wife gave birth to another beautiful girl 2 months
ago. She was born with a small congenital hole on her back. The doctor re-
moved the hole or rather covered it through a minor surgical operation. She
still suffers the consequences of the surgery due to her fragile body and we have
to change her sutures every day. Please pray for her health. I am afraid that
she would be paralyzed or something like that.

We responded with our congratulations, so happy for good news that filled
his life. We knew he needed good news. We also prayed for his little daughter and
expressed our empathy as fathers as he and his wife nurtured her fragile body.

We corresponded throughout the next months. He'd update us and would
inquire about our children, especially. He would often write around the time of our
holidays. Greetings and best wishes would come not just for our Christian holiday
of Christmas and Easter, but also for Valentine's Day, St, Patrick's Day and the
Fourth of July. He even wrote on the anniversary of September 11:

Let us pray for peace and for the victims of September 11 attacks 13 years
ago . . . It was a horrible day . . . My heart ached for those who died under
the ruble, for those who threw themselves off the high towers and for those
who lost their lives while feverishly trying to rescue others.

Then, another message filled with grief:

. . . my little daughter passed away last Thursday. Deep sadness pen-
etrated my heart and I am experiencing an unbearable pain in my soul now.
Please help me embrace pain and burn it as fuel for the long journey of my
healing.
. . . my sadness will no doubt fly on the wings of time. Thanks for your kindness.
I am trying to fill my empty heart with gratitude for those who are still in my life.

It broke our hearts. We expressed our profound sorrow for him and his family. He responded:

Would you be willing to talk with me on the phone?

The conversation was brief. He thanked us for calling, for being supportive of him. We told him how very sorry we were for his little daughter's passing. He began to sob and couldn't talk. The phone call ended abruptly. His grief was too acute for him to continue.

We sat silently for a few moments, reflecting on the emotion of the call. We simply didn't know what to say after he had hung up.

The intensity of his plaintive grief and his many messages to us evoked feelings that we will never soon forget. A father's deep, profound love, his anguished cries of suffering, bore directly into our hearts. When you lose a beloved father, when you lose a treasured child, it doesn't matter where you live or what your religious background is. The loss hurts so much the same. His cries and his words were the same words any loving son and any devoted father would express. Time zones, cultures and faiths don't separate us when we are in deepest grief and pain. For the three of us to be able to transcend our different environments is a tremendous privilege. To be resting upon common human ground, as children of God, is a gift of supreme sacredness.

It is also how compassion moves us to be. Compassion is the living embodiment of what the church is called to be—an open heart to those who feel rootless and need a home, an outstretched hand to those who are lonely and lost, a source of acceptance to those who are seized by overwhelming demons and fears, a common place of safety and comfort for those who are deep in torment and affliction.

The church is not a museum when it exhibits "in the mess or madness of it all, . . . a sacred potential—a possibility for wondrous redemption in the embracing of all that is." It is what we want the church to always be.

Accompanying the permission he gave for his story to be included in this book, he wrote us this lovely, heartfelt message:

Dearest Michael and Tom,
How nice and kind of you to include my correspondences with you in the coming book, I'm elated beyond the words can ever say. I also appreciate your good gesture and great efforts to do so, and it's my pleasure to be known to your friends and readers around the world.

My eyes filled with bittersweet tears as I was reading the email once again almost five years after sending it to you.

The Cure for Loneliness

"She had more courage in the face of death than I had in the face of life."
-A MAN WHO LOST HIS WIFE TO MULTIPLE MYELOMA

*W*ELL, MY WIFE PASSED AWAY *a few weeks ago. Painful. I wonder if Someone To Tell It To is active in the New York City area?*
Peace & Love . . .

It was the day before the Fourth of July holiday weekend. We had completed several meetings about an hour's drive from our homes and stopped at a beautiful park to make the call. We found a bench in a quiet area of the park. As we watched the ducks splash and swim, we invited him to open up about what the past few months had been like.

He was very open about the events leading up to his wife's death and his feelings of grief and sadness. What struck us most was the loneliness we heard in his voice. He never used the word; but it was clear—he was incredibly lonely. He had been married for 30 years. Now, he's a widower in his 50's.

He left his job as a counselor to be at home with his wife during her last year. He ambles around the apartment they had together, suddenly too large for just him, expecting to hear her voice, to tell her some important news, to watch the sunset together over the Hudson River from their living room vista. In the silence, he misses her more than he can say. His best friend. His partner. His life.

He described the day she died. A trip to the emergency department, which began marked by hope, turned stunningly desperate with the words:
"We think you should come back to see her . . ."
There was nothing more they could do. He was given time to say a final good-bye and then she was gone.

His loneliness was so palpable.

He said, "I just want someone to come and sit with me. I might cry sometimes. But just be with me."

We quietly whispered to each other, "We could do that."

We asked him about his support system. Who in his life can sit with him, and walk along side him so he's not all alone? We knew he was a person of faith and we asked about his church. He answered, "I give myself space and I walk gently through all of this. The church knows who I am, but doesn't truly know me, because of its size."

We knew we could explore his loneliness further when we'd meet face to face. We sat silently for a moment after the call, letting what we both heard penetrate our hearts. The loneliness he was feeling was powerful and quieting. We imagined ourselves in his circumstances. Lost in our own homes. Adrift in our own lives. Disconnected from everything enriching.

It is a solemn privilege to be invited into the depth of another's most emotionally intimate moments. It is sacred. We hope we responded with the sensitivity the conversation deserved. We were both subdued for the rest of the afternoon. His loss reminded us of the fragile nature of life and the relationships we hold dear.

We thought about the holiday weekend. We each had plans to celebrate with our parents, siblings, wives and children. We were looking forward to seeing them and to have some extra time to step away from work. He, on the other hand, wasn't going to celebrate. He had no family in New York to enjoy. He no longer had a job to step back from. The holiday was just another day. Another day of hurting. Another day of darkness. Another day feeling lost.

We emailed him the next day:

> *We are so glad we had the opportunity to talk with you yesterday. It was a meaningful conversation. We are so sorry for the loss you have experienced. We know it's excruciating. We pray for God's compassionate arms of comfort and peace to embrace and surround you. May God's tender care carry you through this season of sadness and grief . . .*
>
> *We look forward to seeing you in NYC soon. . . we send our love.*

It didn't take long for his response:

> *Thanks a lot for your email. You are conveying that you care. This is so important for me right now, being that I have so few friends and/or family, particularly in the New York City (NYC) area. **I haven't received a phone call in what seems like days.** But, I'm "hang'n in there.." . . What's so hard to get used to is the silence. I guess in many ways, I was so dependent on her. While she needed so much, particularly after she became so sick (over the past year), she became the center of my life. On the other hand, she tried to look after me too!*
>
> *There is nothing like going to bed alone; and, then, getting up alone. She*

and I greeted each other in the evening; and, we greeted each other at sunrise. I'm getting used to it though. I need to take care of myself.

I took my bicycle into the repair shop yesterday: new tires, inner tubes and a "tune up." I picked it up today. Hey, it rides nicely.

I've had a couple of people knock on my door yesterday and today. But, they both wanted something. . . My work is meeting the needs of others. I just need to carve out some time for myself.

Thanks so much and GOD BLESS!

Peace & Love . . . P.S.(1) Here is a quote that I've given to a few people: "She had more courage in the face of death than I had in the face of life."

P.S.(2) I'm hang'n in there, though!

Arriving in New York City, a few weeks later, he met us near Times Square, the vibrant heart of the city. He had an "itinerary" planned and we started walking.

"Let me show you where she worked. It's only a few blocks away."

Slowly, we ambled through the crowds. People were hustling around us. But he didn't hurry. Unhurriedly, deliberately, we strolled. Time seemed to stand still. We focused intently on his words and on the passionate love he was conveying, as he told their story.

The traffic, the omnipresent noise of Manhattan, and everyone else on the sidewalks faded into the background as we listened. It was unlike any visit to the city either of us had ever experienced. Neither of us had ever been so unaware of our surroundings before. We had never been part of such an intimate, profoundly personal conversation with someone on those busy and crowded sidewalks. We had never walked those streets slowly, ignoring the energy of the people and vehicles.

It was personal. He took us through one of the beloved and special neighborhoods he and his wife enjoyed, it was as if we were sitting on their front porch and he was introducing us to the surrounding town. The rest of the world was blocked out. It was so simple, so human. Three guys connecting in a way that rarely happens. As we walked we could see much-needed peace filling his spirit. He continued to point out the sights that were part of his life with her.

"Oh, the coffee shop there. She loved it! She went there all the time!"

"Yes. There, across the street. We'd often meet at that place for lunch. I'd get the bus or the Lexington Avenue subway line from my office."

"Look up to the right, where her office was. I still haven't been able to go in the building yet. Still too painful."

Block after block we walked, stopping every few yards as he pointed out another favorite juice place, eating spot or a park or attraction they'd often visit together. He lingered, savoring the memories and delighting in the lives they lived in the frenzied neighborhood.

He also stopped often to greet people experiencing homelessness. He'd stoop down, as they sat on the sidewalks, look them in the eyes, grasp their hands, and ask them about their situation. He'd reach into his pocket and pull out a handful of cash, giving each of them some money before he moved on. He formerly worked with and ministered to people experiencing homelessness and his compassion for them was evident. He'd ask: "How are you doing, brother?" "What can I do to help you, friend?" "What happened to bring you here today?"

We realized quickly how his outreach to those who were in such a vulnerable place was helping him to reach into his own place of vulnerability. When he greeted someone we saw the person and him light up. We saw the darkness they both were experiencing melt away for a few sacred moments.

Those conversations were helping to heal him, to deliver him outside his own hell and desolation. He was a wounded man, touching other wounded men and women with his spirit and grace.

Lunch time approached, he suggested a restaurant where he and his wife both loved to eat.

"I'm buying," he announced. "I'm just so grateful you have come here to be with me today!"

All morning, he had been carrying a bag with him. He indicated he'd show us the contents of the bag at lunch. We were curious about what was inside.

As soon as we ordered, he opened the bag and pulled out a couple dozen photos: him and his wife on their wedding day; her standing in front of a score of scenic and historic lighthouses along the northeastern U.S. coast; and their extended families at reunions and special occasions. With each photo, he offered a commentary about the day it was taken, the visit or the significance. Each photo brought his beloved wife back to life. Each one gave him pause—to smile at a memory, to get lost in a thought or feeling or to wipe away a tear or two from his eyes.

"Our wedding was such a joyful day, you know. We actually got married on a Sunday morning, right in the middle of the regular worship service. There's a liturgy for that in the Presbyterian Church. Our community of faith surrounded us. I loved it."

"I have a passion for lighthouses. I belong to two historic lighthouse societies in the region. She indulged my passion. She was such a good sport. I am so grateful to have had these trips with her. We always had fun together and loved to travel. I miss her. I don't know if I'll be able to get back into traveling and lighthouses again."

"Here we are at one of her family reunions. A lot of good people. But not everyone has kept in touch since she's gone. It hurts a lot."

We sat at the table with him in quiet wonder. As we listened to his stories, as we laughed at a few of them, and as we allowed him to prick open his melancholy and speak of his emptiness, we were in the presence of the holy. The words of old hymns came to life as we felt the spirit of God at work:

> *Breathe on me breath of God, fill me with life anew . . .*
> *Precious Lord, take my hand, lead me on, let me stand, I am tired, I*
> *am weak, I am worn, . . .*

Over lunch, offering us the precious photos of his wife memorializing her and the life he cherished and once knew, he was allowing God's spirit to breathe new life into his tired, weak and worn soul.

He repeated these words over and over during the meal: "She had more courage in the face of death than I had in the face of life."

We have no doubt she had tremendous courage in the face of her disease and in her dying. As he recounted their story, he described a woman of faith, strength and grace. But we believe he underestimates his own courage.

On the sidewalks of New York with us, he walked straight toward many of the places they enjoyed visiting together. He acknowledged them, reminisced about them, and faced the memories. He confronted the fact that his life will never be the same. He didn't shy away from allowing tears to flow. He opened up the internal vault in which his anguish was most poignant and raw. He confronted the brokenness defining his life since she died.

He's still trying to figure out what his new life will be like, what work he'll do, whether he'll stay in their spacious apartment, and how he'll reconnect with society. It takes courage to pick up the pieces of a broken and shattered heart and start all over again. We saw his courage come to life. Walking by his side and sitting with him gave him the support he needed to begin to heal.

After lunch, we stepped back onto the busy, hot sidewalks, in the middle of Times Square. Sirens blasted, traffic rushed, and megawatt video screens bombarded our auditory and visual senses. We walked, listened, and continued to greet those without homes, many of whom were slumped against walls for support. He searched his thoughts for what might be next in this new chapter of life. He talked about reconnecting with others in his church, nurturing supportive relationships, and following the passions he has for ministering to others in their anguish. We knew that he could use his grief, eventually, to minister empathetically to others in theirs. We had already witnessed it happening on the sidewalks that day.

A few weeks later an email came with a very specific invitation:

> *Would it be possible for the two of you to spend the day with me on the 28th? I really do not have any "credible" (excuse the term) person who could stand by and support me . . . Maybe, you could be here for the service. And, maybe you could stay with me for a few hours thereafter (my head is going to be "reeling").*

His wife's ashes were being committed to a columbarium in their church. He wanted us to stand on either side of him during the short service, during what he knew would be a profoundly emotional experience. Without hesitation, we said yes. We were deeply honored to be asked.

He invited us to stay with him in their apartment the night before, to gird himself for the following morning. He talked late into the night, reminiscing, looking ahead. On the bus ride to the church the next day, he pointed out more sites where he and his wife's lives intersected. We learned more of their history and of the days surrounding her death. The committal was short at the intimate columbarium. We all stood as her pastor commended her ashes for perpetuity, the two of us on either side of him. He held up commendably.

Afterwards, the three of us walked slowly up Fifth Avenue, where the church was located, to the edge of Central Park. It was just about noon. He wasn't hungry, but needed to quench his thirst on a stifling August afternoon. We went into the venerable Plaza Hotel, where he had never been before, where its landmark Palm Court, just off the lobby, was opening for the day. Since we weren't eating, we were seated at its beautiful bar and we ordered something to drink, the only patrons there. For the next hour we had one of the most touching, intimate, searing conversations we've ever had with someone. As tears drained down his face and onto his suit, his emotional cries about the finality of it all wracked his soul. His inability to picture what he would do now without her tortured him. On either side of him we sat, saying little, simply accompanying him as he began to take the first steps in the long, laborious process of trying to figure it out.

We sat with her in a small private room of a coffee shop.

Familiar carols played softly in the background. Tiny Christmas lights brightened the room. Tastefully chosen decorations all around us reminded us of the holidays. There were signs of the season everywhere.

But the season was a nightmare to her.

She had lost her teenage son in a tragic accident, in the heart of the season, more than a dozen years before. This day was the anniversary of his death.

We had originally met her at a book signing a few weeks before, a few days prior to Thanksgiving. The particular Barnes and Noble wasn't especially close to any of our homes. It wasn't the most lucrative signing we'd had. We only sold a handful of books and it almost seemed as if it was a waste to have given up a Sunday afternoon away from our families to do it. Meeting her seemed, at first, as if it was a quite random occurrence. But, maybe it wasn't.

The afternoon of the book signing was a complicated one for her. The man whom she was dating and who had brought her there was in midst of calling off their relationship. It was a confusing day for her. We had noticed her several times, walking by our table at a bit of a distance, quickly glancing at us, but definitely avoiding eye contact. But when she noticed us packing up to leave, when our allotted signing time was up, she seized the final opportunity left and quietly approached us,

"You wrote a book? Can you tell me what it's about?"

"We'd love to," we replied, and began to tell our story. "It's a book of essays, many of them about our relationship and some of the hardships we've faced in our lives. It also has many other stories of others and their relationships and brokenness. We wrote it in large part to help people know they are not alone in their distress, whatever they are."

"So, you've written about some of your own trials? How complicated was it for you?"

"It's not always easy. Putting some of the more personal and messy stuff out there for the world to read is intimidating. We never know how others might react. But so far, it's been very positive."

"How much is the book?"

We told her and she paid for one, we thanked her and thought she was about to say goodbye. When suddenly, tears welled up in her eyes,

"It's the start of the holiday season, you know. I hate this time of year. I hate it every year." "We're so sorry. What is it you hate about the holidays?"

"My son died 13 years ago, in December, in a car accident. He left the house happy and full of life . . . and he never came back. Suddenly, he was gone. I felt as if I was gone with him too. It's been the most awful experience of my life. Even my memories hurt, still today."

Beyond "We're sorry," sometimes there's not much more to say in moments such as these. We gave her a hug. We asked if we could arrange a time to speak with her, hoping she would be open to it. She was. She gave us her number and said to call. A few days later, we did.

"I've read your book. I finished it already. The story about the mother who also lost her son in a car crash shortly before Christmas resonated with me. It brought back so much."

She found it impossible to feel the spirit of hope, joy, love and peace the season was supposed to be about.

At one time she was part of a church community and held an active faith. But now she doesn't. She can't find a church home. God seems impossible for her to find, to believe in. Her family lives many states away. She lives far from her son's grave on the other side of the country. The life she had when he was alive is now long gone, buried with him.

There is no one who will talk with her about her son. No one wants to listen. His death is too far in the past. For her, though, it's still very much in the present.

The loneliness is the heaviest thing she feels. It seems when no one wants to talk with her about him, it's as if he never existed. She has no one to acknowledge the existing grief she still has; it's as if it isn't there, as if it isn't allowed to be real.

So on the day of the anniversary of his death, we invited her to remember him with us. We knew it was going to be an excruciating day for her. We thought she might not want to be alone, drowning in her sorrow, despondent at his absence. She readily accepted.

She came into the coffee shop carrying a folder. Lovingly, tenderly, she opened it. "Would you like to see photos of my son?"

One by one she took them from the folder and handed them to us. A score of snapshots. A photographic narrative of his life. Each one told a story. A baby, held in welcoming arms, his entire life yet before him. A young boy in his pajamas, at Christmas, excited and expectant. A young man, just days before he died, handsome, smiling with one more year left in his teens, relaxed, so full of promise and hope.

It was a sacred afternoon.

In those moments his life was real again. By imparting this chronicle of his life he was remembered. With joy and with sorrow. In such a sacred act her pride and her tender feelings, her torment and her longing, were exposed. In this sacred act, if even for a few moments, she did not have to carry all of it alone. That's what made it sacred. If only for a moment, her loneliness could be softened and the ache of her heart relieved.

We felt as if we were part of her family in those moments. It was sacramental to be invited into her longing, her grief, her pride. We believe we are all family; we are all connected in such common human emotions. On that day, in that moment, her longing was our longing, her loss was our loss.

None of us should ever be in it alone. Whether it's grief, anxiety, insecurity, disease or loneliness, none of us should ever be in it alone. We are all part of a shared humanity. We need each other, especially in those moments, to remind one another of our sacredness, of our inherent, God-given regard.

We never fully know what someone else is carrying. But if we are willing to invite others to open up and be heard, we allow them to invite us in to a sacred place where our common humanity resides. There is nothing more profound. We see the face of God, a face of love and compassion and peace in those moments.

While it can be intimidating to sit with someone in pain, with someone who is so broken apart, it can be the most important gift we can give.

By recognizing her and inviting her on an anniversary day, by looking at her treasured photos and not shying away, we tried to be ambassadors of Christ's comforting presence. Of Christ's healing love.

Recognizing and sitting with another in moments of distress is something each of us can do too, for those in our lives. All of us are capable of experiencing these sacred times with another. It can mean the world to someone who needs to know life doesn't have to be solitary, desolate or without assurance of an accompanier who is with us to help soften the harshness of unbearable days.

First World Problems (Tom)

"There's a lot of ugly things in this world, son.
I wish I could keep 'em all away from you. That's never possible."
-Harper Lee, *To Kill a Mockingbird*

"I have three things I'd like to say today. First, while you were sleeping
last night, 30,000 kids died of starvation or diseases related to malnutri-
tion. Second, most of you don't give a shit. What's worse is that you're
more upset with the fact that I said shit than the fact
that 30,000 kids died last night."
-Tony Campolo

"Over and over, when I ask God why all of these injustices are allowed to
exist in the world, I can feel the Spirit whisper to me, "You tell me why
we allow this to happen. You are my body, my hands, my feet."
-Shane Claiborne

WHEN LUKE WAS FIVE his questions and his prayers were so innocent. Every night when I entered his bedroom to say goodnight, we'd say our prayers together. But before we did, I tried my best to explain who or what we were praying for . . .

"There was an earthquake in the country of Nepal today," I tell him. The questions start coming. "Where is Nepal?" Luke asks tenderly. With my limited geographic knowledge, I illustrate where the country is located. "Can I see it?"

I show him a picture on my phone. "Dad, what's an earthquake?" "Sometimes the earth shakes." He starts shaking his bed.

"So my bed would shake back and forth like this, right?"

"It would shake a lot like you're doing, but probably even more."

"Would it go side to side or up and down?"

"I'm not sure exactly. I've never experienced an earthquake before. Sometimes buildings collapse."

"Can I see a picture of the buildings collapsing?" I show him a few pictures of the aftermath. "Did people die?" He asks. "Yes, over 5,000 people died."

"How many is 5,000?"

"It would be like the number of people who attended the hockey game we were at. "

"Whoa, that's a lot of people."

The conversation shifts for a few moments to his T-ball practice that was cancelled earlier in the evening.

"Dad, maybe the people didn't make it to our practice tonight because they thought it was going to rain."

"Maybe buddy, I'm not sure." "Daddy, why are their earthquakes?"

In the moment, I'm sure I could have given him a brief scientific explanation, although I'm not a scientist, but I thought about giving him the honest answer:

"I just don't know buddy. I don't know." "Does God make earthquakes?"

I thought about passing the buck and telling him to ask his mother in the morning. But I take the bait and answer the question, knowing many more questions would result.

"Sometimes bad things like earthquakes just happen." I answer. "But the important thing for us to remember is God is always with us no matter what. God is with us even when things are bad. And we know things can be bad for all of us, right?"

"Yeah." he says. "I wish things didn't have to be so bad."

"When things are bad, it's when our belief in God is so important." I remind him.

Our conversation continues for another minute or two.

We have been fervently praying for a few individuals from our church. He reminds me, nearly every night, to pray for them by name.

His prayers are simple, yet profound. We finish. "I love you, buddy." "I love you too, Daddy." A Rich Mullins song he recognizes from church comes on Pandora. We sing along.

> Our God is an Awesome God He reigns from heaven above, With wisdom, power, and love, Our God is an Awesome God.

The stanza repeats. I leave his room. I can't get the chorus out of my head.

The irony is staggering. Here we are singing about our God being an "Awesome God," and yet, there is so much horror and distress happening around the world.

I don't want my kids to grow up. I want them to stay young; I want them to stay naïve to the world's suffering. But then again, I don't. I want them to be the hands and feet of Jesus.

Several weeks have passed since then. The headlines haven't changed. Still so much misery and affliction.

The alarm breaks the silence and stillness of the night. Morning has broken. I head downstairs to the kitchen and grab the coffee jar. The jar is empty. "Come on!" I grumble. Opening the fridge, I look to see if we have any eggs. No eggs.

"Come on! No eggs!!" I grumble some more. I turn on my computer and glance at the day's headlines: *Nepal Earthquake. Beheadings in the Middle East. Riots in Baltimore. NFL Player Tom Brady Cheats.*

The last headline grabs my attention because I am a sports fan. I open the article and read about Tom Brady, quarterback of the New England Patriots, who is accused of deflating a football during a championship game last season and about the resulting suspension and fine to follow. I read the article as if it somehow fits with the rest of the horrors happening elsewhere around the world.

I turn on Facebook. The walls of Facebook are inundated with pictures of Brady, not the earthquake in Nepal, not the beheadings, not children starving in Africa. Just Tom Brady, NFL quarterback. One of the captions indicates how Patriot fans are starting a fundraising campaign on GoFundMe to pay off the fine. I scroll down a bit further. A guy I know who works as a missionary in Haiti posted a comment about the story.

> *I have kids in Haiti who I still can't get a $30/month sponsor to help feed them and send them to school . . . and NE Patriots fans are giving money to a GoFundMe account to help the Patriots (worth over $2 billion) pay the $1 million fine the NFL gave them . . . ladies and gentlemen, America in 2015!*

I laugh at his comment and look at the clock. I'm running late so I head upstairs to take a quick shower. It's hit or miss these days whether or not we will get a hot shower in our house. Today is a miss.

"Come on! No hot water!!!" My grumbling continues. I run out of my body wash. I have to use Sarah's. It smells like spring flowers.

I leave to go to the office. I pull out my laptop computer. It doesn't work.

"Come on! Are you serious right now!!!" Grumbling has officially taken over my day.

Later in the afternoon, I'm in the middle of writing a story for this book. I take a break to read the latest headlines and weather reports.

"**Another 7+ earthquake in Nepal.**" I pause to say a very quick prayer. "**Lord, have mercy.**" I keep writing.

The day ends and I head home. Traffic is heavy. It's 85 degrees outside and I don't have air conditioning in my car. The car sat in the sun all day and now, inside, it feels as if it's 105 degrees. We come to a standstill. The sweat starts pouring down my face.

"Come on! Why is it so hot!!!" More grumbling.

I turn on the radio. The car antenna picks up one station, a political talk show I have no interest in at the moment.

"Come on! Can't there be one good station to listen to?!!!"

I arrive home and walk through the door. We have a leaky kitchen, but now I see a leak in our living room too. Water is seeping through the ceiling tiles. I sprint upstairs to the bathroom. Sarah is rigorously throwing towels down, one after another, to try and sop up the mess.

"I was making dinner for 10 minutes. Ten minutes!!! The twins decided to plug the drain in the sink and the leave the water running."

Rapidly, I head back downstairs to sop up the mess in our living room.

"Come on! Seriously, come on!!! This is the last thing we need in our life."

We get the mess cleaned up and sit down to dinner.

"Are we eating chicken again?!" one of the kids whimpers. This time they are the ones moaning and groaning.

"We need to be thankful for what we have. There are many people around the world who don't have food to eat for dinner."

I say it emphatically, as if our young children can comprehend the magnitude of the problem.

Later on that evening, I start reading an article about how Christians hold the largest amount of wealth, something crazy like 55% of the total world's wealth.

I continue reading. The World Bank estimates that 1.2 billion people live in absolute poverty, living on less than a dollar a day.

The magazine article hits me like a 2 x 4 between the eyes. I reflect upon my day and realize how much of my day was spent grumbling and complaining about all the petty "problems" I was faced with when so many others around the world have it far worse. Our family has coined a phrase for our petty problems here in the western world. We call them "First World Problems." "First World Problems" are those things that are problems for us only because life is comfortable. For example, a leaky roof, a limited dinner menu, no A/C in the car, a computer working slowly, no milk or eggs in the refrigerator or coffee in the pantry and deflated footballs are all "First World Problems." None of them are life-altering issues. Today my "First World Problems" controlled much of my day, too much.

"Lord, have mercy," under my breath I whisper this prayer for a second time today. I close the magazine.

The kids are restless. Its bedtime again and I enter Luke's room. His innocent questions and prayers continue.

Once again, I explain the day's headlines and who or what we can pray for. I tell him about the second earthquake in Nepal.

"Did more people die?" "Yes, Luke. More people died." "Dad, do you think God can stop earthquakes?" I chuckle because his questions are so perfect.

"God is very powerful. But there are a lot of things happening and they don't have a good explanation for why they happen. Earthquakes just happen. Do you remember what I told you a few weeks ago after the first earthquake in Nepal?"

"I do. God is with us."

"You got it buddy. God is always with us. Always. When life is hard and doesn't make sense, God is with us. You want to know something cool? "

"Yes!"

"The cool thing is that we are given the chance to be God's hands, God's feet, God's body in the world. We are given the gift of being able to show people who are having a hard time—God's love. It's awesome!"

"It is awesome!"

"So people like those who are suffering after the earthquake, or starving children, or grandmothers who are lonely, or bullies at school, all have the chance to see and feel God's love because of us. How cool is that; God gives us a job to do for others?!"

The song "Awesome God" comes on Pandora again.

We sing together.

> *Our God is an Awesome God. He reigns from heaven above, With wisdom, power, and love, Our God is an Awesome God.*

How do we teach our kids about "First World Problems"? How do we teach ourselves about "First World Problems"? How do we talk about "leading a compassionate life" without talking about those who live in poverty, those who have been disenfranchised, those who have been malnourished, those who suffer, those who live in loneliness, those who feel brokenhearted—those individuals for whom life is terribly, profoundly severe?

As author on parenting issues L. R. Knost, has written, "It's not our job to toughen our children up to face a cruel and heartless world. It's our job to raise children who make the world a little less cruel and heartless."

We can't lead a compassionate life without showing compassion to those who need it most. There is a reason more than two thirds of the Bible talks about easing the needs of those who live in poverty. For most of us, when we think of alleviating the needs of those living in poverty we think of sending a check to support a worthy cause, serving in a soup kitchen around the holidays, or going on a week-long mission trip to some far off country to build houses. Certainly those are noble and worthy efforts. But Jesus asks so much more of us. He invites us to be a part of a revolution of love to those who need it most. Jesus said,

> *Whatever you did for one of the least of these brothers and sisters of mine, you did for me.*

Shane Claiborne, author of *The Irresistible Revolution*, quoted Saint Mother Teresa: "Calcuttas are everywhere if only we have eyes to see. Find your Calcutta."

Where is your Calcutta?

Compassion calls us all to identify the Calcuttas around us, those places into which we can go to embody the grace and love of God.

Where can we be the eyes, the arms, the legs, the feet, the mind, the heart and the ears of God? How can we see Jesus in everyone around us, in everyone we meet?

Whom can we invite to dinner whom otherwise would eat alone tonight? How can we show our children the importance of creating community for others who need to know they are valued and loved?

When we send a check to a charity, perhaps we can also send a letter with it, for those who will receive our money—to remind them we see them as real people, not merely a distant figure far away. How about fostering a relationship with them, even from a distance, so they feel the greater power of our awareness and kindness?

How about visiting a neighbor who is homebound? Sit down next to her and ask her to tell you about her day, about her favorite things, about her opinion on an event in the news. Let her know she has a friend and her life, feelings and opinions are of interest to you.

These are Calcuttas. Where can you see more of them?

Forgiven

"On October 2, 2006, my firstborn child, whom I'd cradled in my arms, overseen his first steps, taught to love and serve God, watched grow into a gentle, hard-working man, a loving husband and father—this beloved son walked into an Amish schoolhouse with an arsenal of guns. Before it was over, five precious young girls were dead, five more were seriously injured, and my son had taken his own life.

"Suddenly I had a new identity: the mother of the Amish schoolhouse shooter. I cannot describe my devastation, the gut-wrenching pain, the nights of anguish. All those sweet young lives, families, our own family— changed forever because of a single senseless act of evil and rage committed by my own dear son.

"I would survive this tsunami."

-TERRI ROBERTS

T HE SCENE WAS BUCOLIC. The small white frame schoolhouse. The white picket fence surrounding it. The Amish children playing in the yard. As it came into view, the significance of our visit really hit us.

A half-mile beyond was her home, with its pastoral setting and view.

En route, we passed the ubiquitous souvenir shops and Pennsylvania Dutch restaurants, the horses and buggies and Amish boys on bikes who ride the highways with tractor-trailers and SUV's. We saw countless Amish farms and the acres and acres of fields surrounding them. Even in winter's starkness, the trees bare, the fields barren and snow from a recent record storm remaining where the sun's melting power is slowest to penetrate, the vista was beautiful. Peaceful. Calm. Iconic.

How could such a place hold the memory of such a painful day?

Her smile and warm greeting made us instantly feel as if we were in the company of an old friend, our spirits connecting on a deeper level than would be expected for someone we were meeting for the very first time. She welcomed us into her beautiful sunroom and offered us hot cups of tea.

"This is where I spend most of my time. It's my refuge. I love it so much." Above the door to the room there hung a large wooden plaque reading: *It is well with my soul.*

Windows on three sides framed the countryside beyond them—a neighboring Amish farm, a row of evergreen trees, the multiple bird feeders providing sustenance during the fallow winter months. The walls' yellow color provided a constant reminder of the sun on sunless days. A cushioned window seat held her laptop, a lifeline to the world, especially to the communities of people with whom she endures a uniquely awful kind of loss. On the seat were a few stacks of books, including the two we had recently sent her—a cancer devotional written by Michael as well as our first book written together.

We commented on the comfort and beauty of the sunroom.

"Do you know how we got it? Three days after the shooting, an Amish builder came to visit us. Previously, we had talked with him about adding it on to the back of the house; I'd always wanted one. But the expense was more than I thought we could handle, especially because we had already designated our savings. The money was for the Christmas Disney Cruise our family would take to give the children a new focus for such a major holiday.

"About five or six weeks later he asked if I still wanted the sunroom to be built. I couldn't believe it. When I told him building it probably wasn't the best thing to do, especially in light of the expense and what had just happened, he responded 'You need this.'"

"So, they came and built it! We paid for some of the cost. But a large portion of it was a gift. Can you believe such graciousness? We've been blessed with generous spirits such as his throughout these last nine years. The Amish community has been simply incredible."

"Your story—and the Amish response within it—inspires us so much," we replied.

A few weeks before, we had heard her on a radio interview. She talked about her book, *Forgiven: the Amish School Shooting, A Mother's Love, and a Story of Remarkable Grace* and about the metastatic stage four cancer she was living with. Her extraordinary story is powerful, persistently stubborn to shake—both in its pathos and in its redemption.

We reached out after the interview and asked if we could meet. We knew instantly when we had heard her we had a strong and common bond in common—a belief in the absolute importance of taking our brokenness and wounds and allowing them to be used as a source of hope and healing for others. She is doing it through the horrific events surrounding the loss of her son and through the cancer challenging her physically, emotionally and spiritually every single day, including the day of our visit. She agreed, noting depending on her strength on the day of our scheduled meeting, she may have to postpone our time together. Thankfully, in spite of her notable discomfort that morning, she was still able and willing to meet. We were exceedingly grateful for her graciousness and generosity of time and spirit.

In talks to groups and media interviews, including in a TEDx talk to prisoners at Pittsburgh (PA) State Prison, she describes the two gifts given to her husband and her on the day of "the happening," as the Amish community calls it. Among the many family members and friends who flooded their home to offer consolation, the first gift was their neighbor Henry, an Amish man. After massaging her husband Chuck's slumped shoulders, Henry spoke to him, "Roberts, we love you. We don't (hold) anything against you. We forgive. We forgive your son . . ."

Such unexpected, amazing grace helped her husband and her to realize on that very day they would heal. The second gift was a counselor, named Betsy, whom they had never met before, who came to their house along with a pastor. Betsy asked her if she had good memories of the almost 33 years they had together with their son. Of course, in spite of the horrific events of the day, she did have many good memories. Betsy encouraged her to think about those memories, to take her mind back to the wonderful memories of her son Charlie. She reminded her whatever our worst day might be, that day is not our whole life. It is simply one moment of our life. This insight helped her so much, she recalls. She believes God gave them Henry and Betsy on the very first day to give them hope for all the difficult and confusing days to come.

It was absolutely the darkest day of her life. She cried out to God in bed at the end of the day,

"This is so awful. It's as bad as it gets."

Never had she heard of a crime worse than what her son committed. She prayed to be given a way to use the day for God's glory, for her son's actions to be redeemed. She remembers the prayer, her request, every day now as she strives to redeem the awfulness and the horror.

She told us about one of her surviving sons—Zach—who declared on the night of his brother's death, "I will not be coming to my brother's funeral. I hate him for what he has done. I will not honor him by being there."

She knew Zach would regret it some day, his refusal to come to his brother's funeral. In the days following, she asked everyone who came into their home to pray for a "heart change" for Zach. One of their Amish friends (the builder) asked what he could do for them; she asked him to pray, as well.

"Can I give him a call, too?"

He didn't get to talk with Zach directly when he called. He left a message on Zach's answering machine. Whatever the message said, it changed Zach's heart. The day before his brother's funeral, he called to say when he could be picked up from the local train station. That change of heart was another gift to their family.

Many more gifts came the next day. At her son's grave, as he was laid to rest, 30-40 Amish people attended the service. They formed a protective barrier around her family, shielding them from the cameras of the news reporters out on the road at the edge of the cemetery. They offered the gift of their presence and of privacy, to give her terribly shattered family some peace in the final moment with her son. Following the committal, the first to greet and embrace Chuck and Terri were the parents who had two young daughters die at the hand of their son. Another moment of amazing, remarkable grace.

"Forgiveness is a choice we make," is the mantra she tells us and every other audience to which she speaks. "It is not a feeling. It is not an emotion. It is a daily, conscious, intentional choice. Once the choice is made the feelings and emotions will follow."

Even the Amish community admits forgiveness is not an easy choice. They too acknowledge a decision has to be made every day to do it. "Forgive and you will be forgiven." These words of Jesus, in Luke 6, compel them to obey.

Theirs is an example for all of us to follow.

Five young girls died by her son's hand. Five more received injuries that have taken years of healing, and the healing continues. One of those girls, the most severely injured, Rosanna, is 15 years old as we write this. She is nourished by a feeding tube and is dependent on a wheelchair. Rosanna cannot talk, but is able to make sounds that can be interpreted and understood. Rosanna's family has welcomed Terri into their home to help nurture and encourage Rosanna. For years Terri spent every Thursday evening with her. Now to conserve her strength because of the cancer she lives with, Terri must limit her visits to every other Thursday night.

The first few visits left Terri "an emotional basket case." After them, she pleaded with God, "Okay. If you want me to do this you need to be my strength."

The visits got easier. Today, Rosanna and Terri are intimate friends. Terri is utterly thankful for this gift. She is thankful for Rosanna's family and the community embracing her and her family. Their relationship is one of the most fulfilling relationships of Terri's life and the most endearing one to emerge from "The Happening."

"Now she comes and visits me."

The tears in her eyes and the catch in her voice as she describes their special relationship touched our hearts. Powerful.

We asked her if she and her family have received many hateful, harsh expressions from others about that day. She said, very few. Nearly all of the things others have said to them have been supportive, kind, gracious. We wondered why does she think it's so?

"It was the Amish community's response" she replied without hesitation. "Forgiveness frees us. Their forgiveness freed others to let go of the destructive anger, bitterness and condemnation. It freed us too."

In interviews she says her son built a prison in his mind.

"Any prison in our mind is worse than any cancer. It's worse than any walls we can live in. We do not need to allow these things to bind and blind us."

She described very openly for us the events of the day, in 2006, which so dramatically changed her life forever. How she heard the news. How she fell to the ground in a fetal position, wailing in utter horror and disbelief in her son's yard, feeling as if everything inside of her would be expelled. How the Amish community responded with an unearthly word of forgiveness. How her relationship with that community has only deepened and grown throughout the last decade. How she has traveled to other places of horror and devastation to meet with other mothers and fathers and brothers and sisters and children and friends in places that have become all too much a part of the American, and the world's, lexicón—places such as Sandy Hook and Aurora, and many others.

Both she and her husband Chuck immediately thought they would have to move away. Amish farms and families surrounded their home. They thought they could never face those neighbors again. But it never needed to happen. The community surrounding them made it unnecessary. So did the faith they hold dear, which helps them to be grateful and to seek joy.

She chooses every day to seek joy in the midst of her trials. While "The Happening" was the worst thing to ever come to her life, she is a survivor. It was a tsunami of incredible force. Yet she knows it's not the only event in her life, not the final word, not the sum of her experiences.

"There are so many things in life that tear us apart. Where do we choose to forgive and bring even our enemies into our lives? That choice is a gift."

Terri Roberts feels it's more important than ever to recount her story of loss and forgiveness . . . and of finding joy amid the sorrow.

"To my dying day," she said, "I will keep telling this story."

As we prepared to leave, she gave both of us both a copy of her book, first signing it and inscribing it with a reference to this beautiful and poetic biblical passage, Philippians 4: 6-9:

Do not worry about anything, but in everything by prayer and supplica-
tion with thanksgiving let your requests be made known to God. And the

peace of God, which surpasses all understanding, will guard your hearts and your minds in Christ Jesus. Finally, beloved, whatever is true, whatever is honorable, whatever is just, whatever is pure, whatever is pleasing, whatever is commendable, if there is any excellence and if there is anything worthy of praise, think about these things. Keep on doing the things that you have learned and received and heard and seen in me, and the God of peace will be with you. (NRSV)

Those ancient words define her life. We expect they always have. But never more so than since "The Happening." Terri Roberts impressed us deeply. Her spirit of graciousness and gratitude, of forgiveness and joy no matter what the circumstances, is a spirit we pray will continually grow in our lives. It is this spirit we strive to express to the world. For it's what the world needs to rise above the challenges of our present day.

Terri Roberts passed away on August 20, 2017, just as the final edits were being made to this book The cancer's invasion finally ended her physical life several years after the medical community predicted it would.

Terri's faith and compassion were never stronger in those final years. She died as she lived, with courage, with trust, with amazing grace as her guiding lights. Her legacy lives on. We were privileged to have known her.

GOD IS WITH YOU (Michael)

"It is when we notice the dirt that God is most present in us;
it is the very sign of His presence."
-C.S. Lewis

"God whispers to us in our pleasures, speaks in our consciences,
but shouts in our pains: it is His megaphone to rouse a deaf world."
-C. S. Lewis

I T WAS A HOT AUGUST EVENING in Rehoboth Beach, Delaware, a Friday, at the height of the summer tourist season. We joined a family of good friends and headed to a popular steak and seafood restaurant. We were hungry; but we resigned ourselves to the 40-minute wait. We stood in the line snaking out the door and opted for first-available seating.

Waiting with Matthew is never easy. He loses patience, especially when he's hungry. When he's hungry he'll hit, pull hair, squawk, growl, and generally make a scene that attracts a lot of curiosity. So we were relieved when the hostess finally seated us in a big booth by the restaurant's bar.

The bar was dark and loud and full of energy. The activity held our attention as we waited for our food. We watched an old gentleman sitting at the bar who bellowed sporadically to no one in particular. His words were puzzling to understand and everyone around him ignored him. We guessed he might be a regular there. "He's drunk," we concluded as we collectively rolled our eyes. We were simultaneously entertained and disconcerted by his behavior. His "drunkenness" was essentially confirmed in our minds when he slid off his barstool and staggered around the bar continuing to bellow unintelligibly as he went.

He suddenly approached our table, captivated, no doubt, by the unintelligible bellows of someone else—a hungry, impatient Matthew. We tried not to make eye contact as he staggered over to us. He stopped and talked with our son David, who was sitting nearest to him.

We were curious. "What did he want?" we asked after the old man left. "He wanted to know what Matthew was drinking," David replied. "What he was drink-ing!? Why did he want to know that?"

Matthew was drinking his favorite beverage of choice, chocolate milk, a staple nearly every time we went out to eat. The old man wanted to buy him another one, as if he was buying a round of cocktails at the bar. We watched as he spent the next 15 minutes attempting to get a server to pay attention to him. Finally, he got one to listen to his request and another cup of chocolate milk was delivered to our table. The old man beamed, triumphant. Matthew beamed too. It was a suddenly touch-ing moment.

But what happened after dinner as we got up to leave was even more touch-ing.

When the old gentleman saw us preparing to depart, he once more slid off his stool, staggered over to us, and in his loud, unintelligible voice, repeated something three times until we finally understood, "God is with you." "God is with you." "GOD IS WITH YOU."

As he stood close to us, we realized this man was not drunk. Instead, like our son, he was a wounded soul, with disabilities, himself.

His staggering was actually a limp. His bellowing, garbled speech was actually an impediment. His unusual behavior was not the result of too many beers, after all, but the result of his disabilities. The gesture of buying our son another cup of choco-late milk was truly a gift from one wounded soul to another, a recognition they were two connected spirits. His proclamation—"God is with you"—was essentially just that—the truth. We were reminded once more we were not alone in our life with our son. Our unrelenting responsibilities with him, our constant work to keep him healthy and safe and our desire to give him the best life we could give, were not ours to bear in isolation, by ourselves.

The man was the embodiment of the goodness of God to us on a hot summer night. The man, with his own disabilities, responded to another of God's children with disabilities, and his response lifted, encouraged, and reminded us we and Mat-thew are not alone as we grappled to lead a good, happy, normal-as-possible life. We were also reminded about understanding and empathy, by a man who came to us an angel of encouragement and of hope.

Living with the many persistent marks of disability, it's easy to feel over-whelmed and alone. But every once in a while a light shines into the darkness of discouragement and doubt. It pierces the shadows of our misconceptions and illu-minates a gift in our midst sustaining us and helping to carry us through.

We will always be grateful for the old gentleman at the bar. He reminded us of a truth we will never forget. He reached out to us in a way so few could do as poignantly as he could. His message compelled us to look beyond outward appearances to see into another's soul. His gift was not only chocolate milk. It was a greater gift reminding us of an eternal truth—God accompanies us all throughout our lives. God is with us in all of it.

My Painful, Confusing Past Was Never Far Away From Me

*"To live by grace means to acknowledge my whole life story,
the light side and the dark. In admitting my shadow side I learn
who I am and what God's grace means."*
-BRENNAN MANNING

*"To me, having the courage to tell your own story goes hand in hand with
having the curiosity and humility to listen to others' stories."*
-SARAH KAY

H IS SPIRIT is compassionate and gentle. We could tell immediately upon meeting him he had a heart for listening to others. There was something about him exuding love and grace. Once we heard his story, we knew why. Once he exposed the memories of the shame and abuse he received from his older brother, we knew where his humility and curiosity to listen with intention to others came from. Out of his own brokenness emerged his compassionate, gentle spirit. Out of it came a desire to help others find healing and release from the demons threatening them. We honor him for offering it here. In his own words, this is his story. May it offer all of us an opportunity to learn how pain and confusion can begin to be redeemed, even when we continue to wrestle with our demons . . . .

I do not have a good recall when it all began. It was at a very young age, maybe five or six. How my older brother learned to do what he did to me puzzles me, when I look back on this nightmare.

I always shared a room with him growing up, which led to frequent occurrences. Since it started so young I did not even realize it was not what was supposed to happen, until I was heading into my teenage years. It caused such confusion on my part in regards to not only my identity but being raised in the church.

My brothers and I were teased as little boys from some of my dad's acquaintances and friends. They would call us names and my father just stood there and laughed with them and never stood up to defend us. I would always

252

*wonder why he would not come to our rescue. Was there something wrong
with me?*

*My father was always absent; his job took up a lot of time. When he did
have free time he spent it mostly with his friends at the golf course or at a local club drinking. When my father would drink he had a very short fuse and
the smallest of things would set him off. Occasionally this would lead to him
becoming very physical with my brothers and me. I would walk on eggshells
when I saw he had been drinking.*

*I felt as if I was there to produce things to please him and make him
proud. It was always on my mind—to seek approval so I felt he "liked"
me. No matter what I did, in my mind, it was flawed in my father's
eyes.*

*When I was a teenager I started dating girls, but the situation with my
brother did not change. I was always dealing with such shame and guilt,
wondering what God thought of me. I honestly felt God was disgusted and
did not really want anything to do with me. I continued to struggle with my
identity and wondered about what lifestyle I would take into adulthood. I
started being sexually active with girls to try to bury what had happened to
me over so many years. I labeled myself a fake!*

*I felt as if I was a disappointment, deserving God's wrath and punish-
ment.*

*I was afraid of relationships. I was afraid they would end and I would
be hurt. I was afraid to open up to trust anyone and be vulnerable. I would
be superficial and purposefully keep people at a distance. Because I was constantly feeling hurt, I resisted any thoughts of commitment.*

*In college I was introduced to drugs and drinking and I embraced it with
open arms. I was able to escape my past and the thoughts invading my mind.
I felt so free and alive, but it was temporary and not real.*

*During college I did not want anything to do with church or religion. I
would avoid going home so I would not disappoint my mother by not going to
church. A voice would constantly remind me of my past and how that defined
me now and in the future.*

*Like a lot of single people, everyone was trying to fix me up with other
single women. I resisted for months before I gave in and dated one particular
girl. I fell in love and we were married very quickly. Soon after we were married, my wife and I began having a family. My focus was on my wife and
children even though my painful, confusing past was never far away from
me. My wife and my immediate family are—and have always been—the*

rocks keeping me grounded and motivate me to persevere and continue to fight for my own wellbeing.

I started being involved in church again for the sake of my family; I was awakened through a pastor who I would learn to trust and love. It was a great few years. I felt security and peace because I was no longer constantly reminded by my thoughts of the past. But, security and peace did not last because my past was still with me.

With the age of technology came the temptation and opportunity to dive into images reminding me of my past and acting as a medication for my wounds. But doing so resulted in a deepening of the confusion of my self-image and definition.

I got to the point where I started losing hope of ever being free of my past. It held me captive. In my hopelessness I started feeling like living was not really worth the pain and I contemplated leaving this earth. I was sitting at a men's Bible study, and after it was over the pastor leading it came up to me and asked me if I needed to talk to someone. I was shocked because I hid so well; how did he know? I told him I did need to talk to someone. I shared with him how I was feeling and about my past but I left out all the details.

Soon after my meeting with the pastor, God put into my path a few men who I got to know. Because of their willingness to be vulnerable, I began feeling as if I was in a safe place. I started testing the waters and revealed little pieces of my past that I felt would not disclose my deep struggles. The men seemed to simply listen, not rushing in to try and fix me. They actually seemed to enjoy being around me and I began to think they looked at me as a good friend. I continued over time to tell a little more, but I never revealed my deep secrets.

My older brother died. I was sad. But a part of me was relieved. I was not able to grieve. Several weeks after his death, I visited the mountains of Colorado. In the middle of the night I could not sleep. So I got dressed and hiked into the woods. I was alone and crying out to God. I could not find the words to say, so I began saying out loud, "I love you God."

I felt I heard God say, "I know you do."

I felt God telling me, "You need to forgive your brother."

I struggled with the thought of forgiving him. But after much weeping and talking with God, I finally was able to tell my brother I forgave him. God was not done with me. I felt God telling me, "Now you need to tell your brother you love him." I finally told him I loved him. God then said to me, "Now you can grieve your brother."

I wept for what seemed like hours. I came back down off the Colorado mountain, looking very much like someone who had been crying and had not gotten any sleep. When asked by the men I was with what had happened, I was able to share what God had done for me during the night.

I was doing really well for a short time after forgiving him, but for some reason it did not last. The original group of men I was with by this time had all gone their separate ways, so again I felt the lack of commitment and abandonment. No one is ever in it for the long haul.

God graciously brought another group of men to surround me. In this group there is still a core group who has stuck with it. I was able to go deep with two of the men in particular. We spent several days sharing together away from the normal surroundings and just enjoyed each other's company. Their intent was to bare my soul with them, so they could better understand me and walk with me in this journey. God knows how I need to see God in the flesh through other men speaking in my life. These men, one in particular, continue to walk with me today.

But I just seem unable to shake off the self-image that I have carried all these years.

So the struggles still continue. I do not think I will ever be rid of them. I hope the day comes, and soon, when I can fully accept God's grace and love in me the way I believe it for others.

We believe God creates us all out of love. Because we are so loved we also believe God wants us to love one another—and to love ourselves as well. We wanted our friend to know this truth, to love himself because he is a beloved child of God. His painful, confusing past doesn't have to define him or hold him captive anymore. Those who have hurt much, have the wondrous potential to love much by giving and receiving grace.

Author Brendan Manning has written, "Perhaps the simplest, though certainly not the easiest, place to start is with myself. Carl Jung, the great psychiatrist, once reflected that we are familiar with the words of Jesus, 'Whatever you do to the least of my brethren, that you do unto me.' Then Jung asked a probing question: 'What if you discovered that the least of the brethren of Jesus, the one who needs your love the most, the one you can help the most by loving, the one to whom your love will be most meaningful—what if you discovered that this least of the brethren of Jesus . . . is you?' Then do for yourself what you would do for others."

His Brothers' Love (Michael)

*"Here is what love is like—genuine love. God's kind of love. It's patient.
It can wait. It helps others, even if they never find out who did it. Love
doesn't look for greener pastures or dream of how things could be better if
I just got rid of all my current commitments. Love doesn't boast. It doesn't
try to build itself up to be something it isn't. Love doesn't act in a loose, im-
moral way. It doesn't seek to take, but it willingly gives. Love doesn't lose its
cool. It doesn't turn on and off. Love doesn't think about how bad the other
person is, and certainly doesn't think of how it could get back at someone.
Love is grieved deeply (as God is) over the evil in this world, but it rejoices
over truth.*

*"Love comes and sits with you when you're feeling down and finds out
what is wrong. It empathizes with you and believes in you. Love knows
you'll come through just as God planned, and sticks right beside you all the
way. Love doesn't give up, or quit, or diminish or go home. Love keeps on
keeping on, even when everything goes wrong and the feelings leave and
the other person doesn't seem as special anymore. Love succeeds 100 percent
of the time. That, my friend is what real love is."*

-DAVID SANFORD,
(LOVE: A PARAPHRASE OF 1 CORINTHIANS 13, EXCERPT)

OH, THE DARK PLACES our minds can take us sometimes, revealing where
our most powerful fears lie.

Kathy and I hadn't realized the anxiety we had generated for Adam and David
when we asked them both if they could come home from college for the weekend.
There was something we needed to talk about with them.

I had decided, with Kathy's support, to step away from actively pastoring a church.
The growing responsibilities related to Matthew's needs, Kathy's health concerns and my
own spiritual and professional life were making it increasingly complicated to manage
well without making some significant changes. I didn't know exactly what I'd do next.
But I knew I couldn't be available for what was needed at home and still serve in the
church full-time. Before we told anyone else, we wanted the boys to know.

They reacted well to the announcement. They certainly understood. In fact, they were relieved. Greatly. They admitted to us they feared we were going to tell them we could no longer support Matthew at home anymore. They were worried we were going to send him to a group home, away from our family, giving others the responsibility of having primary and day-to-day care for him. They were concerned how such a move could weaken our family structure and the bond we all had with him and with one another. They were afraid his living conditions would diminish and he wouldn't be loved as well by others, or as completely, outside of our home. Those are realistic concerns, most definitely.

If there was ever-stronger evidence they loved their younger brother deeply, intensely, unconditionally, it was this moment. Their reaction told us how committed Adam and David were to Matthew. They announced to us that day how they were unwavering in their desire to take responsibility for him, along with us in our home and in their homes after we could not. There is no greater joy for us than in knowing their devotion and compassion for their brother, who depends on the love of others to keep him safe and secure.

> *Love comes and sits with you when you're feeling down and finds out what is wrong. Love . . . sticks right beside you all the way. Love doesn't give up, or quit, or diminish or go home. Love keeps on keeping on, . . . that, my friend is what real love is.*

I cannot begin to express in any sort of adequate way how grateful I am for Mathew's older brothers and for whom they have grown up to be. I cannot begin to convey how unmistakably proud I am of them. They stick by us and with Matthew all the way, when so many siblings in similar situations do not.

Having a sister or brother with disabilities, one who takes an inordinate amount of their parents' time and energy, has the very real potential of causing deep resentment—toward the sibling as well as the parents. The potential for bitterness, for feeling as if the brother or sister with such profound needs gets all the attention, is strong. To our knowledge, Adam and David do not have such resentment, such bitterness. If either of them does, they have never expressed it to us, nor have we ever seen it. I cannot begin to tell you how grateful Kathy and I are for the strength of character they possess. Both of them have never been anything but loving—extraordinarily, generously loving—with Matthew and about Matthew from the very beginning of his life.

Love, as David Sanford's paraphrase of 1 Corinthians 13 states . . . *sticks right beside you all the way. Love doesn't give up, or quit, or diminish or go home.*

From the beginning, Adam and David accepted and cherished Matthew as part of our home—an integral part of our home—and they never ran away from the realities, from him. He is a major aspect of their inspiration and their motivation as husbands, fathers and sons. The connection they each have with him, inspires them in their connections with their young families at home.

When they were in high school, I used to get several long weekends off every year while I was a pastor at our church. Kathy and I made certain one or two of those weekends each year would be set aside just for Adam and David, for the four of us to do something relaxing and fun without the responsibility we had with Matthew. We would always go places where it would not have been possible to go with Matthew. Often we'd go to New York City overnight; we saw several Broadway shows, a major league baseball game, visited a number of historical museums and toured behind the scenes at Madison Square Garden. Kathy and I felt those weekends were important, one small way to remind Adam and David we believed they were just as important to us as Matthew is. He got so much of our energy; we never wanted his brothers to feel as if they were less important to us. It was an opportunity for all of us to do something without the limitations and added responsibilities inherent with Matthew. We could focus only on our older sons and it would allow all of us to let our guards down for just a few days.

We were never so touched as the time when one of these special weekends approached; we talked with the boys about what they might like to do with the upcoming weekend. We offered several options, places and activities that would have been complicated to include Matthew. They, instead, responded,

"No. This time we want him to go with us. We want to do something he would like too. We want all five of us to be together, somewhere he'd like too."

They offered—without prompting and to our surprise—an option including him. They didn't want him to stay at home. Instead, they wanted him to come along. I'll never forget how I felt hearing their response—how pleased and touched and elated I was. They so obviously loved and delighted in their brother.

Love sticks beside you all the way.

When Adam lived in Germany for those couple of years, he paid for Kathy and me to fly over to visit for 10 days. My mother also came along. During the trip when we were away, David and Janelle—who were married and had no children yet—stayed at our house with Matthew. This was both boys' gift to us for our 30th wedding anniversary. A generous offering. A few years earlier, before both of them were married, they banded together to send Kathy and me to Hawaii, where my brother Steve and his family were living. They took turns staying at our home with their younger brother so we could make the trip. Another generous offering. We will be forever thankful for their sensitivity. We're a team, the four of us. A good team, and stronger as a family because of the shared experiences we have had with Matthew.

It takes a team to love and not *give up, or quit, or diminish or go home.*

When he was a senior in high school, Adam wrote a few articles about life with Matthew, for his football yearbook and for the ARC of Dauphin County (PA), where Kathy works as an advocate. Here are excerpts of what he expressed,

> *The most special thing football has done for me has been the formation of a special bond between myself and my youngest brother Matthew. He is not one for showing affection and unless he identifies you with something he enjoys or something he wants, he will ignore you altogether. Matthew became a football fan the moment I brought my equipment home the summer preceding my freshman year of high school . . . As I was trying on my equipment, Matthew came into the room and gave me an ear to ear grin of approval. From that moment until the season began, Matthew started carrying my helmet around wanting me to put it on for him . . .*

> *Because Matthew cannot walk very well, my family and I cannot often do things we would like to do. Taking him on trips is usually difficult and when we do he usually breaks something. He also does not like to be away from home for long periods. My brother David and I have spent many nights watching him to give our parents a break . . . Everybody in our family has made huge sacrifices. My father's decision to move to Hershey was greatly influenced because Matthew had doctors at the Medical Center . . .*

> *By living with Matthew, I learned to be patient with people with disabilities. I have also learned that no matter how hard it is to figure out what he wants, it is even more frustrating for him. He has brought our family closer and I think he has caused me to put family first. I think he has prepared me for parenthood more than anything else I could possibly experience. Matthew has also shown me that I should not get caught up in petty things.*

> *As for living with Matthew, I believe I could make it through anything in life, because the experience has made me a better person.*

Adam and David do not shy away from changing Matthew's diapers, from feeding him, from helping to get him dressed, from picking him up, literally, when we cannot. They often volunteer to take him with them when they sense us needing a break.

I poignantly remember the week when Matthew was in the hospital for spinal decompression surgery. The week had been a draining one. Matthew had several

MRIs. The surgery was changed and delayed a number of times. Waiting was a burden. We were emotionally exhausted. After a phone conversation with Kathy, as he called to check in on specifics of the changing circumstances, Adam could sense acute weariness in Kathy's voice. The next thing we knew, David was calling. He offered to come directly to the hospital, to stay with Matthew so we could get a break and go home. He suggested we go have lunch somewhere and not eat hospital food, for a change. The boys had quietly talked with one another and knew how the stress of Matthew's sudden decline was beginning to get to us. Their concern was yet another confirmation for us of how they are very loving brothers and sons.

Both young men were insistent Matthew be a full participant in their weddings, dressing him in the same colors and neckties of their groomsmen. It was vital to them for him to be included as much as he could be. Adam and David were each other's best men, one testament to the unbending ties, which can bind a family with a member who lives with disabilities. They both married remarkable, understanding young women who readily accepted Matthew as an integral part of their own families—knowing they may be helping to watch over him for the rest of their lives. Adam and David loved having Matthew with them at all their football and baseball games growing up. David wanted him included at the ceremonies and in the photos at each of his swearing in ceremonies as the Pennsylvania Department of Aging deputy secretary. Adam flew home from Germany, where he was working at the time on a two and a half year project, to be present at Matthew's high school graduation.

One day they will be responsible for him, fully, when we cannot. One day beyond, most likely one of their children may be Matthew's guardian when Adam and David cannot. Our hearts already warm to see their very young children relate with aplomb and without fear to Matthew's unusual movements, noises, peculiarities and disabilities. Nothing helps us to rest more assured than knowing this. Adam and David raising their children to love their unique uncle - to not be afraid of him, as nearly every other kid is, to accept him for who he is as a valued part of our family—brings great peace to our souls.

That, my friend is what real love is.

Let-Me-Show-You

"Not being forgiven can be a very dark and confining place. And not being able to forgive can create its own kind of claustrophobia. We're called to seek forgiveness and to forgive others. When people are able to forgive there is a sense of release, a sense of openness and light. This is resurrection."
-Br. Mark Brown

"To forgive is to set a prisoner free and discover that the prisoner was you."
-Lewis B. Smedes

"Then Peter came to him and asked, 'Lord, how often should I forgive someone who sins against me? Seven times?' 'No, not seven times,' Jesus replied, 'but seventy times seven!'"
-Matthew 18:21-22 (NLT)

S HE INVITED US to chronicle a part of her ongoing journey out of deep discomfort—toward forgiveness. She knows it can help her to redeem her past and its damage. She prays it can help others to find a way to redeem theirs too. In her own words, this is what she wants others to know:

I felt the arms of Jesus wrapped around me that day and His gentle whisper in my ear, "Oh child, I love you so; I know the depth of your agony and I'm here with you. I've always been with you. We can do this!"

I told Him that I wanted to forgive, for him, for me, but that I was afraid and didn't know how. His response was simple, "I know."

So I asked Him how to do it. Again, His response was a simple one,

"Let-me-show-you." *I got out my notepad a few days before Christmas, and started writing him a letter. With tears streaming down my face, saturating the pages in front of me, I wrote:*

"God loves you more than you could ever imagine. He loves you into the very depths of your soul. You are forgiven, and given the total freedom of any

hate, anger, or words thrown in your face. I'm forgiving the inexcusable in you because God has forgiven the inexcusable in me too. You are loved!"

When I was in eighth grade my brother put a gun to my head and proceeded to take advantage of me.

He raped me.

When the gun became present in the room, the only thing I could think was I'm not going to see my dad again. My dad was my best friend. My only choice was let him rape me or let him shoot me. I guess I kind of subjected to him at that point because I wanted to see my dad again. The gun was not an option for me. I had no good options.

There was a wonderful counselor at school who noticed my behavior patterns changing after the rape. I started skipping classes and missing assignments. She invited me to eat lunch with her one day—as you guys did today—and my world has forever shifted. I started exploring with her, as I'm doing with the two of you, about the darkest, most horrific moments, of my life. What a scary, but much needed relief. It was the first time I ever admitted any of it with any other person, the first time I felt comfortable enough to do it. Light and resurrection was happening.

In Matthew's Gospel, one of Jesus' best friends, Peter, approached Jesus asking Him a sincere question:

"How often should I forgive someone who sins against me?" His question is the same question I have asked Jesus—every day—literally every damn day.

As I meditated on the actual word Forgiveness, breaking it down in my head, I noticed three distinct parts to the word.

The first part of the word is the word FOR. Who is forgiveness for? I asked Jesus.

Forgiveness is, for, ME, was his response!

For the longest time, I thought forgiveness was strictly for the other person—and that bothered me. Why should he get off that easy!? People kept pressuring me to forgive because it was the "right thing to do." "Life is too short to hold on to resentments," friends and family members would say. Had they ever been through all I had been through? Did they have the right? They didn't understand the depth of my pain. That one act has forever changed my life!!!

There's the second part of the word—GIVE. ForGIVEness is a gift from God and a gift you give yourself, allowing the burden to be lifted from your heart and spirit. I have come to learn that true forgiveness is a wonderful *gift that enables me to move on, to begin to heal, to allow light into my life again.*

One Sunday morning my pastor offered a quote by an anonymous author, "Holding resentment is like drinking poison and waiting for the other person to keel over," he read.

Something clicked. For so much of my life, I was drinking poison and hoping he would die; but in reality, I was only killing myself. I resented my brother so much.

Let-me-show-you.

Forgiveness is a gift; it's a gift you give to yourself, certainly, but it's also a HUGE gift you are giving to the one who hurt you.

I thought that I was ready to volunteer at the rape crisis center in town. I sat with other girls who had been raped or abused. But I wasn't ready. It was too soon, too raw. My emotions were shredded. I needed to back away from that. Until I had found more healing and worked through this thing called forgiveness even more, I knew that I couldn't be any good to others who were still so raw and in such deep pain too. I was still a mess.

At the end of the word forgiveness are the letters 'ness'. As I stared at the word that day, with tears in my eyes, I misread the letter (n) with a letter (m).

'Yes! That's it. Forgiving is MESSY', I shouted!

There are so many days when I don't want to forgive—and in those moments I need to beg God to show me how.

Let-me-show-you.

Forgiveness isn't a one-time deal, especially when so much of my life has changed because of what happened to me. Every day, literally every damn day, I have to ask God to help me forgive him. Forgiving my brother doesn't change my past, but it does change my future, and it starts in this moment—EACH moment.

Here are a few principles I live by because I have to: Forgiveness is not the following:

An automatic friendship or relationship

An Erasing of the pain

Okaying the damage that's been done

Allowing the other person to repeat a hurtful act again and again.

Forgiveness is messy. One of my favorite authors is Glennon Doyle Melton. She writes: "Life is so hard; with God and with other people, life is still so hard. What I am learning though is that hard part of life can transform me. But it can only transform me if I refuse to run from it or numb it."

I refuse to run from the pain and no longer try to numb it with the poison. I just give myself an extra amount of grace on those days when I am resentful. I don't try to control my emotions, I simply let them run their course, and I beg God to love through me . . . because there are many moments when I simply can't. You don't just forgive the words and actions that happened to you. You forgive the everyday after, the tears, the moments of asking why, the way it affects your relationships and marriage, your parenting skills, the bitterness you toss to innocent people. All of it! Last year, several of our family members got together for Thanksgiving dinner. My brother and I sat across from one another at the dinner table. It was one of the most awful things I had ever had to do. God, what the hell am I doing here!!! I can't believe this.

Let-me-show-you. *My brother and I currently do not have a friendship, or even try to be brother and sister. That's okay! Forgiveness does not call for that.*

Love yourself enough to forgive, for you.

Sometimes I feel so alone, especially in crowded rooms and situations. I remember what it felt like on both my wedding day and on Thanksgiving Day with my brother sitting across from me, feeling as if no one else there could understand just how utterly unsettling it was to be there with him.

It would be oppressive to have as much grace if I had to see him every day. I might leave God out of the picture and not have God between me and my brother. My thoughts and responses might not be so gracious. I need the space from him to help me hold onto forgiveness, to not let what he did keep punching me in the face, in the heart.

In our earlier book we related a story about the Dutch Christian author Corrie ten Boom's experience in Munich, Germany following World War II, speaking in a church basement about the need to forgive after the horrific violence and destruction of the war. ten Boom detailed her own concentration camp imprisonment as the result of her family's exposure from their covert work of hiding Jews so they would not be imprisoned. She traveled throughout Germany witnessing to the importance of releasing the agony, anger and guilt over all she—and the German people—had experienced and lost.

Following her talk on a cold, dark night, a man approached her whose appearance caused her instant horror when she saw him. He was the most feared, cruel guard in all the camp where she was held, the one who had most terrorized Corrie and her sister Betsie and so many others. The former guard reached out to her, following her admonition to forgive, and asked for her pardon for the evil he had done.

Corrie hesitated for what seemed like an eternity, not certain if she could actually practice the forgiveness she preached. But something came over her and compelled her to reach out her hands to his and she relates an electric charge went through her as powerful as anything she had ever felt:

> *For a long moment we grasped each other's hands, the former guard and the former prisoner. I had never known God's love so intensely as I did then.*

We related this beautiful redemption story during an autumn preaching tour at several churches. The reaction following our sermon about the call and need to forgive, at one of those churches, stands out powerfully to us.

A man raised his hand during the prayer time after we finished speaking: "I am 94 years old. The concentration camp you talked about, I was there to help liberate it. I saw the graves. I saw the ovens. I saw the people who remained. It was a terrible sight. I saw what they did. I'll never forget it."

The silence was electric. In our very presence was an eyewitness to that horrific time and place. We didn't have words to respond. He continued:

"I struggled, mightily, to forgive what I saw—to forgive the Nazis who did what they did, to forgive the townspeople who closed their eyes to what was happening right there in their midst, to forgive the world leaders who turned a blind eye, too, to what was happening. Forgiving evil of such magnitude is nearly impossible. At this age, I'm still working on it. Something like that doesn't leave you. I have great respect for someone like the woman you talked about. I need to let her example help to show me how my forgiveness can be complete."

His words brought a perfect coda to our message, better than any we could have given. He personalized the story. He was witness to the horror, a link to that awful past.

What's also important to remember is that we can and need to invite others to help us to move toward forgiveness. It's often nearly impossible to do the work by ourselves. We pray all of us can have the presence of at least one other person in our lives who can encourage us not to give up when the way is long, meandering and uncertain. We need to allow others to be the earthly presence of Christ in our midst, to point toward the way of forgiveness and peace. Whether it's a counselor, a pastor, a mentor, a friend in faith, a teacher, a respected elder or a someone whom we respect, the person can help us to remain committed and determined to walk the path toward embracing the forgiveness we need for living an abundant life.

Let-Someone-Show-You.

. . . Our Daily Bread (Tom)

"You have not lived today until you have done something for someone who can never repay you."
-JOHN BUNYAN

"That's what I consider true generosity: You give your all and yet you always feel as if it costs you nothing."
-SIMONE DE BEAUVOIR

W E WERE EN ROUTE to a speaking engagement in what seemed like the middle of nowhere. We rolled down the windows to savor the fragrances; the Pennsylvania wildflowers were in full bloom. Things in the car were a bit "stuffy" and fresh air would do us both good. In the back of our minds, we were having a hard time justifying accepting the invitation, expecting the crowd to be a small one, with no set honorarium to cover the cost on our time and travel, let alone the affirmation of our gifts.

I remember saying to Michael, in a very cynical tone, "We may need to stop saying 'yes' to these types of events because they don't seem to help further our mission very much. This trip is costing us a lot. This month our donations have been down and I'm concerned we may be short paying our bills. It's a Tuesday afternoon. I can't imagine too many folks are going to be in attendance. Couldn't we have used this time to do something more 'productive'?"

Michael, in his "glass half-full" demeanor, responded, "I understand your concern. I do. I have the same concerns, sometimes. I know this isn't ideal, but this group seems to relate well to our ministry. Even if there are only a small number of folks here today, I'm sure it will spark some good conversation . . . and maybe we can sell a few books too! Now that we're on our way we have to trust there is a reason we are here today."

His words, although the "right words," weren't the words I wanted to hear in the moment, making me feel even more pessimistic.

Winding through the mountains for another hour or so, we finally reached

our destination, a tiny country church. To my surprise, the parking area was completely full.

Getting out of the car, a woman spotted us from a distance, elatedly yelling our names. We were taken aback with her enthusiasm, "They're here! They're
here! She came over to us and gave us each a big bear hug—it actually felt as if a bear
was hugging us. A few others in the parking lot started excitedly waving too, "Michael and Tom are here!" I remember thinking, "This isn't what I expected, but it is
nice to be noticed!" For a brief moment, very brief, we felt like celebrities about to
walk the red carpet.

Inside the small church narthex, which looked more like an oversized walk in
closet, we noticed a simple stained glass window with an image from the biblical
story of the poor widow with two small coins in her hands.

The woman from the parking lot guided us a few steps to our right, through
the creaky wooden doors, leading to the sanctuary. Opening the doors, we were
overwhelmed by what we saw inside. The church was filled to well more than capacity, standing room only. There were many more people than we expected. We
thought we were speaking to a women's group. But there were a number of children
and a surprising amount of men in the audience too.

It was a picture of the kingdom of heaven—a beautiful mosaic of the children
of God right there before us. We began to be overwhelmed at the sight.

We don't remember exactly what we talked about. But what we do remember
is that we felt God was definitely in our midst. God showed up. People were open
and vulnerable with us. There were some quiet tears. There was a lot of loud laughter. Prayers were offered. It was a wonderful experience.

The most amazing part of the afternoon happened at the end of our presentation. After a final prayer was offered to close the program, the woman who first
excitedly greeted us when we arrived in the parking lot, hopped out of her seat,
creating a loud echo throughout the sanctuary. She grabbed the microphone.

"Before you both arrived today we passed around an offering basket, as a "gift
of love," to help further your ministry. We are so appreciative of you following God's
call and know of the sacrifices, you, and your families, have made. Please accept our
small gift.

$663.46!"

We couldn't believe it. And to this day, we still can't believe it. We never expected an amount of money so large—especially from such a small congregation.

The gift was miraculous. It was miraculous because we knew the kind of sacrifice it took to make it happen. Here was a group of people, many of who were living
on limited incomes, giving all they could with such generous hearts and spirits.

One woman came up to us during the refreshment time following the program and whispered about her life of addiction. She proudly, yet humbly, exclaimed, "I've been clean for two years, twenty-six days, and 14 hours. And two months ago, I gave up smoking. Every day I take the money I would have been using for smoking and put it in this jelly jar. I've been praying and asking God for the right opportunity to give the money away . . . and today was the day! I think your ministry is special and I wish I would have known about it two and a half years ago."

It's a cyclical pattern with me, actually. Something disconcerting happens. I freak out. I can't breathe. I bitch and moan. I vent to a friend. The friend asks, "Tom, where does God fit into all of this?"

"Ugh. Umm. Good question. Where IS God in all of this? If there IS a God, where IS this God? Why isn't God showing up? God, show up. For real."

After brooding for few days about God not coming through, God then comes through. I go through this pattern about, oh, every three or four days.

My name suits me. In the Bible, there is this story about one of Jesus' best friends—Thomas. John 20:24-29 tells us about Thomas (better known by his nickname, "doubting Thomas"). When Thomas first heard Jesus had risen from the dead, he replied,

> "I won't believe it unless I see the nail wounds in his hands, put my fingers into them, and place my hand into the wound in his side." But then eight days later Jesus appeared and the disciples were together again, and this time Thomas was with them. The doors were locked; but suddenly, as before, Jesus was standing among them. "Peace be with you," he said. Then he said to Thomas, "Put your finger here, and look at my hands. Put your hand into the wound in my side. Don't be faithless any longer. Believe!"
>
> "My Lord and my God!" Thomas exclaimed.
>
> Then Jesus told him, "You believe because you have seen me. Blessed are those who believe without seeing me."

What strikes me the most about this story is Thomas was one of Jesus' closest confidants, in Jesus' inner circle or so called "band of brothers." Nonetheless, even though he knew Jesus, spent a great deal of time with him, watched Jesus perform miracle after miracle and answer prayer after prayer, Thomas still questioned. Thomas was still uncertain. Thomas still wondered. After all, all of Thomas' hopes and dreams were dashed just a few days earlier, when Jesus, the long awaited Messiah, died on the cross, cancelling any visions he had for the future. We can't blame him for his skepticism (it's not every day someone raises from the dead). But do we?

One of Michael's and my best friends (whose name also happens to be Tom . . . are you sensing a theme here) finds himself probing—often—too! At 78 years of age, he wants to know the truth about life and its purpose; he does. But he also can't accept things blindly without some sense of reason. He's a rational guy. This presents a problem for him because "faith is believing without seeing," and he knows this. However, he wants to see; so he inquires, often. Does his inquisitive mind make him less faith-ful? We don't think so. In fact, most of us have a healthy dose of skepticism from time to time. One of our favorite authors, Anne Lamott, writes this about her interaction with her friend Father Tom (a.k.a "doubting Thomas"):

> *I have a lot of faith. But I am also afraid a lot, and have no real certainty about anything. I remembered something Father Tom had told me—that the opposite of faith is not doubt, but certainty. Certainty is missing the point entirely. Faith includes noticing the mess, the emptiness and discomfort, and letting it be there until some light returns.*

This might be grossly oversimplifying my doubting spirit, but did God actually know what he was doing when he created me? I often find myself comparing myself to others, completing the following statements:

> *"God, why am I not a better communicator like he is?" "God, why does life seem like it is so much easier for them?" "God, why am I not a superior writer like she is?" "God, why am I not more level headed?? "God, why am so I emotionally volatile?" "God, why am I not a confident leader?" "God, why do things have to be so laborious for me?" "God, why does it seem like you aren't hearing my prayers?" "God, why does it seem like you don't love me, because if you loved me, then. . .?"*

My daily life is a constant flip-flopping between being comfortable in my own skin, to wishing I had a different set of skin, to resting in God's unfathomable love and grace for me, to wondering if God's love is as strong as others tell me it is. This is doubt, for me. Thankfully, the more I read and the more I learn, I understand I'm in good company. There is a whole cast of characters throughout history who doubted. Author Eugene Peterson has written:

> *All the persons of faith I know are sinners, doubters, and uneven performers. We are secure not because we are sure of ourselves but because we trust that God is sure of us.*

There is a phrase, which appears in the story about doubting Thomas I have become especially fond of: *Peace be with you!*

In the middle of Thomas' considerations, deliberations, reflections, and contemplations, Jesus says, "Peace be with you!"

What I'm imagining is Jesus saying to Thomas, "I know you don't get it. I know you want to know the future. I know your mind is working overtime. I know you feel empty on the inside. I know you aren't sure of yourself. But I am offering you rest. I love you. I created you and I knew what I was doing. I wired you with that searching mind and inquisitive heart of yours, and I love it. You want to know me; you do. You want to feel and experience my love. I'll show up and remind you of my love. Just trust me."

And Jesus does show up. He lets Thomas touch his nailed scarred hands. He reminds Thomas of his love and favor.

Michael and I often find ourselves from week to week, praying for God to shed some light into our seemingly dark situation—where we worry every day about bringing in enough income to support our families and our mission. We pray for eyes to see and ears to hear all that God is doing in us, around us, and through us. We pray for simple reminders of God's faithfulness, goodness, love and compassion.

Author Rachel Naomi Remen has written:

> *Perhaps the secret of living well is not in having all the answers but in pursuing unanswerable questions in good company.*

Michael and I don't have the answers, but together, we pursue answers, in good company. We try to surround ourselves with people, like our good friend Tom, who reminds us certainty IS the opposite of faith. To us, faith means asking, probing, questioning, wrestling, wondering, waiting, happening, and yet, believing. It's believing in a God who will show up.

And here is the deal—God does. The gifts and simple reminders, although small sometimes, are what we need to keep following God's leading. In the story of the "Widow's Offering," we find a woman who had almost nothing to give, give her all. Here is how the text reads:

> *Jesus sat down near the collection box in the Temple and watched as the crowds dropped in their money. Many rich people put in large amounts. Then a poor widow came and dropped in two small coins. Jesus called his disciples to him and said, "I tell you the truth, this poor widow has given*

more than all the others who are making contributions. For they gave a tiny part of their surplus, but she, poor as she is, has given everything she had to live on. (Mark 12: 41-44 NLT).

Three Christmases ago, we were in the middle of sending dozens of Christmas cards as a way of expressing gratitude to our donors and their commitment to our mission throughout the year. The same day we received in the mail a card from a woman we had listened to throughout the year. We opened the envelope to find the card and a $20 bill. With it was a handwritten note:

I cannot thank you enough for your kindness and love throughout this year. This small gift does not come close to expressing how much I value what you have done for me. But it's from the heart . . . Merry Christmas!

That gift was like a million dollars to us. We knew she didn't have much money to give. We knew of her fragile economic circumstances, she was living on the brink of homelessness. Just as the story of the "widow's offering" was about a woman who gave sacrificially to support the work of her temple, our friend's gift was given sacrificially. It was generous and warmly given. It was gratefully and warmly received.

In one of her first messages to us, four years ago, she wrote:

Michael and Tom,

I opened my email at 6:00 a.m. and read your note, but didn't have time to respond since I had to leave for work. I couldn't wait to get home to thank you—there are no adequate words to express how touched and grateful I am for your kind response. I cried when I read it. I don't know how it is that I can tell two people I don't even know all these deep dark secrets of my life and actually feel liberated. Or maybe "lighter" is a better way to describe how I feel.

I will most likely tell you more of my story—since I'm now finding that it is a little less painful to tell it when I'm not just talking to myself. It makes sense to do this—there is a purpose. I so did not want to have my life come to an end with all this still inside me.

If you are touching and helping other people like me, you both must be angels sent straight from heaven. And this is from a non-believer (sort of).

Just when we need a word of affirmation that we are making a positive difference in someone's life or a gift that provides us with the money we need to pay a necessary bill, we always—always—receive it. We doubt, so often. We question and we sometimes despair. We go to dark and anguished places internally and we have long discussions about our fears. There are times we toss and turn and can't fall asleep thinking about it. We wake up at three in the morning with thoughts of gloom at the forefront of our minds. We toss and turn some more.

But, after all the doubting, after all the sleepless nights and intense discussions, a small country church takes an offering and overwhelms us with its generosity. A woman who has given up smoking offers us her cigarette savings. Another woman sends us a heavenly message about our impact. And she sends us a gift from the depths of her heart, sacrificially, graciously.

But there's even more. In those gifts and through those words, we are offered a deeper sense of peace, a peace that Jesus offered us through his life, his death and his resurrection. Just when we are wont to despair, God reminds us our daily bread is given, we do not have to starve for anything that we need.

I am reminded once more of Eugene Peterson's words:

> All the persons of faith I know are sinners, doubters, and uneven per- formers. We are secure not because we are sure of ourselves but because we trust that God is sure of us.

It is there, on this foundation of trust, where I need to remember to stand every day. It is there where I find my hope and my help, in the name of the one who loves me infinitely, eternally. It is there where I draw my strength and my faith.

I've learned over the years (and am continuing to learn) being moved with compassion toward myself is most disquieting. Yet, knowing I'm within a great cloud of witnesses who all had their own suspicions, enquiries, and ambiguities, about God and about themselves, gives me great comfort and reassurance. Once again, I am not alone.

Our Human Compassion

T
HE BLINDS WERE DRAWN. The room was darkened on a sunny afternoon. Her downcast posture and demeanor signaled her depression and fatigue.

It was our first meeting with her.

We learned she had stage four cancer, most likely in the end stages. The only times she got out, especially in the icy, cold winter season in which we visited, were to go to the doctor or for her chemotherapy treatments.

She was lonely, defeated and simply worn out.

The cancer had persisted relentlessly for years. The agony wouldn't go away. Sleep was always interrupted and intermittent. Surviving entirely on Social Security, she depended on a local food bank to provide enough food; most months it wasn't quite enough. To make it worse, the holidays had just ended and it wasn't the best of seasons for her. It wasn't just because of the cancer and its plethora of relentlessly debilitating side effects. It was also because of the people she loved the most – her family. She had spent most of the season alone. Stuck much of the time at home, she had very few visitors. Memories of celebratory Thanksgivings, merrier Christmases and happier New Years saddened her. She feared there would be no more of them.

Her tears punctuated the telling of her story. Her living room walls were filled with photos of a large extended family; four generations of faces and milestones dominated the room. She spoke of losses and longing, of limitations and lament: Her late husband. Her parents. Her brothers who don't keep in close touch. Those whom she nurtured and to whom she devoted her life often hurt and disappointed her. It was not the way she had imagined her life would be.

Now, in her most vulnerable season, she feared the loneliness her health and age would surely continue to bring.

We asked her what keeps her going, what sees her through.

"My faith," she responded. "It's the one thing I have giving me the strength I need to do what I have to do."

As we were preparing to leave, we asked if we could offer a prayer for her. She was eager for one and so we prayed. Her tears spilled more. She embraced us, grateful. We promised we'd return.

A few weeks later, when we did, we were stunned by who greeted us at the door. It was her. But it was a very different her.

This day, the blinds were open. The room was bright on a sunny afternoon. Her more energetic posture and demeanor signaled her happiness and renewed enthusiasm. She was simply not the same woman we had seen just weeks before. We told her what we saw. We asked her why.

"It's because you came to visit me. It's because you sat here with me and listened. It's because you showed me love. You let me tell you all about myself. You didn't interrupt. You didn't tell me what to do. You let me cry and it was okay. You let me tell you things I never told anyone else before. That's why."

It was simple. It was holy. Seeing the difference our presence had made and having her acknowledge it was very holy too.

Another day. Another woman, alone.

Midway through our first visit with her the phone rang. "I'll just let it go to voicemail," she indicated. The answering machine message came on, with her husband's voice: "You've reached our home. We're sorry we missed you. Please leave a message." The three of us sat there for a moment, silent. He had been gone just three weeks. Yet his voice still lived on.

She needed to talk about him, about the sudden and mysterious illness, right after they returned from a wonderful vacation, that sent him to the hospital over the Christmas season and kept him there into the new year. She needed to process the severity of what happened, the crushing, sudden decisions she was forced to make about his treatment, and his death, still so impossible to accept, to comprehend.

Already, others were telling her to delete his voice from the machine. It made them uncomfortable. They reasoned it had to make her uncomfortable too. But it didn't. In fact, hearing his voice actually was a comfort to her.

"It's the only thing I have left. If I delete it from the answering machine I'll never be able to hear his voice again."

We urged her to keep it on there as long as she needed. If it brought a measure of comfort to her, it needed to remain.

Her burden of guilt was so heavy. Did she pray the right words? Did she ask for the right things? Did she have enough faith to save him? Why didn't a miracle happen for her husband, for her?

We reassured her. To our best understanding, it isn't the words of our prayers or the strength of our faith saving another person's life. We remembered the words of 19th century Danish theologian and philosopher Søren Kierkegaard: "The function of prayer is not to influence God, but rather to change the nature of the one who prays."

Her prayers, whatever they were, didn't contribute to her husband's death, we reassured her. Her prayers, instead, enabled her to open a dialogue between her and the one who, perfectly, completely, could understand her sorrow, feel her anguish and accompany her on this toughest journey of her life. We didn't know why a miracle hadn't occurred. We can never answer that question, nor even try to. We simply hold onto the words of wise people, such as Kierkegaard, who have traveled and contemplated the road before us, and others such as C.S. Lewis, who wrote: Prayer, ". . . doesn't change God, but it changes me."

As is typical when someone dies, people show up and spend time and support immediately after it happens. In fact, often it's not helpful, because it's just too much all at once.

We remember our first conversation with her over the phone. "I don't know what to do. My house is filled with people telling me what I should do and I just don't know which way to turn. It's overwhelming."

Others had moved on from those first weeks after his passing. Their lives continued pretty much as they had before. But hers hasn't. Her world has been radically, permanently upended. The circle of people with whom she can safely open up with is growing rapidly smaller. Others lose patience with her continued tears and with her need to talk about how violently and painfully her life has changed.

This is where we believe our mission falls short. Sure, we can visit and listen and respond to her messages. But she and everyone else like her needs and deserves connections with others who will be compassionately present than we alone can provide. We wish we could talk with her every day—to remind her what she is feeling is quite normal, to remind of God's presence and unwavering love, to show her she doesn't need to go through the valley of the shadow of death alone.

What if each of us saw one another as if we were all family? What if more of us would create a safe space where others could ask those probing questions about God and the painfulness of life, as we tried to do with her? What if all of us would allow one another to walk with grief at our own pace, allowing one another to pause where we need to and still be there no matter how long it takes?

It's not easy to do this, we know. There are no easy answers to another's cries of misery and bleakness. But to allow each other the time and space we need to make the journey through the darkest valleys of our lives, is a profoundly loving and healing gift. It diminishes our grief.

We believe all of us have the capacity to be part of those hallowed moments. All of us can be more intentional about visiting, listening and showing someone her life is of consequence. It's not just something we professionals are able to do. It's something we humans are created to do.

And when we can see just how our compassionate presence can actually lift someone from loneliness and despair, it is a hallowed moment not to be forgotten.

As Nelson Mandela stated, "our human compassion binds us" one to the other and helps draw us from the arid, desolate corners of our lives.

Rescue

"The church should be more like a midwife than an epidural."
-Brené Brown

"Some wandered in the wilderness, lost and homeless. Hungry and thirsty, they nearly died. "LORD, help!" they cried in their trouble, and he rescued them from their distress. He led them straight to safety, to a city where they could live. Let them praise the LORD for his great love and for the wonderful things he has done for them. For he satisfies the thirsty and fills the hungry with good things."
-Psalm 107: 4-9

JANUARY 2014, via email:

> Right after the new year began, my wife of 14 years shared that she wasn't sure if she wanted to continue with our marriage. She informed me that she "needed space" to sort through her feelings. We had just experienced a season of many difficulties: my battle with cancer in 2011; my mom's recent battle with breast cancer; her mom's passing away in the summer of 2013; the death of my dad last month; and to add to all that, I found one of the persons I am working with—dead—in his home two weeks ago.
>
> My wife's request for distance shocked me. I was absolutely devastated.
>
> During the next few weeks, I experienced a numbness that is indescribable. I knew that our marriage had been struggling, but my ability to see "reality" was enveloped in clouds of denial. Sleeplessness, overwhelming feelings of abandonment, betrayal, and rejection created a spiral downward into an abyss of severe depression. I was truly spiritually, physically, and emotionally bankrupt. My life was in total collapse and I felt severely hopeless.

We responded as soon as we could:

> Thank you so much for reaching out to us. It took an incredible amount of courage and we are proud of you for taking the first step.

Your story is filled with so much pain, frustration, and disappointment;
we are unspeakably sorry. We pray for God to meet you in your pain and in
your losses, for you to know you are not alone in this agonizing season. The
simple fact that you are reaching out today shows your openness to finding
healing from the brokenness you are experiencing . . .
    . . . Is there one part of this that is especially painful for you?

He replied:

I am beating myself up pretty bad. Am very hurt—feeling betrayed, sad,
anxious, fearful, and obsessed with the impending season of us "taking a
time-out" of our marriage. As a recovering addict who can be co-dependent,
I feel responsible for everything, but I know that is a lie. I am willing to take
full responsibility for my hang-ups, hurts, and behaviors, but I need to allow
her to do the same. . . if she chooses . . . Also, I don't even know how to con-
tinue the grieving process after losing my dad . . . Pain. Numb. Confusion.
Denial.

We offered to meet him. He was able to, the following week on a Friday, at an
area coffee shop.

The man who walked in looked as if he had been totally beaten up by life. An
indescribable weight was bearing down on him. His appearance suggested someone
who had everything, figuratively everything, in his life "hit the fan"—and it had.
Our immediate response was to each give him the giant hug we sensed he needed.

We chose a table closest to the window. The sun had already started to set.
Winter's gloom—and his despair—invaded the room. The coffee wasn't warming
his spirits, but we hoped the conversation and our presence could, somehow. We
genuinely cared and we listened, as intently as we could, as he voiced what his
wounded heart was feeling. We tried our best not to offer pious platitudes or "quick
fix" formulas. Instead we tried to simply enter into the horrendous confusion with
him. His words were few, and sometimes absent altogether. There were many moments in which the three of us simply sat, not speaking, still, in solidarity with
him.

We continued meeting with him nearly every Friday through the winter and
into the spring. We sent him regular email and text messages reminding him he was
loved. We knew he wasn't feeling loved, especially by himself. Knowing of his deep
faith and intentional reliance on scripture, we sent him passages we hoped would
have meaning to him. There were days when he would call us on his lunch break,

needing encouragement. We did our best to inspire him to stay focused, just to make it through another day. We invited him to take time off of work to go hiking, to see a movie, or to go out to eat—anything with the potential to help him take his mind off the intense hurt wracking his soul. We wanted him to know there was more to his life than the devastation he was experiencing. But for the longest time he wasn't ready. Our conversations were acutely intense because his agony and sorrow were so great to bear.

We also prayed for him. We often felt as if we weren't helping him at all.

Then, seemingly out of nowhere, a new day appeared to be dawning. As winter turned into spring and spring into summer his empty and deflated heart started to show signs of filling up again. For a change of scenery and pace we asked him if he would be willing to meet us at a different coffee shop. He agreed. A new environment seemed symbolic of the beginning of his new outlook.

When he sat down he had a question for us: "I have some big news to share and I would really love your perspective. Someone contacted me from a ministry out west and asked if I would fly there for an interview. I think they really want me for the job and I'm strongly considering it. What do you guys think?"

It was stunning news. We knew he was turning a corner and God was loosening the chains of his misery. But we hadn't realized how much he was changing. We saw a new and brighter light shining all around him. We could see it in his face and we could sense it in his demeanor. God was rescuing him. His life was evolving.

Now, three and a half years since our first meeting, his life has changed even more. Two weeks after he arrived in his new state and at his new job he visited a new church and quietly slipped into a seat. Before the service began a friendly woman, about his age, sat down next to him in the area in which she always sat. They greeted one another and continued a conversation following the service. Learning he was quite new to the area, she invited him to have coffee at a place nearby. He accepted. They kept having coffee and had hundreds more conversations. Daily. Serious. Emotionally intimate. She, too, had great trauma and disruption in her life. Her husband was killed while driving, leaving her a single mom with three adolescent children. The past seven years had been lonely; starting over with no partner, raising the children by herself was an immense responsibility.

They became two wounded souls slowly beginning to help heal one another. They fell in love.

He kept us apprised of developments in their relationship. He introduced us to her and together, the four of us had many conversations. They were perfect for each other, we believed.

Just as we were doing our final edits for this book we both received this series of texts:

> *Good evening, gents, just a quick update—actually, a prayer request . . . we had some serious chats this weekend. We are discussing what moving toward marriage looks like!!!!*
>
> *. . . I'm going to ask her officially tomorrow. Will keep you posted . . .*
>
> *. . . Hey guys! Miracle!!! She said yes!!!!! Any chance you guys can be my Best Men on 7/22? Thanks for everything. NEVER dreamed in a million years that I would see myself as the most fortunate man on Earth—like today. We both love you.*

Yes, God is rescuing—and redeeming—him. We accepted his touching invitation to be his best men. So, we stood next to him in the yard of the bride's home as she and he made their vows before a standing room only congregation of 250 family members and friends in a ceremony that was poignant and redemptive, beautiful in every way.

It took a community to lift them to the celebration of their love. A community providing encouragement, patience, prayer, reassurance and a few well-placed verbal prods to remind him that he was deserving of love—and a new wife and life —again.

It takes a community that clothes each of us in love to show us how love can sustain and redeem us. Their community accompanied them through it all—the losses, the devastation, the loneliness—and joined together to witness the fruit of such love.

A sacred moment of celebration.

We couldn't help but think about being clothed in love as we prepared for the wedding, dressed in our new suits matching the groom's, how it took a community to get us looking our best for the service. New suits were gifted to us by the bride and groom. Bow ties were handmade by the bride's 18-year old daughter, a fashion student and design prodigy. The groom and we had no idea how to tie real bow ties. The only kind any of us had ever worn was the clip on variety, as we dressed in our childhood Easter finest. After dozens of attempts, after watching several YouTube how-to videos, after a half dozen different pairs of hands fussing at each of our necks, and with cameras whirring and bystanders chuckling, bemused by each entertaining, failed effort, our ties were finally camera and wedding-worthy. We couldn't possibly have gotten those bows tied without the community support. It's a small symbol; but an apt one.

The thing is, we all need accompaniers, for the small, seemingly insignificant and especially for the large, momentous moments of our lives. We need them for everything in between, as well.

We need others who can listen to and help hear the deepest yearnings of our hearts. Accompaniers willing to sit with us in the enormity of confusion. Accompaniers willing to listen, especially in the silence. Accompaniers willing to work at it until we get it reasonably right. Accompaniment is willing to bear witness to the character of God to others who need to know love and redemption and rescue can be real.

We were utterly privileged to accompany our very dear friends, by standing with them in the biggest public moment of their lives together. After all we've shared with them, we wouldn't have missed that moment for the world.

Around the same time we were watching him rise out of the abyss of his misery, we received an email from someone else. She also felt abandoned. Her agony was fraught with foreboding. She heard about our work from a close family friend. The title of her first message was "Personal Prison of Fear":

> *I've been afraid for so long.*
>
> *Afraid that the most important people in my life—my husband, mother and father—would die. They did, and within less than 5 years.*
>
> *Afraid I would lose another job. I was among thousands let go from a large company in the 80s. In the last 10 years, I lost three more jobs, all in group layoffs. Two were in the last 3 years.*
>
> *Afraid there would not be enough money after my husband died. There wasn't. Afraid the man I was living with would hurt me. He did. Afraid of losing my house. I did. Afraid I would have to declare bankruptcy. I did.*
>
> *I was afraid after the first robbery. And then it happened a second time. And then a third.*
>
> *I was afraid when my identity was stolen. That freaked me out, but I've done all I can do to prevent damage.*
>
> *I could be real afraid right now, because I don't know where I will be living this fall. In this house where the landlord will take no responsibility if something catastrophic should happen that could cost me thousands of dollars. Or having to move again, which is just one big expensive distraction.*

She too, lived locally; we met her at the same coffee shop. We remember asking her, "How are you still standing today? What keeps you going?"

She asked if she could have a pass on answering the question. She said she wasn't trying to avoid answering it. But she really wanted to take time to process an honest response.

Two days later we received her answer. She was fearful about many things. But, at times she also experienced peace. Her email explained:

> You asked me how I'm still standing after all that has happened to me. What is it that makes some people keep going? I don't know. For me, I think it's pure faith that I will be OK. When I was facing breast surgery in February less than 3 weeks after my abnormal mammogram, I was afraid at first. Every woman is. But in the days before my surgery, I had a strange sense of calm about it. I wasn't afraid. I fully and truly put my trust in God. My realtor, a 10-year breast cancer survivor who has counseled many women with breast cancer, was yelling at me, "You better be afraid. You need to be afraid. You should be afraid." But I wasn't. I think I just trusted in God at that point that it would be OK, and I'm putting my trust with God again that my 6-month mammogram in September will be OK. When you have gone through everything I have the past few years, faith is all that is left. Somehow, this will work out. God's got this.
>
> For now, I do know that I don't want to be afraid anymore. I'm tired of being afraid.

Days turned into weeks and weeks turned into months. We continued meeting with her at the coffee shop. We continued, by God's grace, to provide the presence and intentional listening she needed. We wanted her to now there were others who heard her, others who could sit with her in her fear.

Over time, the "Personal Prison of Fear" she had been living in was beginning to subside, and a new day was starting to dawn. She was ready for a change. An opportunity opened up for her, too, to move to another state. A fresh start and a new beginning—physically, emotionally and spiritually—was exactly what she needed. So, she packed up her life and she went. The deepest gloom she had been living with, the chains that had kept her in bondage for so long, were snapped. God was rescuing her.

> "Lord, help!" they cried in their trouble,
> and he saved them from their distress.

He led them from the darkness and deepest gloom;
he snapped their chains.
Let them praise the Lord for his great love
and for the wonderful things he has done for them.
For he broke down their prison gates of bronze;
he cut apart their bars of iron.
PSALM 107:13-16

It's impossible to dispute; sitting with, listening to and accompanying others through their most excruciating experiences demands much from us. Patience, persistence and kindness are required. Rarely does anyone begin to step out of the morass quickly and easily. Time actually can help to heal wounds. But accompaniment is also needed; others who can listen to and help hear the deepest yearnings of our hearts. Compassion is willing to sit with. Compassion is willing to listen. Compassion is willing to accompany. Compassion is willing to bear witness to the character of God to others who need to know love and redemption and rescue can be real.

When professor and author Brené Brown wrote, "The church should be more like a midwife than an epidural," she described a way of relating to others largely avoided in communities of faith in our lifetimes. Very few of us like pain. Most of us want to mask it, fix it, make it disappear. Much like an epidural given to a mother in the midst of giving birth, we want to numb what hurts and take the feeling away. Instead, Dr. Brown asserts, we would be much more helpful and supportive, especially emotionally and spiritually, if we can accompany one another through our heartache and hurt, sitting in it with each other, not masking it, avoiding it or pretending it's not there at all.

Solidarity (Tom)

"Our hearts of stone become hearts of flesh
when we learn where the outcast weeps."
-BRENNAN MANNING

"When we experience the healing presence of another person,
we can discover our own gifts of healing. Then our wounds allow us to
enter into a deep solidarity with our wounded brothers and sisters."
-HENRI NOUWEN

"I FEEL VERY ILL-EQUIPPED to be giving this talk tonight," I said meekly.

I was seated in the passenger seat next to Michael. We were on our way to speak to a support group for individuals who were living with some form of cancer or supporting a family member or loved one on the cancer journey.

Michael, knowing my sense of uneasiness about the subject matter as well as my general angst at speaking in front of people, addressed me with sensitivity.

"You will do great. We will be great. God has always been with us in our talks!"

Although his words initially calmed me, my apprehension increased the closer we got to the venue. Sensing my discomfort, we spoke more about how I was feeling.

"Do you have any idea what is making you so anxious tonight?" Michael probed.

I didn't know how to respond to his question at first so I gave a surface level answer.

"I guess I'm just tired; I haven't slept well the past few nights."

The answer was partly true, I hadn't slept especially well during the preceding week; I had been home sick with a stomach bug. But, we both knew there was more to it.

I was stalling. I needed a few minutes to ponder the question so I could give an honest, thoughtful response.

Cars raced by. My mind starting racing too. Michael waited patiently.

"I guess I feel a little out of place speaking to this group tonight because cancer hasn't been a part of my story, for which I'm exceedingly grateful. I mean, I know we speak to a lot of people facing cancer or supporting someone who does. But I'm not there right now. Don't you think people will be wondering why I am speaking to them? Won't they be a bit offended?"

Michael responded:

"Those are excellent questions. Let me respond to them first. First of all, this group invited us to be here tonight, so I don't think they are, or will be, offended by our mission or our stories. They approached us. I've spoken to this group before and they are a very warm group. They will love you and I know they will greet you very warmly too. I know intimately how anxious you get before you speak. But God uses you every time you do it. I am proud of you for making yourself available to do this. I know it creates anxiety for you to do it."

He thought for moment, and then went on.

"Let's talk a little bit about the 'identifying with someone else's story' issue you raised. I think it is an important one and I'm glad you brought it up. You are right; you have never had cancer and we can certainly thank God for that. I know several of your friends, even at their young age, who are facing a tough cancer diagnosis and how you are supporting them through it. When you are on those phone calls with them do you ever find yourself questioning whether or not you should be speaking to them? I'm guessing not. You just do what you always do, what we always do together, respond as empathetically and compassionately as we humanly can. At the end of the day, isn't that what the compassionate way of Jesus is all about? Compassion is ultimately about relationships with God and with each other. The only way we can truly have compassion for someone else is to feel, as best we can from a distance, what someone else is thinking and feeling on their own journey. So whether it is cancer, loneliness, grief, loss, depression, PTSD, or anything else, we do what we always do—we listen, we ask good questions, we offer kindness, grace and empathy. We enter the darkness with them. We offer ourselves. It's all God asks of any of us."

"We offer ourselves." I thought more about it as we pulled up.

The event went well, better than we expected it would. People were very engaged as we talked about the importance of having safe people in our lives with whom we can share vulnerable moments. Nearing the end of the evening, the facilitator stood up to lead the group in prayer. One by one she related each person's victories and setbacks:

"Please pray for Joyce. Joyce has just been diagnosed with cancer in her liver."

A collective sigh went up in the room as if everyone was inside a giant helium balloon and all the air was escaping.

"Jeff is here tonight!" she exclaimed enthusiastically. "He just finished his last round of chemo."

Cheers erupted in the room. It was as if everyone had just won the World Series.

She moved on down the list.

"Samuel is back in the hospital so please remember him. Please continue to keep Diane on your radar also; losing her husband last month has been very painful."

The list went on and on, announcements filled with both joys and sorrows. There were tears in the room, but there was also laughter and celebration. The whole range of human emotion was expressed. And, we were grateful, in our own small way, to experience it with them too.

The facilitator ended our time together with a very heartfelt prayer. She gave a benediction with a verse from the book of Galatians in which the Apostle Paul wrote:

Carry each other's burdens, and in this way you will fulfill the law of Christ.

On the ride home, we reflected on the topic of compassion and what it means to immerse ourselves into someone else's situation. I referenced what happened during the prayer time and how I felt a special bond with the group. Michael spoke of the connection between everyone present.

"None of those people in the group could experience exactly what someone else in the group was experiencing," he said. "Certainly, there were parallels on their journeys with the common thread being cancer. But, each situation was unique. Yet, they all, in their own way, understood, as best as they humanly could, what each other was going through. They have community and communion with one another. They are able to express compassion because they were accessing their feelings and immersing themselves in the human condition. What a privilege to be able to witness it happening!"

The next day was a Friday. We were leading our own support group for people who had experienced a major life change. We would discuss the loneliness they each faced. One woman lost her husband unexpectedly to a rare virus. Another woman lost a child, which drastically changed the course of her life. Another woman expressed the sadness she felt after her husband walked out suddenly, destroying her dreams of having a traditional family, a happy home and a partner for life.

There was a common thread of loss in the group, but also the more pressing issue of isolation. As with the cancer group the previous night, this group could express life's sorrows and joys with one another.

Through the afternoon, we were once again privileged to witness genuine community and compassion unfolding in front of us. The women were open and candid about the journey they found themselves on and how life was very different than the one they had anticipated.

Being able to be fully present with people in some of their most awful moments is a sacred gift. We can listen and through our listening we hope, we pray, to help others find the healing and reassurance of God's presence amidst the hardship. But, we have also learned to disengage from the pain so we can fully engage with our families, in every day moments, as well as celebrations like the upcoming holiday weekend.

I gathered my family and embarked on our journey to my parents' home in New Jersey. It was late afternoon and all four kids fell asleep in the car and so did my wife. The radio doesn't work in our van, so I had a lot of time to reflect on the week. I thought about the meetings with the cancer and grief support groups, and replayed my conversation with Michael about how to relate to the group's experiences.

At first, I couldn't release some of the emotions I had experienced when we engaged with each group. The intense feelings of sadness, loneliness and disillusionment from each of the individuals were weighing heavily on me. I would have to work harder to disengage so I could be fully present.

The holiday weekend came and went. When Michael and I got together on Tuesday, we spent some time re-connecting.

"So how did the weekend go for you?" Michael asked.

"The weekend was a good one. We had a wonderful time with our family. Jon, my youngest brother, is moving soon so it was the last time we'll spend time with him for a while and it was good to be together. I'll miss him. We'll all miss him," I said.

I went on about all of the events of the weekend and the discussion went to a very serious place.

"Last evening Sarah worked at the hospital," I continued. "I spent most of the actual holiday yesterday at home with the kids. And you know how it goes— moments of pure grace—but also many moments of anxiety."

I went on. "I was enjoying the day with my kids. But as the evening rolled around, an intense sadness came over me. I thought even more deeply about each of those people we had spoken with last week and the loneliness they face. I thought especially of the one woman who lost her husband at such a young age and the extreme loneliness she feels as she arrives home at the end of the day to an empty house. I thought about how she spends most of her meals by herself, and the fact that she mentioned she no longer has anyone to 'laugh with her' as she watches the evening comedy programs she and her husband used to enjoy."

"I had trouble letting go this time. I felt the weight of their sadness and it was intense. After putting the kids to bed, I lay in my own bed, feeling incredibly, incredibly lonely myself. And I'm not sure why? Even though Sarah was out for the evening, I knew I would see her today. I have four children who provide me with much companionship, which we all need. I have family members and friends, like you, who I can call in a heartbeat. Yet, for whatever reason, I felt very, very lonely. So weird."

Michael quickly responded, "It's not weird at all!"

I continued. "I was picturing myself, last night, as being like one of those women. What if Sarah didn't come home last night? What if I didn't have my kids living at home with us? And some day they will move away. What if I didn't have any family members or friends to call in those lonely moments? What if I didn't have much companionship? I was thinking about what it would be like if I was in one of their situations. After all, it's possible. I mean, even two weeks ago when we spoke to the group of senior citizens, if you remember, they talked about how their two greatest fears are abandonment and a loss of independence. Some day I will get old too. And, I might fear what they're fearing too."

Michael thought for a moment and then responded, "I'm glad you brought this up. Honestly, I think all of us have these feelings of intense loneliness at times. Remember my stories about Kathy's cancer and how lonely I felt knowing I might be responsible for Matthew all by myself? I felt very lonely. Remember how we talked last week about how each of us can be compassionate to others, when we have experienced, to a degree, what someone else is going through? Those times like you had last night can sometimes be a gift, although painful. Those moments can help us to respond, even more empathetically to those who are experiencing a sense of loneliness, because you have felt it too. And because you have felt it, deeply, you can help others find reassurance because you can imagine what they are going through.

Essentially, isn't it what God did for us, through Jesus? Jesus came to enter into solidarity with us, to offer that healing presence, to show God understands."

We both thought about it for a moment.

"I guess the real challenge for us, all of us, is to see a bit of ourselves in everyone we meet," Michael said. "Whatever others are going through, we have to be able to picture ourselves, as best we humanly can, with what they are experiencing. The fact is we can't fix their situations. But what we can do is remind them someone is aware of their circumstances and they aren't alone. It's solidarity."

Unconditional (Michael)

"Love is the doorway through which the human soul
passes from selfishness to service."
-UNKNOWN

EVEN PEOPLE WHO DON'T LIKE or follow sports were talking about it. A few summers ago, the Little League U.S. championship winning team— Red Land, was from a small community just south of where our office is located, in Harrisburg, PA. It seemed as if our entire region of Pennsylvania was talking about it, watching each of the team's games as it made its way to the finals, rooting on the hometown boys. What made it even more exciting was the Little League World Series is played every year at its headquarters just two hours north of us, in Williamsport, PA. The close proximity for the fans of a contending team helped to set record attendance numbers for the games.

In spite of the local team's thrilling journey to the championship, it lost its final game 18 -11, and Japan's team was crowned the Little League world champions for the year.

The local news stations and newspapers, as well as social media, were filled with best wishes, stories, commentaries and excitement over Red Land's accomplishments. For weeks afterward and deservedly so. The news of the team's improbable success was a welcome respite from the overwhelming summer news of a horrific refugee crisis in the Mideast and Europe, an anxiety producing roller coaster ride for the world's stock markets and the circus of a presidential primary season begun all too early and consuming too much money. Finally, we got some news we could celebrate. A huge parade greeted the boys on their return to the area late on the night of their final game. In spite of losing the world championship, everyone declared the team true winners— for their incredible abilities on the field, their graciousness in victory and defeat and their camaraderie and team spirit in reaching an elusive summit in baseball.

As heartwarming as their story is, there was another story connected to the Little League World Series, which touched me personally just as much—and maybe even more.

The day before the world championship game was played, another heartwarming game took place. In the game, televised right before the championship game, athletes with special needs took the field in what the Little League organization calls "Challenger Division" games. In its 26th year, more than 30,000 kids ranging in age from eight to 22, participate in the Challenger Divisions worldwide, according to the Little League website.

In Challenger games, each player gets a chance to bat and to score; yet no score is kept. There are no losers. Some athletes are in wheelchairs and some can run. Some need help batting and some can swing for the fences themselves. Some need prompting to run in the right direction and others know exactly where home plate is and cross it triumphantly. Both girls and boys are on each team. The Challenger players wear the same uniforms, shoulder patches and safety equipment as other Little League players. Each player has a buddy to help him or her in whatever ways are needed.

There was so much pure exuberance and joy on the field during the game. Those players were there simply for fun and to have a great time. It was obvious they did. It was heartrending and poignant how people with special needs—physical and intellectual—were given the opportunity to wear official uniforms, bat, catch, run and cross home plate just as their more physically and intellectually able players did. As each player stepped up to the plate, the screen showed each one's age and favorite food, TV show and major league player. I watched with pride and tears in the corners of my eyes as they joined with one another on the field. I thanked God for the opportunity to watch it. I thanked God for the compassionate people who had the vision for and the drive to organize such a moving event. I thanked God for the tears of pride and joy I felt in seeing such a beautifully imperfect, yet supremely perfect, game.

Everyone is included, everyone gets a uniform, everyone plays, everyone hits, everyone crosses home plate—and everyone is equal. A symbolic embodiment of the kingdom of God.

As the father of a child with profound intellectual disabilities and autism, I couldn't help but love those kids simply for who they are—beautifully imperfect, yet supremely perfect just as they are.

Whenever I see others with special needs, I always view them through the prism of Matthew's special needs. I see him in them and them in him—especially in their passionate expressions, their uninhibited movements and their spontaneous, sometimes overflowing delight in the world around them.

In them, I see love, unconditional. In Matthew, I feel love, unconditional, every day.

I find it impossible to adequately define "unconditional love." In scrolling through the Internet for definitions, there were more than 800,000 results in just one click of the search button. Of the many essays and descriptions I read, none of them were able to define this most beautiful of concepts fully enough. No earthly definition ever will be.

But for the sake of some understanding, here are a few of the most common definitions of unconditional love I found:

- an affection without any limitations;
- love without conditions;
- a state of mind in which one has the goal of increasing the welfare of another, despite any evidence of benefit for oneself;
- love given freely to the loved one, no matter what;
- love infinite and measureless;
- an act of one's feelings irrespective of will;
- separates the individual from her or his behaviors, even the unacceptable ones.

In the Bible, it is defined in terms of God's love for us. God's infinite, gracious, eternal, sacrificial—without conditions—love for us. It's a concept our human minds are quite incapable of fully grasping. If only we could. My understanding is woefully, utterly incomplete. I don't even know how to begin to comprehend how vast and deep and wide and unwavering God's love is for us. But someone in my life—someone created beautifully by God—has shown me a deeper glimpse into just what unconditional love is. His name is Matthew. I've come to see how he is created perfectly too. Having him in our lives presents us with endless opportunities to learn ever more about the meaning and definition of unconditional love. His intellectual disabilities and autism have opened up a world we never could have known without him. It's not to pretend unconditional love is simple and easy. It's complicated. Relentlessly so. It never ends—our vigilance, protecting him, keeping him away from trouble.

When Pope Francis made his historic first visit to the United States in September 2015, I found myself wanting to watch as much TV coverage of the event as possible. His gentle, grace-filled, compassionate demeanor attracted my attention since the beginning of his papacy. Even though I am not a Catholic and don't agree with certain aspects of Catholic doctrine, I resonate deeply with the tone and tenor of his words and actions concerning the worth and dignity of all human beings. Francis exemplifies by his example the love of Jesus.

Throughout his journeys in the U.S., he did something that routinely gave me pause every time I saw or read about it. Whether it was in Washington, D.C.,

New York City or Philadelphia, every time Pope Francis saw a person—especially a child—who was living with a disability, he stopped to pay special attention to him or her. He would kiss him on the forehead, grasp her hands warmly in his, cradle her head gently in his hands and pronounce a blessing on him. Routinely, he would do this. Quietly, reverently, respectfully, he would pause to show he believed they were of sacred distinction.

I respect and am profoundly moved by his expressions of compassion and empathy, unconditionally.

Kathy and I made a decision early on in Matthew's life: we were not going to be bitter and angry about his circumstances—and our circumstances because of his. It took more than enough energy to look after him and the very intensive attention he needed then and still needs today. We didn't have enough extra energy to expend it on questioning why "did this happen?" and who was to blame or why "did God do this to him (and us)?" Somehow, all of the energy to expend on questioning seemed more than we could handle. We simply went about the business of nurturing Matthew's unique needs the best way we could, trying to show his brothers Adam and David we were determined to give them as normal a life as we possibly could. People have asked if we are angry about our circumstances and the responsibilities we have. We honestly never were. Our faith in God has never wavered because of what we live with, nor has it caused us to question God's goodness and love. Speaking for myself, I simply believe God is love—pure, infinite, gracious (crazy) love—and because of such love, we will find the ability to do what we have to do.

I chose from the beginning to learn from the circumstances and to find ways to use them to be the best person I could be in them. It's not to say it's always easy, smooth or good. Some days are terrible. Some moments are dreadful. Some situations frustrate, anger and provoke me to lash out at Kathy or at Matthew. Sometimes it's not pretty at all. I don't want to sugarcoat it or even begin to pretend living with a child with disabilities is all sweetness and light. Everything in our lives is ordered around Matthew's needs. There is nothing we do without taking into account how his care impacts our activities and our responses to all of life's other demands. Yet, Kathy and I are in it together. This realization helps us both to trust in one another and realize we need one another to get through each day in the best way possible.

I can honestly and sincerely say I wouldn't change a thing. We have embraced who Matthew is and isn't and have accepted him simply for who he has been born to be. He has many, many limitations. There is so much he cannot and never will be able to do. In the decision to simply love him, we have freed ourselves from the persistent anger, bitterness and heartache, which can accompany such limitations.

The fact is, we all have our limitations. We all have something—many things, actually—we don't do well. We all have wounds, insecurities, insensitivities, prejudices, blind spots, irrational beliefs, unfounded fears and inconsistent words and actions. None of us is immune. We all have disabilities. None of us has a perfect body, perfect health or a perfect life. We are all challenged, all vulnerable, all destined to die. I don't know why any of is so. Yet I do know the Bible tells us that God values and loves each of us absolutely the same, with our disabilities, weaknesses and imperfections, and all.

Living with a child who has so many limitations has helped me to see how love is immensely stronger than any of those limitations. Because of that discovery, I am trying to grow in being more loving in the face of everyone else's limitations too. None of us can help or change most of the limitations we've been born with. They simply are. It's who we simply are. Yes, some things can improve or change. And isn't one of the purposes of life to grow and change for the better, to become more and more closely in touch with the love and grace of God? Yet, isn't the message of Jesus one showing us how to love one another for who we are, imperfections and all, in contrast to condemning each other for who we are not? I think of every beggar, prostitute, child, leper, tax collector, person with paralysis whom others despised and neglected, marginalized and feared, condemned and left to suffer, whom Jesus encountered. His reaction to every one of them was radical. He met them where they were - touched them, sat with them, made time for them, had compassion for them and loved them for who they were, and didn't damn them for who they were not.

Jesus' love was unconditional. His love calls me to love unconditionally too. Our human tendency is to place conditions on our love. But Jesus' example was different. He never said "I'll love you if . . . you love me back; . . . you agree with me completely; . . . you do everything I want; . . . you are just like me; . . . you change who you are to suit my whims; . . . you are sorry for the times in which you hurt me; . . . you look like me, think like me, worship like me or live like me."

All of us know certain people who are very problematic to love. Loving others unconditionally is an exceedingly delicate dance. We need to wrestle with the common human tensions we feel about some people and Christ's example calling us to love unconditionally. For example, the people who are most trying for both Tom and me to love are those who are more rigid, hardline and unbending, in their opinions, attitudes and theology, especially when they seem judgmental, condemning and dismissive. We work with a lot of people who express to us the profound amounts of brokenness in their lives. Sometimes their brokenness comes from actions they take, certainly. Most times it's because of what others and their circumstances have laid upon them. Regardless of how the brokenness comes about, if we scold people they won't open up to us again. Shame and reprimand aren't what turns people's lives around; they just drive behaviors underground. But in recognizing that brokenness is universal for everyone, maybe unconditional love is easier to achieve.

It is Matthew who helps me to see and feel such a love in the most real and transformative ways. It is through this unconditional love I experience every single day where I am given the inspiration to try to love more unconditionally in everything I do.

Together

"Alone we can do so little, together *we can do so much."*
-Helen Keller

W E MET A MAN who was a patient in the psychiatric unit of a Veterans Administration hospital. A traumatic circumstance led him there. We didn't know what to expect. A friend of ours asked us if we would visit the man, simply to show him other people were concerned about him and his situation and had heard his cries for help.

Making our way to the sixth floor unit where he was being treated, we passed one individual after another in the hallways who was suffering in some way. War had taken its toll on each of them. One man passed us with both of his legs missing. Another man was missing one of his eyes and most of his face was scarred. A security attendant said he would go to get the man we had come to visit. But he forewarned us the man wasn't in a good place emotionally.

When he entered the room, the man immediately started berating us, demanding to know how we knew about his situation and why we had come to see him. It was awkward. For five minutes, he yelled at us, a profanity-laced diatribe. We knew why. He was in deep, deep anguish. When he finally settled down for a few moments, he apologized,

"I'm sorry to react this way. But I'm embarrassed. This is one the most embarrassing moments of my whole life. I didn't want people to know I was here. Not all of my family knows I'm here. Thank you for coming. But I'd like you to leave now."

We were at a loss as to what to say. What do you say to someone whose life is so utterly broken? We couldn't say much. And we didn't. We apologized for making him so uncomfortable and made our way out. We hoped even in the awkwardness and embarrassment, somehow he might be able to see others wanted to reach out to him. Somehow, perhaps, he might come to know he didn't need to go through his distress alone. We hoped he could believe others were willing to continue to be in it with him. It is important for all of us to know someone else can help us carry the burden.

It could have been easy to take his dismissal and rage personally. No one relishes being turned away, feeling rejected or told that we aren't welcome. It is in situations such as those, when we give thanks we are "in the arena" together. As Theodore Roosevelt famously said:

"It is not the critic who counts; not the man who points out how the strong man stumbles, or where the doer of deeds could have done them better. The credit belongs to the man who is actually in the arena, whose face is marred by dust and sweat and blood; who strives valiantly; who errs, who comes short again and again, because there is no effort without error and shortcoming; but who does actually strive to do the deeds; who knows great enthusiasms, the great devotions; who spends himself in a worthy cause; who at the best knows in the end the triumph of high achievement, and who at the worst, if he fails, at least fails while daring greatly, so that his place shall never be with those cold and timid souls who neither know victory nor defeat."

Neither one of us had to carry the weight of such an unsettling encounter by ourselves. But we did enter the arena—which is what is most important.

Driving in the car to our next appointment we were able to process what happened. We both expressed our regret at our presence making the man so embarrassed. We never meant to cause those feelings within him. We felt terrible for him, knowing his torment was so intense and overwhelming it caused him to lash out. We reassured each other his fury wasn't directed so much at us as it was a result of his inner turmoil.

We have subsequently spoken with the man since his release from the hospital. He wanted us to know he was sorry for the way he reacted to our visit. He described how he simply wasn't able to think clearly, how confused he was by the circumstances leading him to the hospital. We understood . . .

One afternoon, we were sitting at a table with a group of pastors at a conference. One of the pastors, when asked what the past year had been like for him, said very vulnerably it had been one of the most unbearable years of his 30-year career. When he was asked why it was so unbearable, he used an illustration from his childhood:

When I was 14 years old, I had a golden retriever named Slider. The dog was my very best friend—my only friend. We lived in the middle of nowhere, so summer afternoons could have been lonely for me without him. My parents worked a lot and I was home by myself for long periods of time. On especially hot days, I would take the dog with me to the creek about a half-mile behind our house. We would splash in the water together. We would play together. We would have lengthy "conversations" together.

Every time I called his name, he came running, excitedly. He made me feel loved. Until one day . . . after running in the creek for several hours, Slider suddenly disappeared. "Slider! Slider! Slider!"

I called his name, louder and louder, but with no response. I kept yelling, hoping he would come running. Aimlessly, I sprinted through the woods, searching. Immense fear came over me. What would I do without my best friend? I started having all kinds of crazy thoughts running through my head. It was getting dark and I wasn't sure how many miles away from home I was. I knew my parents would be the ones panicking if I wasn't home when they returned from work, so I retreated.

Without giving up all sense of hope, I kept shouting as I made my way home. Way off in the distance, I heard a faint whimper. Even though I was tired of searching. I barreled toward the distant sound. In the middle of a patch of raspberry bushes, I saw Slider lying perfectly still. I could see he was in enormous discomfort; every breath and every movement was agonizing for him. Looking down, I noticed he was caught. One of his hind legs was stuck in the jaws of a bear trap. Bending over next to him to help ease his burden, he did something he hadn't done in the 10 years we had him—he bit me. He wouldn't let me get close to him, each time I tried.

It took several months before Slider was willing to allow me to "console" him again. But I believed once the pain subsided, he would be my best friend again... and eventually he was!

"This past year has been one in which I felt much like a dog, trapped, and I didn't even know it. In my three-decade career, I have met a lot of people in severe pain. I have reassured them, as best as I could, just as I was attempting to reassure Slider the day he was trapped. Most people were grateful for the consolation I offered in the moment. Some, because of their immense agony, weren't ready to receive it—and I understood. But for reasons I didn't understand until today, I have been the dog in a trap, hypothetically biting others who were trying to reassure me. Until today, I didn't realize why I was trapped. I have been there because I'm scared about my looming retirement next year. The only thing I have ever known is being a full-time pastor and shepherd. I've always been the one lifting up others and I'm rarely letting others in, supporting me when I've needed it. One of the biggest regrets of my career is I didn't join in my work with others. There was so much I did alone—counseling, visiting, leading studies, providing inspiration. That model actually made me lonely. It wore me out. It made me carry burdens and secrets I couldn't release. Being a leader is extremely taxing. The work is too sensitive to do alone. We're not taught in seminary to be team members. Lip service might be played to it. But the model we see above all others is the model of the individual out there on his or her own. But it wasn't the model that Jesus established for his disciples." . . .

Since we founded Someone To Tell It To, we have made it a spiritual practice to read together—to learn, to grow, and we hope, to share wisdom we've gained to encourage others.

One of the books we have read is by Rachael Naomi Remen, M.D., a moving and inspirational book entitled, *Kitchen Table Wisdom*. One of its stories, especially significant is, "The Container." An excerpt:

> One of the angriest people I have ever worked with was a young man with Osteogenic sarcoma of the right leg. He had been a high school and college athlete and until the time of his diagnosis his life had been good. Two weeks after his diagnosis, they had removed his right leg above the knee. This surgery, which saved his life, also ended his life. Playing ball was a thing of the past.
>
> He refused to return to school. He began to drink heavily, to use drugs, to alienate his former admirers and friends, and to have one automobile accident after the other.
>
> He was a powerfully built and handsome man. Profoundly self-oriented and isolated. At the beginning, he had the sort of rage that felt very familiar to me. Filled with a sense of injustice and self-pity, he hated all the well people. In our second meeting, hoping to encourage him to show his feelings about himself, I gave him a drawing pad and asked him to draw a picture of his body. He drew a crude sketch of a vase, just an outline. Running through the center of it he drew a deep crack. He went over and over the crack with a black crayon, gritting his teeth and ripping the paper. He had tears in his eyes. There were tears of rage. It seemed to me that the drawing was a powerful statement of his pain and the finality of his loss. It was clear that this broken vase could never hold water, could never function as a vase again. It hurt to watch. After he left, I folded the picture up and saved it. It seemed too important to throw away.
>
> In time, his anger began to change in subtle ways. He began one session by handing me an item torn from our local newspaper. It was an article about a motorcycle accident in which a young man had lost his leg. The doctors were quoted at length. I finished reading and looked up. "Those idiots don't know the first thing about it," he said furiously. Over the next month he brought in more of these articles, some from the paper and some from magazines: a girl who had been severely burned in a house fire, a boy whose

hand had been partially destroyed in the explosion of his chemistry set. His reactions were always the same, a harsh judgment of the well-meaning efforts of doctors and parents. His anger about these other young people began to occupy more and more of our session time. No one understood them, no one was there for them, no one really knew how to help them. He was still enraged, but it seemed to me that underneath this anger a concern for others was growing. Encouraged, I asked him if he wanted to do anything about it. Caught by surprise, at first he said no. But, just before he left he asked me if I thought he could meet some of these others who suffered injuries like his. . .

Within a few weeks, he had begun to visit young people on the surgical wards whose problems were similar to his own.

HE came back from these visits full of stories, delighted to find that he could reach young people. He was often able to be of help when no one else could . . . Gradually his anger faded and he developed a sort of ministry.

My favorite of all his stories concerned a visit to a young woman who had a tragic family history: breast cancer had claimed the lives of her mother, her sister, and her cousin. Another sister was in chemotherapy. This last event had driven her into action. At twenty-one she took one of the only options open at that time, she had both her breasts removed surgically.

He visited her on a hot mid-summer day, wearing shorts, his artificial leg in full view. Deeply depressed, she lay in bed with her eyes closed, refusing to look at him. He tried everything he knew to reach her, but without success. He said things to her that only another person with an altered body would dare to say. He made jokes. He even got angry. She did respond. All the while a radio was softly playing rock music. Frustrated, he finally stood, and at a last effort to get her attention, he unstrapped the harness of his artificial leg and let it drop to the floor with a loud thump. Startled, she opened her eyes and saw him for the first time. Encouraged, he began to hop around the room snapping his fingers in time to the music and laughing out loud. After a moment she burst out laughing too. "Fella," she said, "if you can dance, maybe I can sing."

This young woman became his friend and began to visit people in the hospital with him. She was in school and she encouraged him to return to school to study psychology and dream of carrying his work further. Eventually she became his wife, a very different sort of person from the models and cheerleaders he had dated in the past. In our final meeting I opened his chart and found the picture of the broken vase that he had drawn two years before.

Unfolding it, I asked him if he remembered the drawing he had made of his body. He took it in his hands and looked at it for some time. "You know," he said, "it's really not finished." Surprised, I extended my basket of crayons towards him. Taking a yellow crayon, he began to draw lines radiating from the crack in the vase to the very edges of the paper. Thick yellow lines. I watched, puzzled. He was smiling. Finally he put his finger on the crack, looked at me and said softly, "This is where the light comes through."

We offer this story, and others, because they serve as a great reminder—at certain points in all of our lives we will find ourselves battle-scarred from the "arena of life." Deaths. Deceptions. Disappointments. Disillusionments. Disagreements. Whatever it may be, there will be times when we wonder if there will ever be a way forward, if we will ever be able to go on.

We believe one of the biggest reasons most of us shy away from those who are wounded is because we are afraid we won't know how to respond to them.

"What do I do with them?" we wonder. "What should I say?"

"What if I'm told something too personal, too sensitive, to hear?" "What if I react in some inappropriate way?" "What if I make things worse?"

Those are all honest questions. Feeling apprehensive is natural. But having a "partner" with us as we interact with others is profoundly important. It reminds us that we, too, aren't alone in carrying others' burdens.

We often tell people that there is a reason Jesus sent his disciples out in pairs. As Luke 10:1-3 (NLT) tells us:

The Lord now chose seventy-two other disciples and sent them ahead in pairs to all the towns and places he planned to visit. These were his instructions to them: "The harvest is great, but the workers are few. So pray to the Lord who is in charge of the harvest; ask him to send more workers into his fields. Now go, and remember that I am sending you out as lambs among wolves."

We are all wounded people in need of goodwill, dignity and affection. We are all broken in some way and in need of recovery. We need other shoulders to cry on, hands to lift us up, arms to embrace us, and backs to carry us.

In his book, *Here and Now: Living in the Spirit*, Henri Nouwen writes, traveling alone is rarely healthy for our spiritual life; he quotes the physician Luke:

Jesus doesn't want us to travel alone. He sends us out two by two, . . .

Nouwen rarely, if ever, traveled alone on his journeys around the world, to speak, teach and inspire. The community in which he worked and lived—Daybreak—always sent someone with him when he traveled:

> *And what a difference that makes!*
>
> *Traveling together radically shifted the significance of my trips. Instead of lecture trips they became missions, instead of situations full of temptations, they became spiritual adventures, instead of times of loneliness they became opportunities for community.*
>
> *The words of Jesus, "where two or three are gathered in my name I am in their midst," have become very real for me. Together we are well protected against the seductive powers surrounding us and together we can reveal something of God that none of us is able to reveal on our own.*

What would it look like if we actually sent, like Jesus did, disciples in pairs? What if we entered the arenas of lives, the especially frightening ones, with others to encourage us along the way? "Being moved with compassion" may call us into demanding arenas, testing our patience, our endurance, our strength, and even our ability to love. But things wouldn't be so intimidating knowing we are always accompanied in it.

A funeral we led together started off anxiously—and late—because of a young adult son who was angry about with his father's passing. When the son finally showed up at the service he was obviously drunk. He was aggressive. We were warned this might happen, as the young man had announced the night before he very well might need to drink heavily to get through the following day. When he obviously made good on his promise, we looked at one another and exclaimed, "Oh crap. What do we do now? What are we in for?"

The funeral directors and his mother and other family members were definitely on edge as they were awaiting his arrival. It put us on edge too. Now, we all wondered, how would he act during the service? What if he disrupted it with inappropriate comments? How could we help to keep the atmosphere dignified for his mother and the others who were there? How would we respond? Just what would we need to say to help redeem this time of remembrance?

We thank God even though he squirmed in his front row seat and sat restlessly through the service, he was quiet and non-disruptive throughout. Even at the internment, while he talked loudly up to the moment the brief committal service started, when it did, he pulled himself together and was quiet through to the end. Even though he danced along the edge of disruption, ultimately he made it through the services, much to our relief.

His mother was very apologetic to us and gracious, trying her best to keep the services dignified for those who were there and for the memory of her husband.

But, oh how comforting it was for us to have each other by our sides.

We live in a culture in which individualism is held in high esteem. While every individual's needs and dignity are of inestimable importance, we also have been created for one another. We need one another. We are better, stronger, greater, when we work in connection and collaboration with one another. When we compete, we often work against one another. But when we connect, collaborate and work with one another,

"The whole is greater than the sum of our parts," as Aristotle famously declared.

When we speak to groups together we enjoy it so much more when we can tell our story and the stories of others together. We can play off one another, enhance one another's words and be a model for how people—and men especially—can work closely, non-competitively, healthily and organically together. The fact is, one of Tom's least favorite parts of the job is public speaking. It creates great anxiety in him in the hours and moments before the engagement. He'd prefer to do almost anything but speak in front of a crowd. But he also knows it's part of the founders' job; we are the major public face of the ministry. Yet, when Michael, who is comfortable in speaking in front of others, is able to stand with him, next to him, at a podium, on camera or on a stage, he is given the emotional courage and moral support he needs to take on the role. It makes a difficult, in many ways dreaded task, manageable, much more comfortable and even remarkably good.

For two years we worked with a family to help them reconcile from a decade-long estrangement. The work was especially complicated, an intimate work of breaking down the walls of mistrust, disappointment, hurt, regret and grief. Across the table with a meal or a cup of coffee, was when the rebuilding of trust, communication, connection and grace was accomplished.

Every meeting lasted for several hours—we need to give the appropriate amount of time to hear each person's perception of the events leading to the breakdown in their family bond.

Each meeting was exhausting. Each one had a moment when we were certain that all the work everyone had done was "going off the rails" and would be lost, perhaps for good. None of the meetings was easy. The painful disarray marking the family's previous decade would take many probing, uncomfortable conversations and acknowledgements of unintended damaging actions and resentful feelings in order for the healing to begin.

But it did begin. For it, we were exceedingly grateful to God and for the family who desired with all their hearts to start over. They did extraordinary work to begin putting all the broken pieces back together.

We are also grateful in this instance, as in so many others, we were in every meeting, every hour, together. This work was among the most delicate and complicated work that we have ever done. The stakes for the family relationships and dynamics were very high. We really wanted them to reconcile. We wanted to succeed for them—for their sakes and for their confidence in our ability to help them. It is nearly impossible to imagine anyone entering into a situation as delicate as this one, trying to lead the way to reawakening the family's bonds, all alone. Working together gave us greater confidence; there is strength in numbers in situations such as this. It enabled us to have the courage to ask incisive questions, knowing we weren't alone to hear the more painful answers. Listening to such deep generational brokenness together insured that we were catching more of the story, recognizing more of the subtle tones and providing a more nuanced response to the very serious issues at hand. And as always, inevitably happens when either one of us is at a loss as to what to say in response to something we are hearing, the Spirit shows up in the other one of us, giving the right words at the right time to say.

Together. It's a model we want to promote and help others to embrace. There is nothing better, nothing sounder, when we can work in close connection with one another, each of us employing our best gifts to offer our best selves to those who are in need. We are exponentially stronger when we do.

Conclusion

Chains Shall He Break

Truly He taught us to love one another His law is love and His gospel is
peace Chains shall He break for the slave is our brother And in His name
all oppression shall cease Sweet hymns of joy in grateful chorus raise we,
Let all within us praise His holy name
-"O Holy Night" ("Cantique de Noël"), Adolphe Adam

BEAUTIFUL AND STIRRING, evocative and uplifting, the carols and songs, accompanied by trumpets, drums and an organ, create a memorable holiday mood. Familiar and timeless, hope-filled and full of promise, the The Festival of Nine Lessons and Carols offers sage lessons interspersed between musical selections. The service, held every December in a nearby college chapel, touches our deep longing for a world ruled by love, not hate, joy, not despair, and peace, not violence and discord. It is the sanctuary we need and seek in the midst of a turbulent holiday season marked by hatred, condemnation, protest, division, and utter disconnection.

It is mid-December when we write this final essay, only a few days after three horrific terrorist acts killed 129 people in Paris, 43 people in Beirut, and 224 people on a Russian airliner blown apart by a bomb over the Sinai. Hundreds more were wounded in those attacks.

In addition, a long list of breaking news reports highlights racial turmoil and profiling, torture, rape, killing fields, kidnappings, hostages and beheadings, and other violent acts around the world and in the U.S. The general state of the world does not appear to be good, in any way.

Some days, we are hard-pressed, amidst this darkness, to see evidence of the Prince of Peace in our midst. The stirring carols and anthems can begin to ring hollow. The ancient scriptures can sound like platitudes. We wonder, as we celebrate another holy season of expectation, how long it will be before those who walk in darkness will see the "great light" that the prophet Isaiah promised 28 centuries ago.

For many people, today and throughout time, darkness and not light, oppression and not freedom, trespass and not justice have been the defining characteristics of their world and their lives.

Yet, when we look closely enough, we *do* see promising signs, glimpses of the peace and the light about which Isaiah prophesied.

A little more than a year before, shortly before Christmas 2014, leaders of the world's major religions gathered to to sign a shared commitment against modern slavery, calling it a crime against humanity. According to *The Huffington Post*, for the first time in history, major Catholic, Anglican, and Orthodox Christian leaders met with leaders of the Buddhist, Hindu, Jewish and Muslim religions, to commit to eliminating modern salvery by the year 2020. Specifically, the religious leaders called for the elimination of slavery in every form, including child labor, prostitution, organ trafficking, and any act violating the human dignity of the person.

We consider any action which does not treat others as equals to be an abhorrent crime," Pope Francis proclaimed. "God is a love that is manifested in every human being; everyone is equal and ought to be afforded the same liberty and dignity."

This historic convocation was a commitment to compassion for the nearly 36 million people who are considered victims of slavery today. We believe it is a sign, a "wonder," a light in the darkness. It signals hope in what often seems to be a world without hope.

As followers of Christ who approach another Christmas, we remember the promised coming of a Wonderful Counselor, a Mighty God, an everlasting Father, a Prince of Peace. And yet, we are bombarded hourly by images denying us wonder, obscuring the awesome power of God, perverting our Creator's intentions, and violating every condition leading us to blessed peace. It takes intention to turn our gaze away from the darkness and focus on the light.

We received a message from a stranger, in Jerusalem, the holy city, in relation to Michael's son Matthew. The gentleman wrote about an essay from our book, *Someone To Tell It To: Sharing Life's Journey*, which tells a story about Matthew's exuberance and delight each night when the neighbors turn on their Christmas lights during the holiday season each year. He wrote:

> *I was deeply moved by your beautiful story "The Returning Light." I am an Orthodox Jew and live in Jerusalem, where much work has been done with mentally challenged children and adults . . . I also found your message very timely, as it is essentially the message of Chanukah, which begins in two weeks. At a very dark time in Jewish history, the lights that burned miraculously for eight days in the Temple, as well as those that we kindle today, remind us that the light of God, no matter how hidden it may appear to be, is*

*always there. This is particularly relevant to those of us who live in the won-
derful community of Har Nof, where, two weeks ago, four incredibly special
men were shot or hacked to death . . . while praying in the synagogue around
the corner from my home . . . We are still in shock and deep mourning. It is
hard to see God's light at times like this, yet we go on believing it is there.*

*I have no doubt that, in these difficult times, your son is more aware of
God's presence than any of us . . .*

The man's words gave us pause. Is Matthew—and so many, many others like
him—more aware of God's presence in this violent, dark, painful, oppressive world
than the rest of us? Is he aware of God's presence in a world which is so often lacking in compassion? Those Christmas lights, shining in the darkest time of the year,
give him so much joy, more than we can fully describe. His reaction to those lights
remind us light can pierce the darkness and can begin to bring joy and beauty. In
this lies our hope.

The Prince of Peace has come and still resides here among us, shining more
points of light than we can begin to number. When we look away from the darkness
of our world and stop to ponder the lights and point them out, we begin to see how
very many there are.

We simply pray in every season, for all of us, in some vital, life-giving way, to
come to see and feel and know the good news foretold by Isaiah and the reality of
promises come true in the Gospels.

We long for the message of the carols we sing during the holiday season to penetrate our hearts, every heart, and to touch and inspire us in new and lasting ways. We
long for signs, real signs, of the profound love of a generous God breaking forth into
our human hearts, shining healing light into the darkest recesses of our souls.

*Oh holy night! The stars are brightly shining It is the night of the dear
Savior's birth! Long lay the world in sin and error pining Till he appear'd
and the soul felt its worth. A thrill of hope the weary world rejoices For yon-
der breaks a new and glorious morn!*

*Fall on your knees Oh hear the angel voices Oh night divine Oh night
when Christ was born Oh night divine Oh night divine*

We believe, as the renowned carol, "O Holy Night," states, God, in the form
of Jesus, took on flesh to live among us. His name, Immanuel, which means God-
with-us, is the greatest example of compassion we have ever known or experienced.
God, in the form of Jesus, moves into our darkness, brokenness, pain, anxiousness

and confusion, reminding us we are never alone and everything we experience, God has experienced too.

It is in response to this miraculous gift, how we, too, can be "moved with compassion" for our fellow brothers and sisters, as God has been moved with compassion for us.

This is the belief guiding us. This is the vision inspiring us.

Epilogue

"Let us not underestimate how hard it is to be compassionate. Compassion is hard because it requires the inner disposition to go with others to the place where they are weak, vulnerable, lonely, and broken. But this is not our spontaneous response to suffering. What we desire most is to do away with suffering by fleeing from it or finding a quick cure for it. As busy, active, relevant ministers, we want to earn our bread by making a real contribution. This means first and foremost doing something to show that our presence makes a difference. And so we ignore our greatest gift, which is our ability to enter into solidarity with those who suffer."
-Henry Nouwen

I
T WAS LATE FRIDAY AFTERNOON; our workweek was coming to a close. It had been a fruitful week, we had had several intense listening conversations—a middle-aged woman tormented from depression, a teenager battling the same issue, a single mother of three small children churning to keep her head above water, an older man fighting alcoholism, and many others. Each conversation, although unique and important, had the common thread of suffering running through and through.

We wish we could say we walked away from each of those conversations feeling like we had somehow scaled Mt. Everest together, looking down into the distant valleys, seeing how far we had come. But sadly, it's not the case. Quite honestly, more times than not, it is never the case. We didn't leave those conversations feeling as if we had, by listening intently and "suffering with," solved anyone's problems or cured their situations, moving them to a perfectly healthy place, emotionally, physically and spiritually. Nevertheless, we do believe, by our listening and our presence, healing was beginning, however slowly.

Listening is intentional, extremely intentional. Compassion is intentional too, maybe even more so, because it asks so much of us. It takes intentional effort to enter into someone else's situation and pain, to the best of our human capacity, often times without seeing the fruit of our labor.

One semester in college, I (Tom) studied in London. Throughout our trip, we

311

visited many of the famous buildings and cathedrals making England such a special, historic place. I remember walking into St. Paul's Cathedral and being totally overwhelmed by its magnitude. The tour guide talked about how long it had taken to build the structure and how some individuals had worked on it their entire careers, never getting the opportunity to see the finished result. Some worked on just one small section of the cathedral, doing the exact same thing day after day, never privileged to see how their craftsmanship contributed to the whole of the magnificent structure.

Compassion is a lot like an "incomplete" building project. It asks us to sit with someone is her most confusing hour—knowing we may never understand the point of our presence, just as she may never understand the point of her confusion.

We all want our lives to be consequential. We want to leave our mark on the world. But so many of our compassionate responses to the brokenness all around us, aren't quantifiable—and we have to be okay with this fact. It would be wonderful, if each time we offered a compassionate response, to be able to look at the response, as a farmer looks upon fruitful fields of grain, and see all we accomplished. True compassion, as Martin Luther King Jr. declared is:

> More than flinging a coin to a beggar; it comes to see that an edifice which produces beggars needs restructuring.

Restructuring an edifice isn't something that happens overnight. It may never happen in our lifetimes.

But the good news is God doesn't ask us to restructure an edifice by ourselves; God knows we aren't God. God simply asks us to be faithful with the things we are given; to pay attention to the needs of those around us; to respond with grace and empathy; and then to simply "let go."

Jesus gave us the mandate to . . .

> Be compassionate as (our) God is compassionate . . .

. . . knowing very well we are fully human and God is the embodiment of the perfectly compassionate way. When we, as God's imperfect children—with all of our uncertainties, anxieties, brokenness, wounds, insecurities and complexities—think we have this life figured out God surprises us. God surprises us with God's goodness, faithfulness, righteousness, holiness, graciousness and loving-kindness. All of which are marks of compassion.

Writing a book on the topic of compassion may be one of the more complex projects on which we will ever have to work. By no means do we want people to look at us as if we have the market cornered on the topic. There are always countless more examples we could cite, lessons to be learned, and stories to be taught.

One of the most thought provoking questions for us to answer has been—how do we, as middle-class Caucasian Americans, have any right to talk about what suffering looks like when our lives are relatively easy in comparison to so many lives around the world? We have had to continue reminding ourselves, daily, to simply invite God into every moment, asking to be used, in our own small way, to extend God's goodness and mercy to those who are hurting, isolated, vulnerable, estranged and crushed. We have to remind each other—when we have been prone to guilty feelings penetrating our hearts and minds—we are not God—we are simply God's hands, feet, eyes, ears and presence in the world. Imperfectly so.

Three years ago, as we wrote in our first book, we received a phone call from the state police just a few days before Christmas. A couple we had "suffered with" for several years through their cancer journey completed a double suicide. It was a horribly painful time for us as we wrestled with the questions inevitably arising: Did we do enough? Did we say enough? Were we present enough? Were we compassionate enough? Did we express our faith enough?

Compassion, as we learned then and are continuing to learn now, doesn't ask us to have an end goal in mind, it simply asks us to go to those places of suffering and to make a home there. This is what Jesus has already done for us. It doesn't ask us to control or manipulate outcomes, but simply to be "moved deep with our bowels" as Jesus was moved "deep within his bowels" and enter into solidarity with those who are fellow travelers.

We hope and pray by reading these stories you have been "moved to compassion" in your everyday lives.

"So take seriously the story that God has given you to live. It's time to read your own life, because your story is the one that could set us all ablaze." Dan Allender

About the Authors

MICHAEL GINGERICH and TOM KADEN are the co-founders of Someone To Tell It To – www.someonetotellitto.org - a non-profit ministry with the mission of creating a caring culture that accompanies others on journeys toward deeper connections. They are husbands, fathers, pastors and mentors who want to inspire a movement for people to listen more intently and be more compassionately present in others' lives. Their ministry is headquartered in Harrisburg, Pennsylvania.